More Than A Native Speaker

An Introduction For Volunteers Teaching English Abroad

D1300165

Don Snow

Typeset in Gill Sans and ITC Cheltenham
by World Composition Services, Sterling Virginia USA
and printed by
Pantagraph Printing, Bloomington, Illinois USA

Teachers of English to Speakers of Other Languages, Inc.
1600 Cameron Street, Suite 300
Alexandria, Virginia 22314 USA
Tel 703-836-0774 • Fax 703-836-7864

Director of Communications and Marketing: Helen Kornblum
Senior Editor: Marilyn Kupetz
Cover Design: Ann Kammerer

ISBN 0-939791-64-1
Library of Congress Catalogue No. 96-060035

To the staff and teachers of the Amity Teachers Program

Table of Contents

Introduction

It was at the Taipei YMCA in 1979 that I first stood before an English class as a volunteer teacher, wondering how to survive the period with my dignity intact. I was assured of my command of English, but much less confident that I would even understand a jargon-laden question about English grammar rules, let alone be able to answer it. I was also distinctly aware that knowing how to speak English was not the same as knowing how to teach English. What few vague ideas I had about language teaching dated from painful experiences in high school and college foreign language classes, which had convinced me that there had to be a better way to teach language than lecturing on the finer points of grammar, but which had not shown me what that better way might be. Thus, in that first class period, my attention was focused much more on my need not to make a fool of myself than it was on effective pedagogy; my primary goal was to hear the bell ring before I had run out of things to say.

During the next 2 years, as my skills improved and I became more confident, I became less worried about getting through a class period. In this next stage of my development, I tended to judge the success of a class period largely on whether or not students seemed to like a lesson, and rarely persisted in any activity to which students did not quickly respond. As a result my courses evolved into a series of "Greatest Hits" activities that entertained reasonably well and generated quite a bit of language practice but did not have much continuity. It was only after considerable trial and error—and a graduate program in language teaching—that I was able to move from a standard of "Do my students like this activity?" to one of "Is this activity really going to help them learn?" This is not to say that the English courses I taught during my earlier years were a waste of students' time; I no doubt provided my students with good practice opportunities and valuable language knowledge and may have enhanced their interest in language learning by making it more enjoyable than it might otherwise have been. However, as I studied the rudiments of the language teaching craft I learned not only how to teach language lessons more effectively but also how to help students learn to structure more productive language learning experiences.

Every year, thousands of men and women from English-speaking nations go abroad as volunteer English teachers through organizations such as the Peace Corps, Voluntary Service Overseas and myriad other government, church, and academic organizations. As novice language teachers, these volunteers face problems similar to those I confronted and, over time, many learn to be good language teachers. To a large extent, success in teaching is based on qualities such as diligence, patience, and common sense, which many nonprofessionals possess in abundance, and many volunteer teachers make a significant educational contribution to their host nation in spite of their lack of professional training. However, learning the craft of language teaching by trial and error is a process that can take a long time and involve considerable emotional wear and tear on both volunteer teachers and students. The purpose of this book is to accelerate the process by providing a nontechnical introduction to English teaching that is geared toward the special needs of native-English-speaking volunteer teachers working abroad.

The Volunteer Teaching Experience

Because teaching English as a volunteer teacher in a foreign country is quite different from teaching as a trained teacher in an English-speaking country, the assumptions and emphasis of this book are different from those of most introductions to English teaching in several ways:

1 Most volunteer teachers have some experience with language learning as a result of high school or college foreign language courses, have a native or near-native knowledge of English, and have a native understanding of at least one English-speaking culture. However, most volunteer teachers do not have professional training or experience in language teaching, and are not necessarily interested in making a career of language teaching. Therefore, this book is a practical introduction to the range of issues involved in learning to teach English abroad rather than a scholarly introduction to the language teaching profession as a whole. That is not to say that this book is "unprofessional"; it is based firmly on current English teaching thought and research and is informed by the extensive experience of the author as both a language teacher and language learner. However, my assumption is that what a volunteer teacher needs most is a readily intelligible distillation of English teaching theory and practice, explained with a minimum of technical jargon. I also assume that readers are less likely to have the opportunity to follow up on academic footnotes than they are to be interested in buying a few books on English teaching, so I have restricted my references to a relatively small list of readily available books and resources that volunteer teachers might purchase for a small, portable teaching reference library.

2 In contrast to English teachers in English-speaking countries, volunteer teachers abroad are almost by definition working in an environment that is culturally alien to them. This means that the task facing them involves not only learning how to teach English but also learning about and adapting to the expectations, goals, methods, and resources of an unfamiliar educational system and culture. It should be noted that this situation has advantages as well as disadvantages,

one of which is that it provides an excellent opportunity for genuine communication; students are experts in the culture about which the teacher is trying to learn, so many activities can involve students talking and writing about their culture in order to help educate the teacher.

3 Volunteers teaching abroad are trying to cope with teaching while at the same time undergoing the exciting but difficult process of adapting to life in a foreign culture. Although it might be argued that this adaptation process is outside the range of what should be considered in a book on language teaching, I have chosen to discuss it because it not only has significant impact on the life of volunteer teachers abroad but can also affect their teaching, especially their effectiveness in teaching explicit or implicit lessons about culture and about cross-cultural communication.

Teaching situations abroad can differ significantly according to the culture of the host country, students' skill levels, resources available, class size, and a host of other variables. Although I have tried to address as broad a range of situations as possible in this book, the teaching setting I most often assume is a country that is non-Western culturally and less economically developed than most nations of the West. To be more specific, I assume that you will work in a setting that has many of the following characteristics:

The Typical Volunteer Teaching Environment

1. Equipment: There will probably be at least chalk and a blackboard, or some equivalent. Tape recorders, videotape machines, and other types of equipment may also be available, but access might be limited and their availability cannot be taken for granted.

2. Materials: There will usually be some kind of textbook available for most English courses, though in some cases it may be that only the teacher has a copy. Some supplementary reading and listening material in English is available outside the classroom but the range is probably limited. Volunteer teachers are confronted with the dual problems of adapting existing material and creating new material.

3. Class size: Volunteer teachers will often teach classes with 30 or more students, and classes of 50 or more are not unusual. This means that teaching methods that require individual attention to students may not always be possible to use.

4. Skill level: Volunteer teachers teach students at every skill level; some have students who are brushing up their command of the terminology of nuclear physics, others teach students who still don't understand "How are you?" However, volunteers usually face students who lie somewhere between these two extremes, who have adequate English skills for rudimentary communication with a foreign English teacher in class, but who cannot yet communicate fluently. In many countries, you will find that students can read more than they can say or understand in conversation.

5. Program: Volunteer teachers often teach in situations where there is some existing program (goals, curriculum, expectations, evaluation system), but by design or default most programs still leave room for innovation and decision making on the teacher's part. Teachers thus need to adapt to the existing program, and are therefore faced with deciding when to conform and when to innovate, a decision which can be tricky in an unfamiliar cultural environment.

6. School: Volunteer teachers often work in the host country's formal education system, teaching in primary, secondary, or tertiary institutions. However, some also teach in night schools, adult education classes, intensive English programs, TOEFL preparation courses, or various kinds of English clubs.

7. Language environment: Most volunteers will teach in places where English is not widely used outside the classroom. This not only limits students' opportunity for practice but also means that goals and motivation are more problematic than is the case for students studying English for survival in an English-speaking country. For example, in many countries, students study primarily to get high scores on examinations; consequently, they study in ways that prepare them for tests but do not help them develop usable English skills. This, in turn, means that they may lose interest in English study once they no longer have tests to pass. Therefore, volunteer teachers need to be aware of the vital importance their classes have in giving meaning and life to English study. It is often in classes with native speaker volunteers that students first really experience English as a tool for communication, not just an obstacle to examination success.

8. Culture: Many volunteers will teach in traditional societies; that is, societies that look more to their past for values and practices than most Western societies do. In many of these societies, attitudes toward English teaching have been influenced by traditional methods for learning to read the prestige—or even sacred—language of the region, languages such as Classical Chinese in China and Arabic in many Islamic countries (languages that play a role similar to that which Latin played in premodern Europe). Such societies tend to have a high view of the authority of the printed word and of the teacher, to see language learning as knowledge acquisition rather than skill development, and to emphasize study of texts (grammar, vocabulary, and reading) more than speaking and listening skills. In these societies, grammar books and dictionaries usually have a very high degree of authority, and woe be to the hardy fool who contradicts them. Thus, the assumptions of volunteer teachers as to how one should teach and learn language may differ considerably from those of their students and colleagues

9. Relationship to the West: The position of economic, military, and cultural dominance that English-speaking nations have occupied over the past 2 centuries also allows a few generalizations about the relationship between the culture of the volunteer English teacher and that of the host country. First, most (but not all) volunteers will be teaching in nations that are not as wealthy as the volunteers' home countries. Second, the wealth, technology, markets, and cultural power of English-speaking nations often inspires considerable admiration (and much of the motivation for English study) in the host country. These feelings of admiration are, however, often complicated by feelings of bitterness toward ex-colonial and imperial powers, and by resentment of the host country's relative poverty (which often stands in glaring contrast to a more glorious past). In many nations, therefore, volunteer English teachers need to be sensitive and cautious as they teach about their nations. Students may have very mixed feelings about the English-speaking nations of the West, and many volunteers have been surprised at the speed with which a class of students who seemed very enthusiastic about the West rapidly become defensive or even hostile.

Theoretical Assumptions

In this book I stress the idea that language is a tool for communication, and that communicative activity should play a major role in the language classroom. I have taken this stance not only because it is a dominant trend in current thinking about language teaching but also because most volunteer teachers find this approach instinctively appealing and comfortable to work with. At times, however, I also discuss teaching methods, such as text memorization, that are associated with other theoretical approaches. This is partly because I share the belief of many scholars that there is currently no single theory of language acquisition or teaching that can be taken as authoritative.[1] It is also partly because volunteer teachers often teach in environments where noncommunicative methods may be the norm, and whether or not volunteers choose to use such methods they need to be familiar with them. Given the tendency of many Westerners to be highly critical of traditional or out-dated approaches—and the probability that their host colleagues will often use these methods—it is also important that volunteer teachers be able to see that there are reasons why these methods are used and that they are not entirely without redeeming merit. Without this bit of empathy, volunteers may end up alienating both their colleagues and their students.

As is increasingly recognized within the language teaching profession, the English classroom is often not the most important focus of activity. In many cases, the success of students in learning a language depends more on the effectiveness of their strategies outside of class than it does on the skill of the language teacher in class. This is especially true for the many students who are not studying English in full-time programs that allow them several hours a day of language class, and whose success depends on the work they do outside of class or after the English course ends. It is also especially true for students whose native language is not closely related to English, and whose acquisition of English is not speeded by the vocabulary, grammatical, or cultural similarities that accelerate the English study of many European students. Consequently, I have not limited discussion to classroom teaching techniques; there is also discussion of study methods and ways for students to plan their own programs of study.

I have chosen to organize my discussion of language teaching in a rather traditional way, approaching listening, speaking, reading, writing, grammar, vocabulary, and culture separately rather than organizing discussion in a way that is more obviously compatible with whole language approaches. Again, this is a deliberate choice. In discussion of these topics I have not ignored their interrelatedness, but I organize discussion around traditional categories because such divisions are likely familiar to volunteer teachers as a result of experience in foreign language classes. Another reason, as above, is that many of the schools and students with whom volunteer teachers will work tend to think in terms of these categories, and it is wise for volunteers who are learning a new craft in a new environment to begin with what is familiar to both them and students.

In the ordering of topics in this book, I have tried to roughly follow the order in which a volunteer teacher is likely to need the information contained. As suggested above, in my experience beginning

---

[1]See Bowen et al. (1985); McLaughlin (1987); Omaggio Hadley (1993); and Richards (1990).

language teachers experience an EFL version of Maslow's Hierarchy of Needs that looks something like this:

LEVEL 1:
Need to make it through the classroom hour without running out of material.

LEVEL 2:
Need for positive student response to one's lessons (or at least no overt expression of boredom and displeasure).

LEVEL 3:
Need to feel that one's lessons actually help students develop English skills.

Thus the first section of the book, Chapters 1 through 6, are devoted to issues of classroom survival: basic principles of language learning and teaching, and course and lesson planning. Chapters 7 through 14 then discuss the various aspects of language teaching in more detail. Finally, Chapter 15 addresses adaptation to life in the host country; and Chapter 16 suggests future paths for volunteers who decide to become professional language teachers.

Additional Notes

This book is intended for volunteer teachers from a variety of English-speaking nations, but I think that I am more convincing and accurate if I draw primarily on my own U.S. background for language and culture examples. You will also find that Asia in general and China in particular are overgenerously represented in my choice of examples; again, this is because much of my language teaching experience has been in the East. Finally, I must beg your indulgence for my occasional use of the term *Westerners* to refer to people from countries where English is spoken by most people as their first language. The problem is simply that it is too much of a mouthful to consistently refer to "Americans, Canadians, British, Irish, Australians, New Zealanders, and others."

As much as possible, I have tried to use normal English rather than jargon and acronyms. The few exceptions are as follows: *EFL* (English as a foreign language) refers to teaching English in a country where English is not widely used. This is in contrast to *ESL* (English as a Second Language), teaching English to non-English-speaking people in an English-speaking area. I will also allow myself the new acronym *VT* (volunteer teacher) to refer to native speakers of English who are serving as volunteer teachers of English abroad.

To counterbalance my personal idiosyncrasies and the Chinese bias of my experience, I have relied on the help of a number of friends to tame my more questionable assertions. I wish to express my gratitude to Kate Parry and Shelly Chase for truly sacrificial efforts in reading over entire early drafts; to Clifford Hill for suggestions on evaluation methods; to Jack Richards for encouragement and practical advice; and to anonymous TESOL reviewers for their generous gifts of expertise and time. Thanks also go to John Garoutt, Alexis Albion, Fred Elting, Chris Blankenship, and Jim Kwong for their feedback on various portions of the draft. Of course, ultimate responsibility for any nonsense that remains in the final product lies with me.

Preparing
to Teach

The following chapters will address the issue of planning for language teaching.

CHAPTER 1 will discuss some basic principles of language teaching and learning.

CHAPTER 2 will then suggest ways in which you can gather information before planning your courses.

CHAPTERS 3 and 4 will consider the basic elements of a language course, essentially a formula consisting of goals + materials + methods + evaluation.

CHAPTER 5 will discuss the practical issues involved in planning a successful lesson.

CHAPTER 6 will wrap up this section with some examples of how all of this is put together into typical language courses and lessons.

1 Principles of Language Learning and the Role of the Teacher

- ◆ How well students learn a language ultimately depends more on their own efforts than on those of the teacher. Thus, any attempt to understand effective language teaching must consider the issue of effective language learning.

- ◆ Three basic realities of language learning are that a language is a tool for communication; that learning a language involves mastery of both knowledge and skill; and that the struggle to learn a language is a battle of the heart as well as of the mind.

- ◆ The role of a language teacher is not simply to be a transmitter of knowledge; like a coach, a language teacher needs to assist students in understanding the task before them, staying motivated, building discipline, and learning how to pursue the task on their own.

- ◆ The assumptions stated above may not be shared by students or colleagues in your host country, so it is important to make your assumptions explicit to your students and to make sure that your expectations and your students' are not too far apart.

W
hat is a language teacher? Perhaps the first image that occurs to us is of a tidily dressed woman or man standing in front of an attentive class, explaining a grammar point or a new word. Then he or she checks whether or not students understand the point by asking each one a question or two, patiently correcting any mistakes they make. We have all seen this model of teaching in films and on television, and many of us have been in language classes that were taught largely in this fashion; it would therefore be easy to let this model shape the way in which we set out to teach our own classes. In this chapter, my purpose is to challenge some of the assumptions underlying this language teaching model, to introduce a number of basic principles of language learning, and to suggest a different model of the role of the language teacher.

Students at the Center

During the past few years, more and more books on language teaching are placing students rather than teachers at center stage (e.g., see Scarcella & Oxford, 1992). This is due to a growing recognition that whether or not students succeed in learning a language depends more on their own efforts than on those of the teacher, and that a good program of instruction therefore needs to be student-centered instead of teacher-centered.

One reason it is important to view language learning as a student-centered process is that students are individuals who are very different in a number of significant ways. First, students differ in their language knowledge and skills; one student may read well and have a broad vocabulary but be almost incapable of speech, whereas another student may have exactly the opposite profile of skills. Second, students differ in their learning styles and strengths; a study method that may be intolerably boring, confusing, or intimidating for one student may prove comfortable and effective for another. Finally, students differ greatly in their levels of motivation, their attitudes toward study in general, and their feelings toward English study in particular. One student may be basically diligent but resent Western cultural influence in her country; another thinks the West is appealing but has little love for study; a third doesn't care one way or another about English but would like to get a good grade on the final exam. Consequently the reasons for a student's successes or failures have to be sought at a variety of different levels and differ greatly from person to person; it is inevitable that no teacher-designed "one-size-fits-all" lesson or program will meet the needs or suit the styles of all of the students in a class. Instead, as much as possible, students need to take charge of their own learning process, choosing goals that fit their needs and learning strategies that work for them.

A second argument for student-centered approaches is that students will learn more effectively if they are active participants in the process than if they only passively follow the teacher's instructions. This is true if for no other reason than that much language study and practice takes place when the teacher is not around to give instructions or to check up on students; students who view homework or small group conversations as a welcome chance to develop their skills will make much better use of these opportunities than students who merely consider them a chore to be coped with as quickly as possible.

The final reason that the focus in language learning needs to be on students is that few EFL programs of English study are long enough to guarantee that students will have mastery of English by the time they leave the program. In many countries, English is offered in middle school and even primary school—often as a required subject—but students only study English a few hours a week and have little opportunity to practice what they learn. Even those few students who complete a university major in English will still usually have gaps in their English skills when they graduate, and students who are not English majors or who study in some kind of night school have even less English training and practice. Thus, if a high level of proficiency is the goal, students will probably have to continue study of English long after they leave the educational system, and those students most likely to keep making progress toward mastery of English are those who are already accustomed to designing and carrying out their own language study plans.

To sum up, as Brown (1991) notes, not even the world's best language teacher can guarantee success in language learning: "The bottom line here is that, as a language learner, you can—and must— take control of your own language learning and assume responsibility for your success or failure" (p. 6).

There are a great many points one could make about language learning, but I have chosen to focus on three that deserve special attention because of their inherent importance and because they are points that many learners tend to lose sight of: (a) language is a tool for communication; (b) learning a language involves mastery of both skill and knowledge; and (c) a learner needs to give serious consideration to the impact of feelings on language study.

Basic Principles of Language Learning

Language as Communication

Perhaps the most fundamental reality of language learning is that language is a tool for communication. As obvious as this may seem, the implications of this point are not always as clear to students as they should be. We need to remember that many students' experience of English learning trains them to see English as anything but a communication tool. The daily reality of English study for many students is one of memorizing words and rules in preparation for a test and rarely if ever involves using English for communicative purposes. After years of this kind of study, it is only to be expected that students will come to see language learning as an exercise primarily geared toward formal accuracy, especially on tests.[1] Such noncommunicative approaches to English study tend to focus students' attention on form to the exclusion of use and also undermine student interest; few students are excited by grammar and vocabulary study per se.

The study of English is potentially more appealing when English is presented as a key for establishing communication with a new world. This communication can take a variety of forms; it can mean sharing ideas face to face with someone from a foreign country, or gaining access to the knowledge embedded in the world's vast library of material published in English. In either case, learning English means developing the ability to understand and interact with a universe that is largely inaccessible to those who don't know English. Here it is worth pointing out that although learning any language opens new doors, this is particularly true of English because of its growing role as an international language; English is now the language of publishing and speech for most international communication and is often used even by people from non-English-speaking countries when they need to interact with people from other nations.[2]

There are also other reasons to focus on communication in class, one being that it may make language learning easier. Brown (1991) notes that in learning their first language, children tend to focus on communication before accuracy, and suggests that this order of priority should also apply to learners of a second language. Taylor (1987) also suggests that a communicative approach to language learning helps students learn grammar more effectively.

If students are to view study of English as the learning of a tool for communication, and to begin to taste the thrill of discovery that mastery of a new language can entail, it is important that as early as possible in their learning process they actually experience language as communication. In an English class, this means using speaking or writing practice as an opportunity for students to share what they really think, feel, or believe. It also means that when students say or write something, responses should be directed to the ideas expressed rather than only to the accuracy of the language.

Language as Knowledge and Skill

A second important truth of language learning is that language learning is mastery of a skill as much as it is acquisition of knowledge.

---

[1]Although these assumptions are held by students in many parts of the world, especially Asia, they are not universal. Some students (often from Latin America, Africa, and the Middle East) go to the opposite extreme, striving for communication with almost a complete disregard for accuracy.

[2]Kaplan (1986) estimates that 80% of the technical information available in the world is in English.

In other words, it is not enough for students to know word meanings and structure rules; students need to be able to apply this knowledge quickly, even automatically, in order to express themselves smoothly in speech or writing, read at a reasonable rate, or comprehend spoken English rapidly enough to keep pace with the speaker. In order to build these skills, practice is necessary; study alone will not suffice.

Again this point might seem obvious, but we must remember the unintended lessons which many approaches to language teaching leave students with. For many students, learning language has always been about learning grammar rules and memorizing vocabulary in order to be able to successfully figure out true/false, matching, and fill-in-the-blanks puzzles on tests. Many students have had little training in speaking-listening skills that require speed and automaticity and can only be learned through repeated practice. Naturally, many students' perceptions of what is and is not important in language learning are shaped by their experience in language classes, and it is not surprising that in many places most students do not fully appreciate the skill component in language use and are inclined to neglect practice in favor of study.

Because language use does have a heavy skill component, which demands that complex operations be performed not only accurately but quickly, there are some important implications for the ways in which students must learn:

1 Language learners need a great deal of practice. In order to learn to speak well, students need to spend a great deal of time speaking; in order to learn to read quickly and effectively, they need to spend a lot of time reading, and so forth. Almost all teachers would assent to this principle in theory, but in many English classrooms the teacher still talks most of the time. Sometimes this is because teachers feel they need to dominate in order to maintain control in class; sometimes it is because teachers feel that if they aren't "teaching" they aren't really earning their pay. For whatever reasons, stepping off the podium and giving students a chance to speak (read, write, etc.) is more problematic than it may initially seem.

2 Language learners need repeated practice. It generally takes more than one practice opportunity to learn to perform any skill smoothly, and language learning is no exception. Many language skills require a student to do many different things at the same time; for example, speaking involves choosing words, applying grammar rules, attending to pronunciation and intonation—all while trying to decide what to say. It is impossible for a speaker to consciously pay attention to all of these operations at the same time, so it is important that some of them be practiced to the point that they can be performed without much conscious attention.

The problem with carrying out this principle arises from an assumption that students often learn from their classroom experience: the notion that the teacher's job is to cover material in the book, and that once the material is covered students are expected to know it. The implication is that each point should be covered once and once only. (Among students who have internalized this view of language learning, the protest that "We've done this already" is expected to effectively veto an activity whether or not they have really learned the skill in question.)

Language Learning as a Battle of the Heart

A final fundamental reality of language learning is that feelings play a major role in language study and need to be taken seriously in the planning of a successful language learning campaign. As Oxford (1990) puts it: "The affective side of the learner is probably one of the very biggest influences on language learning success or failure" (p. 140). Learners who have a strong desire to learn and who feel good about their progress are far more likely to continue working hard over the long haul required in learning a language.

One of the reasons why emotions play such an important role in language learning is the long haul mentioned above. Learning a foreign language well involves a great deal of effort over a long period of time. The basic rules of English grammar and a survival vocabulary can be learned within a few months, but mastery of the language takes much longer. Students need considerable practice to develop effective skills in listening and speaking, not to mention reading and writing. It also takes a long time to amass a sufficient vocabulary for reading texts and listening to speech (e.g., on the radio or TV) intended for native speakers. On top of all of this, a student needs a solid founding in the cultures of English. All of this is particularly difficult for students in an EFL environment to achieve because they have fewer opportunities for practice and contact with Western culture than do students in an ESL setting. The problem is especially severe for students of English in places such as Asia, the Middle East, and Africa because the native languages, writing systems, and cultures have little in common with those of the English-speaking world, and their English study thus entails far more learning.

Some students are surprised by the amount of time and effort that it takes to learn a language. Thinking back on my days as a beginning Russian student, I remember noticing in my college catalogue that our 3rd-year Russian courses were literature courses. I therefore foolishly assumed that if we were going to read literature in the 3rd year, the first 2 years would be sufficient to teach me daily Russian.[3] Most language students are probably not quite this naïve, but unreasonable expectations are not rare. As Scarcella and Oxford (1992) point out: "students are often unrealistic in what they believe they can and should accomplish in a given period of time, so their self-esteem suffers" (p. 58). Students who feel bad about their language learning are particularly vulnerable to discouragement and the temptation to quit.

Even students who recognize the fact that language study is emotionally demanding often fail to account for this problem in their study plans. Too many students assume that being a "good" student means toughing it out, slugging away at a language until it finally gives in. Again drawing on my own experience, I remember fantasizing that if I could just read one big Russian novel—even if it meant shovelling my way through the book word by word with a dictionary—I would conquer the Russian reading problem forever. The strategy may well have worked had I ever been able to keep at it, but I never could.[4] This tendency to try and take a language by frontal assault, of course, often reflects the manner in which languages are taught, with inadequate attention to the emotional needs of learners.

Another problem arises from a peculiarity of the language learning process—the further students go, the more their rate of progress seems to slow. To some extent this is due to a phenomenon known as *plateaus* which are often experienced by intermediate and advanced learners. For reasons no one quite understands, many learners tend to make progress in spurts more than in a neat step-by-step progression, and between these spurts students often have a feeling that they are making no progress—they have hit a plateau. These plateaus, however, are generally temporary and therefore do not pose a serious threat to students who know that they are a common feature of the language learning experience. (The best thing for a student to do is either just keep on studying or lighten up for a short break before plunging back in.)

A more serious problem arises from the fact that the more students learn of a language, the less visible impact each additional day of study makes on their skills; hence progress becomes harder and harder to discern. In order to understand this phenomenon, the

---

[3]Within a few months I was disabused of the notion that one learned spoken Russian in 2 years of college courses, but the need to complete a language requirement kept me going. Sheer perversity pushed me into a 3rd year, and then I learned that "reading" Russian in 3rd-year courses meant slowly decoding texts with a dictionary. My study of Russian did not last much beyond graduation day.

[4]This suggestion may sound bizarre, but I assure you that I am not the only language learner it has ever occurred to. For example, in chapter 6 of *How to Learn Any Language*, Barry Faber (1991) seriously suggests this approach for beginning readers, using newspapers instead of novels. To his credit, Faber makes it very clear that this approach is not for the faint-hearted.

analogy of a river emerging from a mountain gorge onto a broad plane may be helpful; as its channel widens, the river appears to slow down, although the same amount of water is moving over the same distance in the same time. Likewise, beginning language students can see their progress very clearly because they are making progress on a narrow front. Between Lesson 2 and Lesson 4 in a textbook, their knowledge of English doubles, and every new word they learn significantly increases their ability to communicate. However, as they reach more advanced skill levels, their progress becomes less apparent; successful completion of Lesson 74 does not make as obvious an impact on a student's English skill level as completion of Lesson 6 did, and learning lower frequency words like *manual* and *tome* doesn't enhance their ability to communicate as much as mastery of earlier words like *book* did.

A final reason for which English study can be emotionally demanding is that there are generally few rewards during the first years of English study in an EFL setting. When students reach a level of English skill that allows them to actually use English for practical or personally rewarding purposes, this provides a kind of reward which helps sustain students' interest in continued use and study of the language. For example, for students who can finally follow a radio news broadcast in English, a sense of daily progress in English is no longer necessary to keep them going. However, for students in the middle stages of language learning, whose progress seems to be slowing but who cannot yet do much with their English, it can be very difficult to resist the temptation to chuck the books and go fishing. It may take years for students to develop their speaking to the point where they can converse with an English speaker or learn to read well enough to comfortably read an English newspaper or book, and even when they attain a sufficient level of skill they may find that there are few English speakers to speak with or few newspapers to read. It is hard in such circumstances to sustain much enthusiasm for language study.

Brown (1991) sums up the importance of affective factors in language learning: "The emotions are the foundation on which all your learning strategies, techniques, and gimmicks will stand or fall. . . . Without that emotional foundation, you are fighting an uphill battle at best." It thus makes sense to structure programs of language study in such a way that students get the maximum sense of progress and reward and so are encouraged not to abandon the effort halfway.

The Role of the Language Teacher

As suggested at the beginning of this chapter, we may all be accustomed to a model of language teaching that is heavily teacher centered. To my mind (influenced no doubt by too many years in China) this teacher-centered approach calls up images of the great sage Confucius sitting amidst his disciples, explaining the Way and occasionally asking questions to check his disciples' comprehension; hence, I will refer to this approach as the Sage model of teaching. The Sage owes his exalted position to the fact that he knows more than his students do, and his primary task is to transfer his knowledge to his students. Once the students understand what the Sage is trying to explain, the teaching task has been successfully completed.

It is not surprising that the Sage model is influential in shaping the ideas of VTs about the role of the language teacher. As noted above, this may be the model that you saw in your own high school or university language classes. Also, it may well be the predominant teaching model in your host country, and thus the role that students and colleagues will expect you to play. However, there are also more subtle reasons behind the influence that this model exerts. One is that it is a natural role for VTs because it places a premium on expertise in knowledge of the subject. The primary qualification for Sage status is knowing more than the disciples; the VT's primary qualification as a language teacher is superior knowledge of English. Another attraction of the Sage model is that it places the teacher in firm control of the classroom, with the power to steer away from uncertain or uncomfortable waters and to maintain the appearance of an orderly class.

A certain amount of the Sage is virtually inevitable in your teaching life, and it is not necessarily bad. You do in fact know far more about English than your students do, and one of your roles as language teacher is to convey as much of that knowledge as possible to your students. However, I would suggest that there are also serious drawbacks to excessive reliance on this model. One is that it can be hard to play the Sage role well. For example, setting yourself up as the final authority on English can result in very uncomfortable situations, particularly if you have not mastered the intricacies of English grammar. Although students' command of the rules of English is generally faulty, they often have more explicit knowledge of grammar rules (and the vocabulary used to discuss them) than VTs do. This can prove rather awkward when students ask questions that you can't answer, or even test your grammar knowledge in order to show off at your expense.

Even for VTs who become proficient in explaining obscure points of grammar, the Sage model still presents problems, one of which lies in the teacher-centered nature of the Sage model. In this model, teachers are not only personally responsible for transmitting most of the knowledge students are to learn, but also have the responsibility for deciding what is to be learned and how. One (usually unintended) side effect of this approach is that students learn to be passive, to do what they are told rather than actively finding ways to enhance their own learning. Another unfortunate side effect is that, as suggested earlier, the teacher's role may degenerate into one of covering material during class (i.e., explaining or simply mentioning it briefly), reducing class to a formalistic exercise in which the teacher skims over material primarily so that students can be held responsible for it on the final exam.

A second flaw of the Sage model is that it is often classroom centered; in other words, it assumes that most learning takes place in the classroom and downplays the importance of work done by students on their own. There may be homework, but in the minds of the teacher and students the homework is simply rehearsal for the main show. The subtle message of this assumption for students is that real learning requires the teacher; the temptation for teachers is to measure success by the polish of their classroom performances rather than by student progress.

A final problem with the Sage model is that it assumes that learning a language is essentially a process of accumulating knowledge, and that the battle is won once students understand what the teacher is trying to explain. Unfortunately, as we have seen, this assumption isn't true. Acquisition of knowledge plays an important part in language learning, but acquisition of knowledge is not enough—learning a language is also mastering of a set of skills, and skills are not learned via explanation. Explanation is generally only the beginning of the learning process, and the teacher who plays the Sage role often puts on an impressive show but leaves students to face the real battle alone.

A better model for a language teacher is that of the athletic coach or piano teacher, a model which I will call the Coach.[5] The main advantage of this model is that it assumes that most of the learning process takes place during practice away from the teacher's watchful eye, and that success or failure in the learning process depends much more on what students do outside class than on what teachers do in class. A coach will certainly have some tips on how a basketball player should make jump shots, but it is the player's hours of practice shots which will teach the skill. Likewise, a piano teacher cannot teach a student digital dexterity by explaining it; a student must practice scales many times before they can be played smoothly.

Of course, one role of the Coach is to share his/her knowledge of the subject, but equally important parts of the Coach's role are (a) helping students better understand the learning process, (b) providing encouragement and cultivating students' motivation, (c) helping students build discipline through accountability, and (d) guiding them toward taking initiative and responsibility for their own learning. These are not the only possible roles which VTs could adopt, but they are vitally important ones which are worthy of further discussion. In the following sections of this chapter, we will consider these four aspects of the Coach's role and how they relate to basic principles of language learning and teaching.

[5]I am hardly the first to suggest this analogy. See, for example, McKay (1987) and Stevick (1988).

Helping Students Understand Language Learning

One of your first tasks as language teacher is to help students understand some of the concepts that we have discussed above. In part this is done by talking with your students about these principles (assuming that their listening skills are up to the task). However, if your views are going to have much impact on your students, it is important that what you say about language learning be backed up by the way you teach your courses. In other words, if you stress the idea that students should take responsibility for their own language learning, you need to find ways to structure room for student initiative into your courses. If you argue that language is a tool for communication, you must as often as possible allow students to use language for genuine communication in your courses. If you emphasize that mastery of English involves developing language skills through practice, you need to give your students ample opportunities to practice in class. Finally, if you urge students to attend to the affective side of language learning, you need to show similar concern for the issue in the way you structure class exercises and practice. Students will often learn more about the nature of language and language learning from what you model in your classes than from what you tell them in lectures.

Another important aspect of helping students understand language learning is teaching them to think through their goals and methods. This is especially important for students who have generally been passive participants in the language learning process because without a clear sense of goal, it is difficult to decide what methods will be most effective. When lecturing on English study, one of the questions I am most often asked by students is "How can I improve my English?" My first response is usually to suggest that the questioner study hard, but this invariably brings a groan from the audience and a demand that I stop avoiding the question. I then ask the questioner to be more precise about his or her goal—is it to build a better reading vocabulary, improve oral fluency, or what? Unfortunately, the questioner often has no clear idea of what he or she wants to achieve beyond "improving English", and doesn't seem to realize that I can't be more specific in my directions unless I have a clearer idea of where the inquirer wants to go. Teaching students to consider the question of goals and methods is a major first step toward helping them become better language learners. (See Chapter 3 for further discussion.)

Encouraging and Motivating Students

In the introduction I referred to a stage in the development of a language teacher where whether or not students respond favorably to an activity becomes the primary criterion for deciding whether or not to continue using it. In suggesting that this is not the only criterion by which to judge activities, I do not mean to say that it is not important. It is desirable that students like your class as much as possible because on the whole students tend to learn more about something they like and find interesting than something that holds no appeal for them (Scarcella & Oxford, 1992). Thus a class that is lively and fun is—all other things being equal—usually a better class than one that is boring or tense. It is also helpful if students find you encouraging and friendly, and if the class environment is as nonthreatening as possible (Littlewood, 1984).[6]

Two other important factors in the sustaining of student motivation, a sense of progress and feeling of reward, have already been introduced above and will be discussed in more detail in Chapter 3 when we discuss how to structure language study plans. Here, suffice it to say that praise from the teacher and a good time in class will not go very far if students do not feel that they are making progress or if they do not feel there is any purpose to their study.

Ultimately, it may be that the best way to arouse and maintain student interest in English study is to make your courses as genuinely communicative as possible. Most people enjoy talking about themselves and learning about others, so this provides a natural opportunity for speaking and even writing practice—certainly more interesting than rewriting sentences or parroting a memorized dialogue. Many students are also interested in the world beyond the borders of their town or country, and learning about this broader world provides an excellent excuse for reading and listening. In fact, as a foreigner in your host country you have a powerful advantage as a teacher because your presence in the classroom creates a natural "information gap": in other words, because there are many things you know that your students don't know, and many things they know but you don't know, there is a great deal you can talk to each other about without having to manufacture a topic.

A final way in which you can be a source of encouragement for students is by serving as a role model. Students often have great respect for a teacher who has successfully mastered a foreign language, and this respect may make them more eager to follow the teacher's example. However, it by no means follows that a good language teacher must be a great language learner; in fact, those rare individuals who seem to absorb languages effortlessly are often quite discouraging for struggling students to be around, and they may not make very good language teachers because they don't understand the difficulties that mere mortals face. To be a good role model, what is perhaps most important is that you make a serious effort to learn what you can, and that students see you practicing what you preach. Your effort to learn the language

---

[6]A personal example: In high school I continued with Chinese lessons for 4 years—despite marginal grades—mainly because I liked the class and the teacher.

of your host country will not only make your life there easier and richer, but will also give you a much better idea of the difficulties that your students face and will increase your ability to empathize with them. In general, students will tend to work harder for a teacher who they feel understands them and identifies with them than for one who doesn't seem to share their burdens. (See further discussion of learning the host language in Chapter 15.)

Building Discipline and Accountability

When it comes right down to it, one of the greatest advantages of taking a language course (as opposed to studying a language by yourself) is that a language course provides someone who will hold you accountable for how much and how well you learn. In other words, when you take a course, you must study because tomorrow there might be a quiz, a test, a discussion covering tonight's reading assignment, or at least a teacher who will be disappointed if you don't do what you are supposed to. Thus, as long as human beings are naturally inclined toward procrastination and laziness, a third important role of the language teacher will be to see that students put in the many hard hours of work necessary for mastery of a language, and to help them learn the discipline necessary to keep them working diligently when there is no longer a teacher around.

Many of the ways in which teachers hold students accountable come under the heading of assessment and evaluation, discussed in Chapter 4, but here it should be noted that accountability is not only a matter of quizzes, tests, graded homework assignments, and other measures that students often view as more akin to the stick than the carrot; it also includes praise, encouragement for work well done, or almost any other kind of response which recognizes efforts that students have made. (In fact, positive reinforcement often has more impact on students than negative.[7]) The basic idea of accountability is that you consider students' efforts important and care whether or not they did their work. Some students will only work if threatened; others only need a gentle reminder. Most, however, are a little more likely to work if they know that they will be held responsible for it.[8]

[7]Brown (1991) notes that research in psychology indicates that rewards affect behavior more than punishment does.

[8]Littlewood (1984) points out that excessive anxiety in a situation can hinder learning; however, he also notes that "a certain amount of it can stimulate a learner to invest more energy in the task" (p. 59).

Encouraging Students to Take Command

A final role of the language teacher is to move students toward taking charge of their own language learning—setting their own goals, making their own plans of study, and then holding themselves to their plans—because self-starters are most likely to reach the final goal. It is thus important that even as you plan out your course you think about ways in which you can encourage students to take initiative. There is no end of ways in which you can do this.

- ♦ Have students keep their own vocabulary list.

- ♦ Let them choose their own books for reading practice.

- ♦ Have them choose topics for writing or discussions.

- ♦ Ask them to tape their own listening material (e.g., off the radio).

- ♦ Design and carry out a study plan of their own as a component of your course.

The important thing is that students get into the habit of taking charge of as much as possible of their own study programs.

One aspect of helping students take control of their own learning is exposing them to different learning strategies. As was mentioned above, students are individuals who differ not only in their English skill levels but also in their learning styles. Some students learn language best through careful analysis, others may rely more on instinct; some thrive in free-wheeling group discussion, others in quiet conversations with a partner, and so on. However, in many countries students are only familiar with a narrow range of study methods that are recommended—or required—by teachers, classmates, or tradition, and may use methods unsuitable to their personalities or skills simply because they are not aware of alternatives. One of your roles as teacher is thus suggesting approaches to language learning that students might not have previously considered. Of course, this is easier if you have had experience with a broad range of study methods and strategies, but it is still generally possible for you to make a valuable contribution simply by calling students' attention to the issue—many students have never consciously asked themselves what study methods are best suited to them. The fact that you are from a different culture also means that you are probably familiar with a somewhat different range of study methods from those normally used by students in your host country, and this creates the possibility for useful and interesting cross-fertilization.[9]

---

[9]In the TESOL field there is a growing body of literature that emphasizes the teaching of learning strategies. See, for example, Oxford (1990) and Brown (1991).

Getting students to take charge of their own language study is often more easily said than done. Many students no doubt have no real desire to learn English, and only long for the day when they complete their requirement and can kiss the whole thing goodbye. However, there will also be other students whose whole attitude toward language study will change if you carefully but firmly hand the reins over to them.

The assumptions about language teaching I have presented above would not raise many eyebrows in the Western English-teaching world, but they would not all be taken for granted in many of the nations to which you are likely to go as a VT. In fact, many of the assumptions that I have described above as problematic are the very assumptions that will influence your colleagues and students. A few examples:

Making Your Assumptions Explicit

1. Focus on the student as learner: In many societies, the teacher's social role is much closer to that of the Sage than the Coach; teachers are respected in the community primarily for their knowledge of their field and their word is not to be challenged. In such a society, a teacher-centered approach to education fits the culture better than the student-centered approach I have argued for.

2. Emphasis on the individuality of each student: The emphasis on the student as a unique individual with a distinct learning style may seem rather foreign and Western in some societies. In comparison with the U.S., for example, many societies are somewhat more culturally uniform, have a more standardized education system, and encourage individualism less.

3. Language as communication skill: In many host countries teachers do not emphasize this point, and it might work against their interests to teach language in this way. Some of your host country colleagues may have had little opportunity to develop their English skills, particularly spoken fluency; in contrast, they may be very familiar with the formal features of English, especially grammar and vocabulary. They may also find it safer to teach through lectures that stick closely to the text because this allows them to prepare a limited body of material. This text-centered grammar-analysis approach to teaching plays to their strengths; a highly communicative teaching approach that plays to the strengths of a native-speaker VT might be not only unfamiliar but also very difficult for some of your colleagues to adopt.

It is also important to note that for many students who are in educational systems where test results determine their academic futures and careers, learning how to communicate is not the primary goal; the primary goal is to score well on examinations. In such situations, while it is no doubt desirable to add as much of a communication skill element as possible to courses, it would be irresponsible for the teacher to fail to prepare students for tests, and traditional methods may well be as effective in preparing students for examinations as communicative methods are—or more so.

My point is not to undermine all of the principles that I have argued for earlier in this chapter; those principles are sound and provide a good foundation for language teaching. However, it is important that you not arrive in your host country with the attitude that your colleagues and students are backward and that your job is to reform their English teaching system. A more generous and probably fairer way to look at the situation is to recognize that all approaches to teaching have advantages and disadvantages, and that in many ways teaching methods I have described above as traditional approaches may be very efficacious within their context. However, they also often have distinct weaknesses, and your different approaches to teaching can help round out the diet of language learning approaches offered to your students.

In order to help students deal with discrepancies between your language teaching approaches and their language learning expectations, I would make two suggestions:

1 You cannot assume that students share your assumptions, so it is very important to explicitly communicate your assumptions to your students. Students should know what to expect in your class, and how you perceive your role as teacher. You may sometimes also need to modify your assumptions so that you are more in tune with your class.[10]

2 You need not explicitly or implicitly criticize other approaches to teaching. Instead, present your assumptions as just that—*your* assumptions—rather than as the only acceptable approach to language teaching. As suggested above, some of these ideas have a Western flavor, and you might present them as an alternative approach which you are adopting in class because it suits your teaching strengths and because it is a part of the culture from which you come.

By approaching your teaching in this way you are less likely to come into conflict with the culture in which you will teach and live,

---

[10]Nunan (1989) notes that this may even be necessary in classes in English-speaking countries: "It is not uncommon in adult ESL classes for the teacher to see herself as a guide and catalyst for classroom communication while the learners see her as someone who should be providing explicit instruction and modelling the target language" (p. 84). In such cases, Nunan recommends negotiation.

and it will be easier for you to maintain an open mind when considering the weak and strong points of other approaches to teaching.

A Concluding Thought

When all is said and done, it may be that your most important role is an unintended one, related more to what you are than what you do. Many schools like having VTs less because of your expertise in language teaching than because you are a native of an English-speaking country, and your presence has a number of advantages for an English program. First, you bring a sense of authenticity and reality to the classroom—you are living proof that there really is a place where the peculiar sounds and symbols of English are used by real people for real communication. Second, your presence forces students—possibly for the first time—to use English as the medium of real communication. Unlike your host country colleagues, you probably can't speak to students in any language other than English, and success even in limited communication with you is evidence to students that they have in fact learned something that has a purpose going beyond examinations. This can be a real boost to students' self-confidence. Finally, the opportunity to meet and get to know a native of an English-speaking country often does a great deal to raise students' level of interest in English study. Rubin and Thompson (1994) point out that "Research has shown a definite relationship between attitudes and success when foreign language learners have an opportunity to know people who speak the language they are studying. Such positive attitudes usually help learners maintain their interest long enough to achieve their goals" (p. 6).

The implication of these realities for you is that the professional polish of your teaching is not the only yardstick by which your contribution will be measured. Certainly you should still strive to make your teaching as professional as possible, but you should also bear in mind that simply by offering your presence and your efforts you may be making a far greater contribution than you would have imagined.

2 Getting the Lay of the Land

- *Flexibility* is the key word in preparation before you leave your own country.

- Before beginning to make detailed plans for your courses, try to find out as much as possible about your teaching environment and your students' goals, needs, and expectations.

- The first few days of class are an excellent opportunity to find out more about your students and their English skills.

It is common for volunteer teachers to arrive in a new city only days—or even hours—before the first day of class, and this puts you under considerable pressure to sit down at the first possible moment to begin pulling together lesson plans. The problem with these early plans is that they often have to be scrapped within a few days because they don't quite fit. Perhaps the students' levels are higher than you thought, or they passively but firmly refuse to go along with one of your planned teaching methods, or maybe you discover that their listening comprehension is so poor that they don't understand your instructions. Many false starts can be avoided if you take time before the first day of class to find out as much as possible about your students, school, and new teaching environment. You are, after all, entering a new culture in which many aspects of life—including education—are likely to be unfamiliar, and it only makes sense to allow yourself some orientation to your new situation. This chapter will discuss ways in which you can lay good groundwork for your course planning before leaving your home country, after arrival in your host country, and during the first few days of class.

Before Leaving Home

While you are still at home, there are many ways you can prepare for a stint teaching abroad. One is to find and talk with people who have lived in your host country, especially those who served as teachers there. Through a local university you can often locate either citizens of your host country or foreigners who have lived there. You might even try going to your local host country restaurant and asking around; this may be a place where people who have an interest in your host country gather and are known to the staff. It is also a good idea to begin looking for books about the culture and history of your new host country before you leave home.[1] You may find such books readily available once you reach the host country, but it is not at all unusual for volunteer teachers to discover that the range of these resources available in the host country in English is quite limited, and that many such books present an "ideologically correct" view of the country that you may find unsatisfying.

Another valuable form of predeparture preparation is English teaching experience. Many community organizations and churches run volunteer-taught English classes for immigrants and refugees, and an experience of this kind will help you get your feet wet. Needless to say, teaching an immigrant—or even a small class of immigrants—in an English-speaking country is very different from teaching an English class abroad. Students actually in an English-speaking environment not only have access to a much richer range of practice opportunities but

[1]See Kohls (1984) for a list of information resources covering a large range of countries. The Interact Series of books published by Intercultural Press, Inc. (PO Box 700, Yarmouth, Maine, 04096) also covers many nations to which VTs most frequently go (to date, the series includes Arabia, China, East Europe, Israel, Japan, Mexico, the Philippines, Russia, Spain, and Thailand).

often also have much clearer goals and sense of motivation; after all, their ability to find a job and survive may depend on their ability to learn English. However, even a brief teaching experience is still useful not only for the teaching experience it will provide but also because of the practice it gives you in learning how to communicate with people whose native language is not English. One of the most important skills a language teacher needs is the ability to make instructions understood even by students whose English skills are very minimal, and teaching practice in your home country will help you begin to hone that skill. Another way in which a volunteer teaching experience may potentially be enlightening is that it will put you in contact with people who are undergoing the often difficult adjustments of adapting to life in a new culture. Understanding the culture shock experience may help you as you adjust to life in your host country, and you may need to prepare some of your future students for similar adjustments if they should ever go abroad. (See Chapter 15 for further discussion.)

A final way in which you should prepare is by collecting teaching resources to either mail or take with you. The problem here is that you often have little idea what to prepare for. Of course, your school or sending agency might have sent you a brief description of your new teaching situation, and perhaps even a list of courses that you will teach, but this information is rarely very complete, and it is not at all unusual for teachers to arrive in the host country and discover for any number of reasons that the information they were given bears only minimal resemblance to the actual job. I have known more than one teacher who hauled a heavy collection of literature anthologies across an ocean, expecting to teach a literature course, only to find that (a) the materials were completely inappropriate for the level of the students; (b) the host institution already had the books; (c) the institution couldn't efficiently duplicate material in the books for student use; (d) the course had a required text geared toward a national standardized examination, or (e) the course assignment had been changed. This of course leads to more frustration and bad feeling than would have been the case had the teacher packed the suitcase with pleasure reading and a few favorite snack foods.

Given this reality, the key word in predeparture preparation should be *flexibility;* unless you are absolutely certain that you know what courses you are preparing for it makes more sense to prepare for a variety of eventualities rather than putting all of your eggs in one basket. Appendix C contains specific suggestions as to books you might take with you as a small reference library, but in general the types of materials I would consider highest priority for VTs would include:

1. One or more texts on language teaching: Bring some to help you continue to improve your teaching skills and as a source of teaching ideas.

2. A grammar book: Choose one that you find easy to understand so that you can learn about grammar as you teach it.

3. A writing text: Look for one that contains ideas for assignments and on how to structure a writing class.

4. A book of speaking and listening activities: Bring at least a good list of topic or activity ideas; once you have an idea you can modify it to fit your class.

5. A book of cultural information about your country: Choose one to use for culture lessons.

Also useful are:

6. Pictures of your hometown, family, and country: Use as conversation starters.

7. A tape recorder/short-wave radio with a good microphone: Bring one to allow you access to worldwide English news broadcasts and give you the capacity to tape listening materials. (This may be available in your host country.)

As you choose teaching resources, you need to ask yourself how flexible they are. To be more specific: Can the material be adapted for students at different skill levels? Can it be used for large classes as well as small? Can it be used without involving audiovisual or duplication equipment, which may not be available? If the answer is yes, you have a good candidate.

I have not included any reading texts in my list of suggestions because reading texts generally need to be duplicated in order to be of use and it may be difficult and time-consuming to get materials copied in the host country. There are, of course, countries where duplication is not a problem, but most VTs work in countries where teaching plans that are heavily dependent on duplication facilities are a recipe for frustration for both the VT and the host institution. Relations between more than a few VTs and their schools have been poisoned by running battles over what can be copied on the (expensive but quick) copier and what has to be produced by cheaper, slower, and less effective methods. My suggestion: Rely on locally available reading materials if at all possible. Alternate plan: Mail yourself lots of second-hand paperbacks.[2]

[2]In many countries, there are special low rates for mailing printed matter. For example, in the U.S. books can be mailed quite inexpensively by "M-bag" (mailbag). Check your local post office for current information.

During the first days after arrival in your host country you will probably be busy setting up your new home, becoming familiar with the surroundings, and sleeping off the effects of jetlag. You will also likely be worried about your first day of class, and the temptation will be to focus on preparation for your classes rather than becoming familiar with the situation in general. However, I would argue that no matter how much you want to jump right into preparing those first few lesson plans, it is invaluable to first devote a day or so to getting the lay of the land; time invested in learning about the general situation will rapidly pay off in terms of more effective preparation.

After Arrival, Before the First Day of Class

Asking the Right Questions

Below I suggest a list of questions to which you might try to find the answers as part of your self-orientation process. This questionnaire may seem a bit excessive, but I have decided to be thorough at the risk of seeming a touch fanatic. The questions have been divided into three sections: questions concerning the goals of your courses, those related to methodology and resources, and those concerning your role in the teaching community.

The Questionnaire

Goals

1. **Why are your students learning English?**

Jobs?
Educational advancement?
Going abroad?
Social polish or prestige?
Recreation or social needs?
Required?
Test?

♦ This is one of the most important questions because goals will determine what skills students need most and how hard they are willing to study.

♦ It is especially important to find out what kinds of English tests students need to take, how important they are, and what they are like. In many countries, English tests play a major role in determining which students will be admitted to graduate programs, university, or even middle school.

♦ Not many English programs explicitly advertise themselves as meeting social or recreational needs, but I can assure you that there are such classes and that the social nature of students' goals affects how the class needs to be taught.

2. What are reasonable expectations for the progress of your students in English?

♦ A major consideration is the time and energy students will have to devote to your course, especially to homework. Here you should consider the demands placed on students by other courses, and by other duties and responsibilities your students may have at school, home or elsewhere.

♦ You need to find out what the local norms are for what is considered a reasonable amount of homework; these differ greatly from culture to culture, and school to school.

♦ Investigate how motivated students are to study English— this will have a major impact on progress. Is English required, or did the students choose to study it? Have their previous courses generally been boring? How do they feel about English-speakers? About people from your country? About foreigners in general?

3. What are your students' goals? Your school's?

♦ Your goals don't need to be exactly the same as your students', but if your goals are radically different, you may well meet resistance or at least confusion as to what you are trying to achieve. Knowledge of your students' expectations will help you explain why you choose the goals you do, and will also help you avoid trying to overturn too many applecarts at once.

♦ In addition to finding out what expectations others have, you should try to find out how strong those expectations are. Some schools may give you considerable freedom to set your own agenda; in others, even small deviations from orthodoxy may upset your superiors.

Methods and Resources

1. **What teaching methods is a teacher expected to use?**

◆ As suggested in Chapter 1, the prevailing teaching mode in many host countries is more teacher centered and traditional than the methods you might find more suitable. If there is a discrepancy between your methods and those your students expect, you will need to be careful about explaining why you are doing what you are doing.

2. **What learning strategies and styles are students in the host country accustomed to?**

◆ Your students' study methods might be quite different from methods you are familiar with, and it may well be that you need to teach students how you want them to study.

3. **What kinds of texts, tapes, and other teaching or study materials are available?**

◆ It is very important to find out who has access to such resources and under what conditions; it is not safe to assume that their existence means that you can use them. For example, in countries where resources are scarce, it is much more likely that access is tightly controlled in order to protect them (or protect the person responsible for them).
◆ Check what kinds of materials students can get in local bookstores; this has a significant impact on what kind of self-study is possible.
◆ Resources may not be kept where you would expect to find them, so you need to learn where to look. For example, in China most teaching books for English are kept in the English department resource room rather than in the school library.

4. **What teaching equipment (e.g., blackboards, overhead projectors, slide projectors, videotape players) is available?**

◆ As above, you need to find out not only what exists but also how much access you have. Another Chinese example: Many schools have machines such as videotape players, but they are still precious commodities, so often only the department technician is allowed to actually run the machines. Teaching plans thus have to work around availability of the staff member as well as availability of the machine.

♦ Reliability is another important factor. Lesson plans built around an overhead projector are very vulnerable to blown-out bulbs or electricity stoppages, and you need to know how likely such problems are and how quickly they can be remedied.

5. How readily can materials be duplicated?

How long does it take?
How expensive is it?
How good is the quality?

♦ In the West many teachers have come to take regular use of photocopying machines for granted, and assume that if the host school has a photocopying machine there is no reason not to sail on as usual. This is a very dangerous assumption. The reliance placed on copiers in Western countries is only possible because there are several in each building and a repair shop nearby. Your host school may have fewer machines and much more difficulty getting them serviced; hence, their use may be reserved for a few high priority items rather than for bulk copying of a *Reader's Digest* article for the adult education English class. Bulk copying may be handled via processes more like mimeographing than photocopying.

♦ When you ask your school about copying, the answer may well tend toward the optimistic. Such answers, often intended to be more polite and helpful than precise, can have the unfortunate effect of setting unrealistic expectations. What you need to find out is the normal amount of time, expense, and difficulty involved in getting copies made, and you may need to learn this either from experience or by asking other teachers.

6. What is available in the classroom?

Blackboards? An equivalent?
Movable chairs or desks?
Electrical outlets

♦ Go and look rather than making assumptions.

7. How many students will be in your classes?

Regular students? Auditors?

- In many countries, language classes have many more students than most language classes in the West do. Class size, of course, has a significant impact on methods.
- Try to discover what policies your school has about additional students sitting in on your course. In many host countries, a foreign teacher is a rare attraction, and many people may show up in your class for the sheer thrill of seeing you and hearing a native speaker. You need to know who is supposed to be in your class and who is not; you should also know what to do with guests.

The Role of the Teacher

Most cultures have distinct expectations as to the role of a teacher; even in the relatively easy-going U.S. it is not common to see a teacher wearing shorts in class, and there is at least a moderate social taboo against the dating of students by teachers. Many other cultures have more numerous and stronger expectations, and your failure to conform to these could undermine your effectiveness before you have a chance to prove yourself. If the host community views your behavior as inappropriate, it might diminish not only the degree to which they take you seriously as a teacher, but also affect their respect and affection for you as a person.

My point is not that you must conform to all expectations; in fact, as a foreigner and a guest, you will probably be given more leeway in your adherence to cultural norms than a teacher from the host country would. However, it is still wise to know what cultural expectations exist so that you do not unwittingly eat away at the fund of goodwill usually extended to a guest. Also, as a novice teacher you will probably find that anything you can do to ensure respect and cordiality will help. If wearing nice leather shoes earns you a little more control in the classroom, do it.

1. How much are teachers expected to know?

- In some cultures, teachers are expected to know everything, and you may run into some initial problems if you are straightforward about admitting your ignorance when you don't know the answer to a question. I would encourage you to be relatively open with students rather than trying to bluff, but it would be good to know how much turbulence you can expect while students are adjusting to your style.

2. How are teachers supposed to behave in class?

♦ One major issue is formality. Western VTs are likely to be less formal than teachers in many countries, and although students may find this relaxed style refreshing, they may also find it inappropriate or see it as indicating a lack of professionalism. If your level of formality differs from the host country norm, you may need to explain why you have chosen your particular style. (This might be an opening for an interesting discussion of cultural differences, though you should also point out that level of formality often results from individual choices and styles.)

♦ Find out how students normally address teachers and vice versa. Students may be accustomed to addressing teachers in a rather formal manner (e.g., Mr. _____, Miss _____, or even Teacher _____). If you want to be addressed by your first name, you might also explain the cultural significance for your choice.

♦ In many countries, students are expected to stand when speaking to the teacher in class, or to rise when the teacher enters or leaves a classroom. If you want to change this habit, explain your reasons. Otherwise, enjoy it but try to not let it go to your head.

3. How are teachers expected to dress?

♦ Many VTs are more at home in jeans and T-shirts than suits, but teach in countries where shirts, slacks, skirts, and leather shoes are the norm for teachers. The real potential for trouble comes from the fact that many Westerners—especially those whose previous experience has been almost entirely in student roles—are not very attuned to the impact of dress and how seriously it is taken in many cultures (including professional circles in Western countries).

4. What expectations exist about teacher-student relationships?

♦ Teacher-student friendships are often a big part of the life of VTs. In fact, it may be among students that a VT finds most of his or her new friends in the host country; students are, after all, the group of people a VT is in closest contact with. However, teacher-student friendships can be tricky in any country because it is hard to balance the "friend" role with the power that is an inherent part of the "teacher" role (mainly due to your power to grade), and the issue is even more slippery in a situation where you and your students don't share a common set of cultural norms. In many countries, students would interpret friendship from a teacher as a sign of favoritism, and an invitation to take advantage of that favor. Far be it from me to suggest that you avoid making friends with students; I would, however, advise you to be alert to the possibility of misinterpretation or role conflicts.

♦ A VT in a new country is often lonely, close in age to his or her students, and not necessarily a card-carrying ascetic. Romantic and sexual attraction to students is thus as natural as it is problematic. However, in many cultures romantic relationships between teachers and students are at least frowned upon if not highly taboo, and a good argument can be made that it is questionable ethically to date someone over whom you have the power of the grade. Note also that in many cultures male-female friendships are rare or unknown, and friendly overtures from a teacher to a student of the opposite sex would almost inevitably be interpreted as romantic or sexual interest.

Finding Answers

Having been presented with a formidable list of questions, you might well ask where to go for answers. If you are going abroad through some kind of agency that provides an orientation program, no doubt some of these issues will be addressed before you reach your new school. However, no matter how well such an orientation is done, many things you hear about a new country and culture won't really make much impact on you before you have actually seen and experienced it, especially if you are going through the orientation before departure while concurrently worrying about problems like travel arrangements, packing, and finding out what shots to get. Thus, much of what you hear is likely to go in one ear and out the other, or be half-understood at best.

Orientation meetings given in the host country by your school provide another useful opportunity to gather information. However, the person who serves as your informant will also often be acting as a host, and in most cultures dragging the dirty laundry out is not a normal part of welcoming a guest. The picture that you get of the teaching situation is often thus biased toward the optimistic and you will need to check what you learn against other sources. Another problem is that your host may not know exactly what kinds of information a foreigner needs. In any culture there are many unwritten rules and practices that are taken for granted, and it is not unusual for a host national to assume that these rules and practices are known and followed by all. For example, a host national may assume you know it is improper to teach in sandals that have no ankle strap but okay to teach in those that do, or that teachers should hand out very few grades above 90% (both lessons I learned the hard way in southern China). It is therefore important that you take an active role in the orientation process by being ready to ask the right questions in order to learn what you need to know, rather than relying too heavily on the ability of others to guess what you need to know.

Veteran foreign teachers can also be an invaluable source of information, but their advice needs to be taken with a certain amount of caution. Not all expatriates adapt well to life in their host country, and when seeking advice you need to be alert for bias. Many veterans will be helpful and insightful, but there will be others whose primary interest in orienting you is the opportunity it provides them to get back at the host country. In judging how seriously to take a veteran's evaluation, be careful of someone who is consistently negative, has not spent much more time in the host country than you have, or who shows little evidence of successful cultural adaptation. On the other hand, those whose evaluations are objective and fair, have made progress in understanding the host culture, and who have established a good working relationship with their hosts may well be your best sources of insight.

There are other people who should be part of your orientation process, but who often aren't unless you seek them out. The support staff at your institution (e.g., secretaries, librarians) are very helpful people to know, and dropping by to ask them a few questions can provide a good excuse for you to meet them under nice circumstances rather than only after a problem has arisen. In most institutions the office staff are wonderful sources of information, and their goodwill is vital to your well-being, so take advantage of your early days to make the best impression possible. Also, although students are not usually included in orientations, they are often among your best and most important sources of information. If there is an opportunity to speak with students before your first day of class, you can learn more about their English learning experiences and get a better idea of the level of their communication skills. After the semester begins, you can continue to learn much from them both in class and outside. In fact, by bringing real questions into the classroom, you provide students with an opportunity to use their English skills for a genuine communicative purpose.

Professionalism in English teaching does not necessarily mean having the whole semester's plan laid out in detail before the first day of class. In fact, I generally find that it is wise to leave a fair degree of flexibility in your plans until you have actually met with your students; it is often only after you have had some contact with your students that you can make good decisions about specific goals and methods.

Consequently, your investigation of your English teaching situation should not end with the first day of class; in fact, the first few class periods are an important part of your information-gathering process. Of course it is a good idea to spend time during the first classes getting to know your students' names, where they are from, and so forth. But it is equally important that you get a sense of their English skill levels, what kinds of attitudes they have toward English study, and how easy they will be to work with. To this end it is generally helpful to spend a portion of the first few class periods informally assessing your students. This chapter will conclude with a brief discussion of activities for your first few days of class.

The First Days of Class

Introductions

Traditionally the first day of a VT English class consists of each student standing up, announcing his or her name, presenting a bare-bones biography, and sitting back down. Although not a complete waste of time, this activity is boring in classes where students already know each other, and often not much more interesting even when they don't because students spend most of the class period waiting for others to stumble through awkward little speeches. This activity can be improved in a number of ways:

1 In classes where students know each other, ask students to mention something a little unusual in addition to their names. For example, ask them their favorite food, favorite time of year, or another personal preference which other students in the class might find new, interesting, or amusing. This not only makes the introductions a little more memorable and fun, but also increases the chance that students will listen to each other.

2 In classes where students don't know each other, have students interview each other and then introduce their partners. This livens

the class up by giving students opportunities to talk, and gives them a chance to meet at least one other person in the class. As in #1 above, you might suggest one or two interesting or amusing questions to add to the standard biographical inquiries.

3 If your primary goal is to gather basic information about your students, have them write it down on a card rather than spending a class hour presenting the information orally. Such cards are very useful for reviewing students' names and give you a written database about each student which often comes in handy later in the semester. When possible, having students give you pictures is also a good way to help you match student names and faces. (By taking the pictures yourself, you can add a festive touch to your class.)

Listening Comprehension Exercises

It is very useful to quickly find out how well students understand what you say because you need to know whether they will understand explanations and classroom instructions. A simple way to do this quickly is to ask students to take notes as you orally present a short introduction of yourself or tell a brief story. After the presentation, ask them to write as detailed a summary of what you said as possible. As a formal test this exercise is problematic because it relies on both listening comprehension and writing skills, but if the exercise is used as a quick probe, its dual listening-writing nature actually becomes an advantage, allowing you to quickly get a rough sense of their listening, writing, grammar, and vocabulary skills.

Writing Exercises

One of the main advantages of a writing exercise is that, in addition to giving you an idea of students' writing skills, it is an opportunity for you to learn other kinds of information. Rather than having students write about "My Summer Vacation," ask them to write about something related to English learning or their education in general. Some preliminary topic ideas to get you started:

Why I Am Taking This Course (if they had a choice)
How I Learned English
My Best (Past) English Teacher
Why English Study Is/Is Not Useful
My Experience With Foreigners (Americans, Canadians, etc.)
How (Americans, British, etc.) Are Different From Us

Small Groups

Small-group and pair work are an important part of oral English lessons, so it is usually a good idea to try these approaches out in order to see how well students take to them. It may be that students function very well in groups or pairs; it may also be that they have never done this before and feel very awkward about it. One way to try these methods out is to break students into pairs or groups of three or four, give them a topic (such as one of those suggested above for writing), and ask each group to discuss the question and write down a response. The response could then be presented orally by a group leader, or you could circulate among the groups and see what they have written. An exercise like this helps you quickly discover how willing students are to work together in pairs or groups, allows you to hear them speaking in a relatively low-pressure setting, and again may produce some interesting insights about their approach to language learning.

Individual Interviews

Individual interviews allow you a chance to not only get a very clear sense of students' oral skills but also learn more about the students and begin to establish some individual rapport. Thus, interviewing deserves serious consideration as an activity for the first week or so of class. There are, of course, also some serious problems to consider. One is that students may be absolutely petrified at the idea of confronting the teacher—a foreigner to boot—in a one-to-one setting, and you may learn less about how well they speak than about the grit and determination with which they would face a firing squad. Obviously, anything you can do to put students at ease will help. Suggestions include:

◆ Starting with light conversation

◆ Opening with very easy questions

◆ Meeting in relatively informal surroundings, and perhaps even offering tea or cookies (though these well-intended attempts to create an informal atmosphere may be more confusing than reassuring in some cultures).

The other problem with individual interviews is that they are very time-consuming. In order to have anything resembling a conversation, you need to spend at least 5-10 minutes per interview. Note that you may need to take a minute or two after each interview to make notes. You can interview more students in a limited time by interviewing in pairs or groups, and if your purpose is primarily to establish rapport and get a sense of the general skill level of the class, this may be a viable alternative. (See Chapter 8 for further discussion of interview technique.)

Conclusion

The most important message of this chapter is that you don't need to finalize your class preparations before getting on the plane, or even before the first day of class. Remember that you are not only embarking on a new kind of job; you are also entering a new country and culture about which there is much you don't know. Preparation is certainly desirable, but it is vitally important that you first learn as much as you can about what you are preparing for. As suggested above, it may well be only during the first days of class that the shape of the task before you finally becomes clear. Take time to scout out the lay of the land; time invested in investigation of the situation will pay rich dividends in terms of more effective preparation.

3

Planning Your Course

- ◆ A course needs to have a long-term plan because plans made on a day-to-day basis can leave students feeling that a course lacks direction.

- ◆ The key elements of a course plan are goals, materials, methods, and evaluation measures.

- ◆ Students must learn to make and take responsibility for their own language learning plans. Hence, one of the goals of a course should be to help students learn to do this.

When it comes to planning courses there are two common traps into which English teachers fall. One of these is planning the course one day or lesson at a time, the "I wonder what will work in class tomorrow?" syndrome. This approach often arises from a well-intended desire to keep students interested, and often results in the teacher daily picking through the course textbook or other materials to find something that will work—that is, something students will respond well to. This approach to lesson planning is not entirely without merit, its primary virtue being that it may result in quite a few enjoyable lessons, but it can also be unsatisfying if it leaves students with little sense of direction and progress.

The other trap lies in simply sticking to the book. While most VTs are disinclined toward such a lockstep approach, it is still possible to be drawn into this because VTs often teach in situations where texts and programs have already been decided, and the easiest way to adapt to a preexisting program and feel secure in an unfamiliar environment is to go along with the program. Again, this approach has its strong points, and is especially important in situations where students will face a standardized examination based on standardized textbooks. However, simply moving through a text drill-by-drill tends to be boring, and it trains teachers and students to be passive recipients of direction rather than active creators of their own plans.[1]

In this chapter, I will suggest two major points to consider in your course planning. First, you should have a plan that gives direction and coherence to your course. This is important not only because it will probably improve your teaching, but also because of the sense of direction and confidence it gives students. Of course, your initial course plans will probably be rather general because you are most likely not yet in a position to lay out your daily lesson plans for a whole semester. Even for experienced teachers real life does not work out so neatly, and even for experienced teachers planning is never really completed. However, having at least an initial set of goals and plans for materials, methods and evaluation measures will go a long way toward ensuring that both you and your students know where you are going.

Second, one of your goals in any course should be to lead students toward taking responsibility for planning their own language study. By learning to actively consider the question of their goals and methods, students are more likely to focus their study efforts in a way that will suit their styles, take advantage of their strengths, compensate for their weaknesses, and meet their personal needs. Students who study in this way will probably not only do better in their coursework, but also be better prepared to continue their study once their days in English classes end.

[1]See Abbot and Wingard (1981) and Bowen et al. (1985) for further discussion of these two traps.

If you have done your homework from Chapter 2, by now you should know something about your students' needs, skill levels, study habits, and expectations. You should also have some idea of what limitations—materials, facilities, equipment, and institutional guidelines and expectations—you will have to work within. Below we will discuss the basic elements of a course plan: course goals, materials, and methods. (Another important aspect of course planning—the question of evaluation and grading—is considered in Chapter 4.)

Goals

Goal setting will vary considerably according to situation. Consider the following examples:

CASE 1:
A general English course for high school seniors who later in the year will face a nationwide standardized examination which determines whether they will have the opportunity for further education.

Here, given the importance of the upcoming examination, you have little freedom in setting goals. Obviously, the primary goal is to help students do as well as possible on the examination, so your teaching should be tailored to the demands of the exam. A secondary goal would be to enhance students' interest in English so that some of them may choose to continue studying English even after they have completed the exam.

CASE 2:
A course for a group of middle-aged scholars who are preparing to go abroad for research work in a Western country. The class consists mostly of people who have considerable experience reading and translating English, but very marginal speaking and listening skills.

This group needs a heavy diet of listening practice, especially practice understanding the kinds of English they might hear in daily life. Lack of listening comprehension skills would effectively isolate these people from even the simplest social contact—far more so than will inability to speak—so this should be the overriding concern. A secondary goal should be helping them improve their speaking skills so that they can cope with survival needs and simple social situations. Finally, survival cultural knowledge would be beneficial.

CASE 3:
A general English course in a college where all 1st-year college students are required to study 1 year of English. They have previously had 2 years of high school English and can read simple texts and handle simple conversation. You are required to use the as-

signed text, but the only tests students need to take
are those you design.

In this situation, you have considerable freedom of action. The
main problem is that because your students are required to take the
course, you cannot assume that they have any other reason for being
there. The first goal might therefore be to enhance their interest in
English study. A second important goal is getting students started
designing and carrying out their own study programs; in 1 year there
is a limit to how high a skill level they are likely to reach, and it is
probable that unless they become genuinely interested in English study
their efforts to learn English will grind to a halt at the end of your
course, leaving them little to show for their effort. As to what English
skills to emphasize, you might decide on the basis of what skills seem
to interest them or what skills offer the most promise of being useful
in the future. However, it would be wise to concentrate students' efforts
to some degree rather than simply doing a little bit of everything; if
students can see and feel progress in one skill area, they will be more
likely to be encouraged to continue working on English after the
course ends.

In some cases you will know why students are learning English
and what they will eventually do with it; goals can then be set based
on the types of skills and knowledge which will best serve students in
their later use of English. Unfortunately, in other situations the needs
of students will be neither clear nor uniform. Students in the same
class, especially voluntary adult classes, may have utterly different
needs or goals; one student may be in your course because she needs
to improve her grammar for writing business letters, while the next
one wants to improve his oral fluency for striking up conversations
with tourists. School settings may also be problematic because few or
any of the students have any clear reason for studying English other
than the fact that it is required.[2] Thus it is often difficult to tailor the
goals of an English course specifically to students' future needs.

As should be clear from the examples above, goal setting needs
to take place within a specific context; different situations call for very
different kinds of goals. Discussion below will thus only address a few
of the main issues involved in goal setting. (Goals for the various
language skills will be dealt with in Chapters 7 through 13. See also
Appendix A: The Goals Menu.)

Healthy Balance of Skills

In situations where it is not possible to tailor instruction to a
particular set of needs, it is generally best to help students develop a

[2]Abbott and Wingard (1981) have a wonderful acronym for this type of situation:
TENOR = Teaching of English for No Obvious Reason (p. 12).

balanced, general set of English skills and knowledge. In ideal situations it is no doubt desirable to develop all of the language skills to a high level, but time limitations often demand that you make choices as to what to stress in your classes and that students make choices as to what skills to give the highest priority to. The following observations may be useful as you think through the problem of prioritizing goals:

1 Listening over speaking. Usually it is best if students' listening skills are somewhat more advanced than their speaking skills. Even native speakers of a language can generally understand more than they can say, and there are many situations (watching TV, listening to the radio, listening to lectures, etc.) which depend entirely on listening skills.[3]

2 Reading over writing. Students are far more likely to need to read than to write, if only because it is through reading that students gain so much of their vocabulary in EFL settings. Again, even native speakers can generally read better than they can write, and read more often than they write.

3 Communication over accuracy. In most situations, communication is more important than accuracy. This generalization needs to be qualified because there are situations where accuracy is very important (tests, formal writing). However, in general an English learner's primary need is to understand and be understood.

4 Vocabulary over grammar. For listening and reading, it is more important to have an extensive vocabulary than to have a thorough knowledge of English grammar.[4]

Given these general features of a good balance, one way to decide where to focus your efforts is to assess your students' levels and then place special emphasis on those areas where improvement is necessary in order to bring students up to a good balance.

Basic Skills and Knowledge

A second all-purpose suggestion is that it is often best to emphasize fundamental knowledge and skills rather than situation-specific knowledge or skills, for example, stressing general communication skills more than the fine points of job interviews, emphasizing grammat-

---

[3]Scarcella and Oxford (1992) claim: "Listening in almost any setting is the most frequently used language skill" (p. 139). This statement may be true more for English learners in a foreign country—where learners may read more than they listen—than for those in an English-speaking country, but the emphasis on the importance of listening skills is still well taken.

[4]See Lewis (1993) for development of this argument.

ical accuracy in writing more than the art of the memo, or building reading speed more than skills in literary criticism. One obvious problem with situation-specific skills is that they are of limited value to students who never find themselves in the right situation. Another problem is that the speed of change in the modern world means that a situation for which you prepare your students may no longer exist by the time they finish your course. I am reminded of a class of Chinese university students who were being prepared to work in trade companies. Because of their future job needs, the department wanted me to teach the class telex writing (a request I ignored mainly because I didn't know how to write telexes). Despite the apparently uniform job needs of these students, when I interviewed them a year after graduation I found that most never needed to write telexes, and since that time telexes have been largely replaced by the fax machine.

Content and Skill Goals

A third bit of generic advice is that in a course it is often best to have a mix of skill goals (listening, speaking, reading, writing) and content goals (vocabulary, grammar, cultural information). Some students are better at memorizing, others at communication, and others at grammatical accuracy, so by including both skill and content goals you give students with different strengths an opportunity to demonstrate their ability, thus increasing the chances that there will be some aspect of your course in which they can shine.

VTs often emphasize language practice in their courses, thus providing a skill focus that is a useful corrective in programs that tend to emphasize mastery of content, but it is probably wise to also include some content goals even in your course. Students who are accustomed to studying grammar rules and memorizing vocabulary may find your course frustrating or demoralizing if you suddenly change the rules of the game by only focusing only on language skills. It thus makes good sense—both educationally and politically—to have a content mastery aspect to your course in order to increase the chances that there will be some portion of your course in which they will feel comfortable.

Attention to Affective Factors

It may be that the most important reason for having explicitly stated goals is that it can make students feel better about their language study, thereby improving the chances that they will learn willingly and be able to sustain that willingness over the long haul. To this end, it is helpful to have both general long-term goals and specific short-term goals.

General long-term goals enhance student morale by giving a sense of direction and vision; goals such as improved listening comprehension or increased reading speed offer the promise of a reward worth striving for. Without a sense of long-term goals it is too easy for class exercises to seem to be an unrelated series of activities that are ends in themselves or that only serve to prepare students for the final test. Of course, in order for long-term goals to have a beneficial effect on student morale, it is necessary that students be made aware of the goals—not only once at the beginning of the term, but on a regular basis. It is easy for teachers to overestimate the sense of vision and purpose that students have in language learning, particularly if they are taking a required language course, and it is also easy to overestimate how well students will remember a lecture on goals given on the first day of class. To many students, a speech given on Day 1 of class is a blur of half-understood language, often listened to while wishing that class would end soon. It may thus be desirable to remind students of why they are doing what they are doing as a part of almost every class. (My rule of thumb is that once students start chanting my little "We are doing this because. . ." speech along with me, they have probably internalized it.)

However, as Stevick (1988) suggests, long-term goals alone are not enough. Long-term goals "are the hoped-for banquet at the end of a long hike. Your hikers also need snacks and water to sustain them along the path" (p. 128). Thus, underneath the broad goals it is also important to have some goals that are specific and short-term, goals toward which students can make observable progress in the duration of your course. For example, if the broad goal of a course is improvement of listening comprehension, more specific goals might include learning to understand the most common reduced forms of English words (*want to* = wanna, *don't you* = dontcha, and so forth), or memorizing the names of the world's major countries and cities as an aid to understanding radio news in English. These latter goals are more finite than the broad goal of improving listening comprehension, and it is entirely possible that students can achieve them within a semester course, giving students the satisfaction of being able to point to a task successfully completed.

Finally, enhancing students' interest in English study should in and of itself be a major goal. It is a natural tendency among English teachers to assume that students should be motivated to study English, so we may need to remind ourselves that students often have no personal reason for being in our English classes; they may be there purely because the course is a required part of a curriculum. In these cases it is natural for students to only be interested in what will get them past the test, and you cannot assume that their interest will go beyond such pragmatic concerns. If you want them to become genuinely interested in English study—as they must if they are to go on and eventually master the language—you will need to make this a goal to work toward rather than an assumption to work from.

Materials: The Book

Unlike goals, the problem with materials is usually not one of overly abundant choice. You may be fortunate enough to find a well-stocked library in your host school, but more often the issue of materials boils down to how you will deal with the assigned course text. In an ideal world, this would be a new book with a bright catchy cover, sturdy glossy pages, and loads of exciting readings, activities, and other goodies. However, you are less likely to be disappointed if you expect a book that is well used, possibly decorated with notes from previous users (though maybe in a language you can't read). The book may either be one written and produced in the host country, or an old book from the U.S. or Britain—perhaps some kind of poorly done reproduction. In either case, the cover is probably done in two tones instead of color, and the pages may be slightly yellowed. On first glance the contents may not seem particularly inspiring, and this impression may not change for the better even when you study the textbook more carefully. In short, your instinctive response may well be "I can't work with this!" The question you then face is what to do with the book.

Again, if you have done your investigative homework well you should have a clear idea of how much freedom you have to stray from the material presented in the book. If the book is part of a prescribed curriculum—especially one leading to standardized tests—you are under an obligation to teach the course material as best you can whether you like the materials or not. Even if there is no such examination, you may still be more or less forced to stick closely to the textbook if the students or your host institution feels strongly about the issue. However, what should you do if you find that you do have the freedom to either retain or abandon the book?

Clearly, there is no single correct answer to this question: a great deal depends on how bad the book is or how much you dislike it. However, I would argue that on the whole it is best to try to make use of the course textbook rather than abandoning it, perhaps supplementing where necessary. My reasons are as follows:

1 Having a course text saves time in lesson preparation. The freedom to throw away the book and make up your own lessons is exhilarating at first when you are fresh and have a lot of good ideas. However, as the semester wears on you may find your creativity wearing out, and then cooking up each day's lesson from scratch can become a real burden.

2 The book provides continuity to the course and helps prevent it from degenerating into a series of entertaining but unrelated activities.

3 Having a book makes it easier for students to review. The alternatives are for you to invest considerable time in producing handouts, or for students to spend class time copying material from the board.

4 Use of the textbook can help students feel better about their English study. Lewis (1993) notes: "Teachers who like to teach without a coursebook sometimes forget that students may need the reassurance of a programme, and the feeling of 'getting somewhere'. Working through a coursebook—perhaps omitting bits, and almost certainly supplementing it—is almost always better than working entirely without a coursebook" (p. 182).

One final issue to consider is the age-old problem of finding a better textbook. Many teachers fully agree that there are significant advantages in having a text—they simply don't like the one that is offered and want to find a better one to replace it. When this is possible, it is obviously the best solution to the problem of a bad textbook. However, this alternative is often less realistic than VTs think. Textbooks brought in from outside the host country are often prohibitively expensive and involve considerable administrative hassle. They may also not be well designed for your teaching situation; for example, most English books produced in the U.S. are designed for students studying English in the U.S., and often make assumptions about the background and needs of students which would be inappropriate in an EFL setting.

Textbooks found in the host country are generally a more realistic option, but VTs are often unpleasantly surprised to discover that their administration is not very enthusiastic about helping procure a new textbook for a course. The problem is frequently one of perspective. The VT is virtually always a short-term person in the department, and for the year or so that the VT spends in the host country the advantages of having a somewhat better textbook—or a textbook that is better suited to his or her personal tastes—are significant. To a long-term administrative staff, getting a new textbook every time a new VT arrives at the school is simply a headache, and often produces no improvement in teaching that is visible from the school office. (I am reminded of a campaign in the Taipei YMCA to get our textbooks changed. The supervisor listened patiently to our complaints, then pointed to a shelf loaded with new copies of the text in question and told us that the book we wanted to get rid of was the one last year's VTs had made them buy.)

Methods

Given the extensive attention specific teaching methods will receive in Chapters 7 through 13, here we will make short shrift of the issue with two brief observations.

The first is a basic rule of thumb: The best way to develop a skill is to practice it, and the more the practice method resembles the actual application of the skill, the better. Simply put, the best way to learn to speak is to practice speaking; the best way to learn to read is to practice reading.[5] This might seem obvious, but in many cases students (and even teachers) simply use methods passed on to them from an earlier generation of students and teachers. The result is that the methods do not always fit the goals. In China, for example, one practice method commonly used by students to develop their speaking skills is getting up early in the morning to spend half an hour or so reading lessons from their textbook aloud. This practice method is not inherently bad—it provides useful review of material previously studied—but reading aloud from a book is a very different process from organizing one's own ideas into sentences, so reading aloud is at best a very incomplete form of speaking practice. Problems created by inappropriate practice strategies can be avoided if students learn to think carefully about what is involved in the skill they wish to develop and then practice in ways that faithfully replicate that skill.

A second observation is that while methods should be chosen on the basis of pedagogical soundness, you also need to consider the question of what methods will be acceptable to your students. It is entirely possible that methods which are educationally sound would not work in your class because students would find them too uncomfortable, too unfamiliar, too dubious, or simply too weird. In EFL settings you need to pay particular attention to this problem because the students in a class will share a great number of common beliefs and customs concerning language study, and you may run into united resistance if your proposed methods conflict with your students' ideas too much. The question you need to ask yourself is: To what extent am I willing to invest time and effort in persuading students to reconfigure their approaches to language learning? It is impossible to predict how strongly a group of students will resist new and different methods for language learning—they may even be delighted to try a new approach. However, in general the more your methods differ from those students are used to, the more time you will need to spend explaining and selling the methods. Failure to do adequate PR work may result in increasing resistance and decreased cooperation from the class, so it is best when you are planning your course to take a good look at your reserves of patience and only take a radically innovative approach if you are also willing—if necessary—to invest time and effort in selling your program.

Student-Designed Plans: The Breakthrough Approach

As indicated at the beginning of the chapter, your ultimate goal is not only to plan a good course for your students; it is also to help them learn how to effectively plan their own language learning. Students who only obediently do what the teacher tells them to will not be very well prepared for the day when they are on their own. While they are in formal language courses, they need to begin developing the habit of designing and carrying out their own language learning

[5]There is some debate on this point within the language teaching profession. For example, Nunan (1989) points out that both *real-world* tasks (practice activities that resemble actual use) and *pedagogic* tasks (activities like grammar drills that

plans because this is what they will need to be able to do when they leave formal language programs.

Students usually have only a limited amount of spare time to devote to language study. The best kind of study program is not an overly ambitious one with vague (and unreachable) goals, but a program that is realistic within the amount of time and energy available. Below I suggest an approach designed for situations where time and opportunity to practice are limited, and that I have found in my own experience to be workable.

As was argued in Chapter 1, one of the main reasons that students fail to learn English—or any foreign language—is that they become discouraged and give up. Brown (1991) points out that "Failure among adult second-language learners is frequently due to our perverse knack for letting ourselves be overwhelmed by the enormity of the task that lies before us" (p. 32). In my experience, surrender is especially likely when learners:

1 Do not feel that they are making progress. This is very common when learners have little time for language study, and is even worse when this limited time is not focused. Unrealistic expectations also exacerbate the problem.

2 Have no chance to use their language skills. As noted in Chapter 1, this may result from an absence of opportunities to use English in the host country, or the fact that learners' skills are still too limited to allow them to take advantage of such opportunities as exist.

3 Cannot do anything enjoyable with their language skills. As much as we wish it were otherwise, language study is often more work than fun. For most people it only begins to be more enjoyable once they can do something that they like to do anyway using the language.

Learners are therefore more likely to stay with a study program if it is focused narrowly enough that it allows them to see progress, and if the program as rapidly as possible allows them to develop one or more skills to the point that the learners can do something useful or enjoyable with those skills. Notice that using these guidelines, choosing a program of study is a very individual matter—what a learner finds useful or enjoyable depends on the learner's personal tastes and interests, and on the situation in which the learner lives. There is no universal right goal or right method.

The assumption on which the approach I suggest is based is that for the use of most language skills there is a breakthrough point, that is, a point at which the learner can actually begin to use the skill

isolate one specific aspect of a skill) can be useful. I emphasize real-world tasks in part because the skills and inclinations of VTs are generally more suited to realistic communicative tasks than to pedagogic ones.

for a useful or rewarding purpose.[6] For example, in the development of conversation skills this might be the point at which one learner can strike up and sustain conversations with Western tourists without being so embarrassed that she beats a quick retreat. For a second learner, the breakthrough might occur when she can understand English novels well enough to find reading more fun than work. For a third, it could be the point at which his listening skills are good enough that his monolingual boss begins using him to translate when foreign guests come to the office.

Of course, the breakthrough point in all of these cases may not be a particular instant in time; it may be a longer process. But there is a distinct and important change that happens to language learners once they can begin to use their language skills, either for personal reward or practical benefit, and once this point is reached the learner's continued language learning takes on more momentum because the learner can use the language in contexts other than language study. Referring again to the examples above, the conversation skills of Learner 1 will continue to improve as she enjoys chatting with tourists, the reading skills of Learner 2 will get better as she reads for pleasure, and Learner 3's listening skills will be further honed as he continues to translate. From this point on, the continued use and improvement of the skill takes on a life of its own.

A student who wishes to work toward a breakthrough needs to choose a goal carefully. The first attribute of a good goal is that it be narrow and specific. For example, "learning to understand radio news" is a better goal than "improving listening." In this case, focusing on a particular kind of listening allows the learner to more rapidly become familiar with the unique features of that particular kind of language use (e.g., the high frequency of place names). For reading, another way to narrow a focus is by topic or author, focusing for example on the works of a particular author so as to more rapidly become accustomed to his or her style. This narrower focus allows more rapid improvement, which in turn encourages the learner to continue.

A second thing to consider in choosing a goal is whether or not there is opportunity to use the target skill in the learner's particular environment. A learner in an area where there are virtually never any English-speakers but where there are English radio news broadcasts might choose to focus first on comprehension of the radio news; a learner in an area where there are no English newspapers but novels can be had occasionally might choose to focus on the latter; and a learner working in a company where English-speaking foreigners frequently visit might well choose to focus on conversation. This is

[6]This is very similar to the notion of a threshold level proposed by van Ek (1987).

simply a commonsense way of ensuring that once the skill is mastered it can be used.

Finally, a learner should consider his or her own personality and desires. Learners who prefer detective stories to great fiction in their own language would be well advised to read Agatha Christie rather than Charles Dickens; learners who prefer chatting to reading might be wiser to focus on conversation; and learners who are avid followers of world events should probably work toward ability to read newspapers or listen to radio news. This way the learner's natural interests and desires will work for the language learning process rather than against it. This might also seem to be common sense, but this rule is regularly violated. Over years of language study, students have often internalized the idea that enjoyment is simply not a part of language study, and even after leaving formal programs they spend hours reviewing grammar books or trying to read classic books in which they have no interest. In classes where I have given students a choice of books to read, I am always impressed at how guilty they seem to be if they choose a popular novel rather than a literary masterpiece— and at how often the students who choose the masterpieces fail to finish reading them. (To be fair, I should also note that I have also had students who took to Victorian classics like a starved wolf to meat.)

To apply this approach in a language course, ask your students to settle on a limited personal goal and study plan that they can carry out concurrently with your course. To provide accountability, have students tell you—either in writing or orally—what goal they have chosen, why, and how they plan to work toward it. Having students set their own goals can be a little difficult because many students are unaccustomed to the notion that they should set goals for themselves, and the goals they set initially may be very vague and not very carefully considered. It is therefore often necessary to spend time with students going over their proposed goals, helping them narrow those goals and think more carefully about why they were chosen. If you have the time and energy, you might even choose to monitor their progress by checking in occasionally, or even include fulfillment of their plan as part of the evaluation of the course. Although your becoming too involved in students' plans may defeat the whole purpose of the exercise, providing some kind of accountability might also be necessary lest students get the idea that you really aren't serious.

Toward the end of your course, a good way to increase the chances that students will follow through with their own study program after leaving your course is to talk with them about how to set up and carry out their own future study plans. Again, you might even have them write down a plan which you can then go over with them.

In my experience as a language learner and teacher, once a learner has reached a breakthrough in one area, the reinforcement and encouragement of that success is likely to motivate the learner to continue working toward other successes in English—and perhaps even toward study of other languages. The time and effort you spend working with students on this is very well invested because you are making a contribution that goes far beyond what you might teach them about English in a few hours—you are giving them a fighting chance to find a path of language study that might continue to work for them long after your class ends.

4 Evaluation, Grading, and Backwash

♦ Evaluation is valuable not only for determining students' skill levels, but also as a way of holding them accountable and encouraging them to keep working.

♦ *Backwash* is the impact that your evaluation methods have on what and how students study, and is a very important factor to consider when deciding how to evaluate.

♦ In your host country you will need to learn the local language and culture of grading; otherwise, your grades may not communicate what they are intended to.

♦ When grading a group of students, it is often necessary to strike a balance between *criterion-referenced scoring* (measuring student progress against an objective scale) and *norm-referenced scoring* (comparing students' performance to that of their peers). The former is more fair, but can be more difficult to do well. The latter is more convenient and also often more readily understood, but is less fair.

Discussion of evaluation and grading at this point may seem somewhat premature; after all, you are probably still thinking primarily about what will happen during the first few weeks of your course. However, your evaluation methods have tremendous power to positively or negatively affect the ways in which students will study, and you need to make good use of this impact in order to encourage students to study and practice in productive ways. You need to at least begin thinking about evaluation when you are planning your course rather than waiting until the middle or end of the semester and then wondering how you can put together a midterm or final exam. Failure to carefully consider your methods of evaluation means running the risk of having the intentions of your course completely subverted.

First, a note on terminology. *Evaluation* may seem to be an overly technical euphemism for *testing*. However, they are not quite the same thing. What we will consider here is broader than testing alone, and consists of graded homework assignments, notes made of classroom participation, and compositions written for a portfolio just as much as it consists of final examinations. In short, evaluation consists of any way in which you measure and judge students' knowledge or skills.

Tests and other evaluative measures come in a variety of colors; tests alone can be broken down into four or more major categories.[1] However, the underlying purposes of almost all classroom evaluation fall into two major categories:

1. Diagnostic: One reason to evaluate is to determine how well students are doing in their studies. This information is useful to students in assessing how much progress they are making and where they are weak and strong. It also helps the teacher determine how effective a course is in facilitating student learning. We should also note that the scores and grades that result from testing are often intended as much for others—school authorities, for example—as for students.

2. Motivational: The most obvious motivational effect evaluation has on students is that it gives them an incentive to study harder, but this is not the only reason evaluation can have a positive impact on student motivation. Madsen (1983) points out that evaluation can also give students a sense of accomplishment by helping them see what they have learned, and this can translate into more positive attitudes toward study.

[1]See Hughes (1989) and Madsen (1983) for further discussion.

Discussion of specific methods for evaluating English skills will come in the following chapters devoted to those skills. The purpose of this chapter is to raise general issues involved in evaluation and grading so that you can begin thinking about how you will deal with this aspect of your courses.

What Is *Backwash*?

The Backwash Effect

A critically important issue to consider when planning evaluation methods for a course is something called the *backwash effect,* that is, the effect of your evaluation methods on students' study and practice methods. Put simply, the idea is that students tend to do what they are rewarded for, and not to do what they are not rewarded for. Thus, for example, if your tests and quizzes frequently include a listening comprehension section, students are likely to work on their listening. In contrast, if you only evaluate a course with written tests, students are not likely to invest much time in developing speaking skills, no matter how important you say oral practice is. The backwash effect is most significant in situations where grades are very important to students, but even when grades aren't important a backwash effect can still occur because students, quite understandably, assume that the evaluation system reflects the teacher's sense of priorities.

The backwash effect can have either a positive or negative affect on learning, depending on how closely the evaluation methods reflect the skill students are supposed to develop. For example, if the goal is for students to develop the ability to express their ideas in English, but their exercises are graded primarily on grammatical accuracy, the backwash effect will pull them away from the goal; in contrast, grading on effectiveness of communication will push them toward the goal. Well designed evaluation methods ensure that the best scores go to those students who have studied and practiced in the desired manner, and will thus encourage students to use good study methods. Backwash becomes a problem only when students are forced to choose between study approaches that develop usable language skills and those that prepare them for a test.

Perhaps surprisingly, teachers sometimes don't give adequate attention to the backwash effect because of failure to appreciate the importance of grades to students. Teachers hand out grades almost daily, and can't possibly treat the assigning of every individual grade as a momentous event; students, of course, tend to feel the consequences of grades more keenly. It may be good from time to time to remind ourselves that the power grades often have over students is not an illusion of students' imaginations. In many nations, opportunity for academic advancement is limited, and examination scores and grades frequently determine who goes on and who does not. Scores and grades may also determine job placement, scholarship allotments, and less tangible rewards such as respect and pride. Students cannot be expected to ignore these realities, and can thus hardly be faulted for gearing their study to result in the best grades possible.

Ensuring Positive Backwash

Below are a number of suggestions as to how to ensure that the backwash from your evaluation measures is positive:[2]

1 Be sure to test the skills you want students to develop, even if testing these skills is not always easy. This advice might seem self-evident, but in practice this rule is often violated. As Hughes (1989) notes: "Too often the content of tests is determined by what is *easy* to test rather than what is *important* to test" (p. 32). For example, the difficulty of providing oral interviews for large numbers of students means that interviews are not included in standardized tests such as the TOEFL exam, and the result is that oral proficiency receives minimal attention from students preparing for such exams. The bottom line is that if you want students to practice a skill, you need to include it somehow in evaluation.

2 Use direct testing measures as much as possible. A *direct measure* is one that requires students to do more or less what they would need to do in real life. For example, an interview is a direct measure because it requires students to engage in real conversation. An *indirect measure,* in contrast, assesses only one discrete portion of a skill. For example, a test in which students only pronounce words in isolation would be an indirect measure.[3] The importance of this distinction is that the more direct an evaluation measure is, the more likely it is to have a positive backwash effect on students. Direct measures require students to practice skills in a way which is similar to the way in which the skills would actually be used; indirect measures inevitably push students toward practicing discrete-point skills which in real life are virtually never used in isolation (how often do we fill in blanks with correct verb tenses?). This is not to say that all indirect testing is bad. Properly used, it provides a rapid way to check on and encourage important aspects of language learning such as pronunciation and vocabulary acquisition. However, it is important that evaluation for a course not rely on indirect measures alone, and it is generally best if direct measures carry more weight in determining grades. (For this

[2]See also Hughes (1989, pp. 44-47).

[3]This distinction is similar to that between integrative and discrete-point testing. See Bowen et al. (1985) for discussion.

reason, most of the evaluation measures suggested in this book are direct measures.)

3 Ensure that students know in advance how they will be evaluated. Students who are surprised by the way a midterm or final examination is designed are not only likely to do less well, but also have more good reason to be resentful. In contrast, using in-class practice, homework, and quizzes to prepare students for an examination is not only more fair but also more likely to ensure that they study in productive and appropriate ways.

Tests

Methods of Evaluation

The backbone of evaluation in many educational systems consists of tests, especially the familiar midterm and final examination. In fact, testing is so often the primary form of evaluation that there is a tendency to assume that testing and evaluation are virtually synonymous. Thus, I would like to begin this discussion of testing by pointing out the many disadvantages of primary reliance on tests.

Many problems with tests derive from the fact that they judge the work of several weeks or months on the basis of a single, brief performance. One undesirable result of this is considerable pressure and anxiety for students, often more than is productive. Because of the unusual amount of pressure that tests generate, they are especially likely to have negative backwash effects, one of which is that they tend to encourage students to engage in short intense periods of cramming rather than regular study and practice.

Another common problem with testing derives from the types of tests commonly used in classrooms. Indirect testing with heavy reliance on true/false, fill-in-the-blank, and multiple choice items is common. The prevalence of this kind of testing is not surprising because there is a long tradition of testing language skills in this way and these kinds of items are used heavily in standardized tests like the TOEFL. However, the backwash effect of this kind of testing is generally negative—students are forced to become experts at guessing how to fill in blanks rather than learning how to really use language. Also, as Hughes (1989) notes: "Good multiple choice items are notoriously difficult to write" (p. 3), and he concludes that most multiple choice tests used by schools are "shot through with faults" (p. 61).

Despite the problems, it may be neither possible nor desirable to abandon testing entirely. Midterm and final examinations are deeply embedded in educational systems of many countries, and you may have no choice in the matter. Another reality is that students may be confronted with other tests after leaving your course, and lack of experience in test-taking would put them at a disadvantage. Finally, well-designed testing can motivate students to study and review productively. In short, the question is often not whether or not you should give tests, but how to make sure that tests have the best possible backwash.

Test design and administration is a topic normally addressed by a chapter or an entire book; below I will only suggest a few of the most basic points to which you should attend.

1 Again, use direct testing as much as possible. Direct testing tends to have a better backwash effect than indirect testing, and a serviceable direct test is generally easier to design than are good indirect test items because there are fewer tricks involved.

2 If you must use multiple choice questions, true/false items or the like, be sure that there is an adequate number of these items. When tests only have a few items, each counts for a large percentage of the final score and luck plays too large a role.

3 Check a test before actually administering it. It is not unusual for even a carefully crafted examination to have serious flaws that escape the eye of the test designer. One good way to minimize the possibility of problems is to have another teacher look over your test beforehand.

4 Use quizzes and practice tests to introduce students to your testing methods well before the midterm. This familiarizes students with the test format, gives you an opportunity to find and correct flaws in your approach, and maximizes the possibility of positive backwash by giving students a clear idea of how they should prepare.

5 Make your tests cumulative. There is little sense in requiring students to learn the material in Unit 8 for the midterm, only to rule it out of bounds for the final. By promising not to test students on material covered earlier in the term, you reduce language learning to a game and increase the chances that students will lose sight of the ultimate goal.

6 Investigate local testing expectations and practices before designing your examination. It may be that nobody else will care how you test your classes, but this is not always the case and it is better to find out before running seriously afoul of local custom. You should also remember that if your class is part of a larger system that includes other school- or nationwide tests, one of your testing duties may be to prepare students for those examinations.

Although it may not be possible to get away from testing entirely, "it is advisable to evaluate students in a number of different ways rather than to rely almost exclusively on formal exams" (Bowen et al., 1985). Concentrating the evaluation process in a few major examinations increases pressure, test anxiety, and the temptation to cheat or cram rather than really learn material. It also maximizes the role of chance—one bad headache can seriously affect a student's grade if the grade is based mostly on one test. Tests are best used in conjunction with other evaluation methods.

Quizzes

Your view of quizzes may be jaded by nasty memories of pop quizzes that seemed to be given more for their punitive value than for any educational purpose. It may therefore come as a surprise that I advocate quizzes as a major part of any package of evaluation measures. However, I have my reasons. First, because quizzes are shorter than tests they can be given frequently, thus spreading the evaluation process out over time rather than packing it into a few exams. This tends to lower test anxiety and minimize the role of chance in determining grades. Frequent quizzes also help students get into the habit of studying on a regular basis and discourage reliance on infrequent bouts of cramming as a learning strategy. Finally, quizzes "have even been known to help improve attendance, punctuality of arrival, and discipline at the outset of the class period" (Bowen et al., 1985, p. 357).

A few suggestions on use of quizzes (see also the suggestions above for tests):

1 For maximum positive impact, quizzes should be given often rather than only once or twice. Unexpected pop quizzes may do more to alienate the class than motivate study. Predictable, frequent quizzes are fairer and more likely to promote study.

2 Quiz formats should be as much like the formats of your exams as possible. Otherwise, they may mislead students as to how to prepare for tests.

3 Quizzes should be kept short. It is only because of their brevity that you can find time to give and correct them regularly, and a short quiz is often all it takes to give students the extra push to do an assignment.

Homework and In-Class Work

An obvious and important alternative to testing is evaluation on the basis of homework assignments or in-class work. For example, writing can and should be evaluated on the basis of many compositions rather than one supreme in-class effort at the end of the semester. Likewise, speaking can be judged in part on the basis of performance in many small exercises over the course of the semester rather than on one intense interview alone. Such an approach reduces fixation on examinations and shifts student attention to the daily work of study and practice.

Portfolios

Another alternative to a final exam is a portfolio, that is, a selection of students' best work presented for a final grade. This approach works most naturally in writing courses in which students can be evaluated on revised versions of their best compositions. However, with a little creativity the basic principle underlying this approach—the idea that students get to choose their best work for evaluation—could be adapted to other kinds of work as well. For example, reading could be included by having students read books, write reviews, and then turn in their best reviews. In a speaking course, students might be asked to write dialogues or do role plays, tape their best work, and submit the tape. Major advantages of portfolios are that they draw on all of the work a student does during the semester rather than reducing judgement to one all-important test, and they also encourage students to assess, revise, and improve their own work.

Self-Assessment

You may not want to go to the extreme of letting students determine their own final grades, but it can be very beneficial to involve them in some level of assessing their own work. This helps remove you from the role of final judge and jury; more important, it forces students to take more responsibility for their own work.

Consider one example of a self-assessment method for an oral English class.[4] Students are given the following three-item form to fill out at the end of each class period.

Such a form gives students a chance to assess their own effort and serves as a regular reminder that their English progress depends largely on how hard they work, not on how well the teacher performs. It also allows students an opportunity to give the teacher feedback on a range of issues, and helps the teacher stay in touch with students' responses to and feelings about the course.

[4]This form was generously provided by Jay Lundelius from his courses in Kinjoo Women's College, in Nagoya, Japan.

Self-Evaluation Form

1. I tried _____% to use English in class today.

90-100% I tried my best to use English today. (I prepared well for this lesson before class, and I used only English with my partners.)

80-89% I tried hard to use English today. (I prepared for this lesson before class, and I used English with my partners almost the whole time.)

70-79% I tried to use English today. (I prepared a little for this lesson before class, and I used English with my partners most of the time.

60-69% I tried a little to use English today. (I didn't prepare for this lesson before class, but I used English with my partners over half the time.)

0-59% I didn't really try to use English today. (I didn't prepare for this lesson, and I used English with my partners less than half the time.)

2. Today I think I learned:

- ❑ a lot of English
- ❑ some English
- ❑ a little English
- ❑ almost no English

3. Comments:

Other forms of self-assessment might entail:

1 Having students check their own work. For example, after a listening exercise you might give a copy of the text to students and have them check their own answers or summaries.

2 Requiring students to present a short critique of their work. For example, at the end of a composition they might be asked to state one or two of the strong and weak points of their composition. (This, incidentally, can make it easier for you to give feedback.)

3 Having students submit a tentative grade for their work, along with a rationale. The necessity of stating a rationale should help prevent students from taking this as a joke, and provides a point from which you can give students a useful reality check. It may also be very instructive for you to see what students think about the quality of their work.

Grading

The first problem with grading is that many VTs would prefer not to do it at all. It not only goes against Western egalitarian ideals, but it also seems to be a nuisance which doesn't do much to further education. Most of us will grudgingly admit that grades can help motivate students to study harder, and accept the reality that grading is a deeply rooted part of most educational systems (including our own), so we are willing to do it when we have to. However, dislike can tempt us to treat the grading process with less respect than it deserves.[5]

Grading is not an inherent part of evaluation. In fact, if the only purpose of grades were to help students diagnose their strengths and weaknesses, grades could easily be dispensed with. Grades themselves are only number or letter codes indicating whether something is good or bad, so comments and suggestions would be much more helpful to students. The purpose of grading is in part to motivate students to work harder, but grades are also used to determine which students will be given priority in selection for good jobs, further educational opportunities, and the like. When they are in a system that uses grades in this way, students will take the grades you give very seriously, and these grades will be a potential point of conflict.

If a grade is essentially a message indicating your assessment of a student's performance, it is important to ask yourself what messages grades send to your students and school authorities. As you consider this question, there are two special issues to which you need to pay attention:

1 Working in a foreign culture, you need to make sure that your grades communicate the message you want them to. This may be more problematic than it seems because a particular grade or score may not mean the same thing in your host country as it does at home.

2 You need to consider the kind of standard you use for determining grades, and the message that your choice of standard sends to your students. It is common for institutions or teachers to feel the need for a nice-looking grade curve, despite the fact that this means a student's score is determined as much by the scores of other students in the class as it is by his or her own performance. This approach to grading tends to focus the attention of students on their class standing rather than on personal improvement. This, in turn, may have a negative effect on the motivation of weaker students in the class. These two issues will be examined in more detail below.

[5]Surprisingly, many books on English teaching—including almost all of those listed in Appendices C and D—don't even have a section on course grading.

The Language of Grading

One problem with grading in a new country is that the grading system may appear disarmingly familiar, only to turn out to be quite different from what you expect. For example, the A-F grading system familiar to Americans is also used in other countries, but apparent similarities in the system do not necessarily mean that grades mean what they would in the U.S. Different patterns of grade distribution may mean that an A- has quite different significance in one country from what it has in another.[6]

Consider the contrast between the normal grade curve in China and the U.S. In China, most university English students get scores in the 70s and 80s, a distribution not unlike that in the U.S. The story, however, is different at the upper and lower ends of the scale. Scores in the 90+ percentile are rarer in China than in the U.S., and are consequently an indication of greater achievement than the same score in the U.S. would be. In contrast, scores in the 60th percentile are more common in China than in the U.S. It might seem that American VTs could easily master the grade distribution in China merely by using the grade distribution they are familiar with but then lowering everything a few points. Unfortunately, it is not quite this simple. Failing grades are much rarer in Chinese universities than U.S. universities (because very few Chinese university students, having made it through a rigorous set of tests to enter university, are allowed to then fail and waste the training that has been invested in them); thus at the lower end of the scale American VTs need to grade higher than they would in the U.S.

The point is that in a new country, you need to learn both the code used for grading and the normal pattern of grades. Questions you should ask in trying to determine how the host country grading system works include the following:

1 What kind of marking system is used? Grades? Scores? Something else?

2 What does a normal grade curve look like? What is the most common grade?

3 How do students view any given grade? What grade causes rejoicing? What is considered to be failure?

4 What grades indicate truly outstanding performance, and how often are they given out?

[6]Even within the U.S., the same grade does not mean the same thing in all contexts. For example, for U.S. undergraduate students, a C grade means *average*—or a little below. For graduate students, who are required to maintain a B average, the same grade is a failing mark.

5 What grades are officially considered failing? How does the system handle failing grades? What are the consequences of failing grades?

6 How much latitude do individual teachers have in determining their own grade curves? How do students and other teachers view a teacher whose grade curve is unusually high or low?

Unfortunately, it is not always easy to get a clear picture of the grading customs of a community. Often there is at least some difference between the official picture and what most teachers actually do in practice. For understandable reasons, it is not at all unusual for teachers and administrators to describe their grading practices as being stricter than they really are. This disparity causes few problems for members of the host community; from experience they know how things really work. In fact, they may not even be consciously aware that there are two distinct systems. However, for a newcomer this presents difficulties because directing a few questions to a school official may not get you all the information you need, and if you take an idealized description of strict grading policies at face value and began giving grades that are markedly lower than those being given by your colleagues, you could rapidly become unpopular.

Consequently, it is important to be persistent in trying to get as accurate a picture of the system as possible. It is often necessary to ask a variety of people, including students (preferably from someone else's class), and to ask indirect as well as direct questions. To the extent possible, you need to find out what people actually do rather than what they say they do.

Choosing a Standard for Grading

It is probably not too much of an oversimplification to say that there are two basic approaches to grading. The first and more common is to see a grade as indicating a student's level of ability at a given point in time, and this is generally determined by comparing the student with his or her classmates. The other approach is to see the grade as indicating how much improvement a student has made over a period of time, in which case the student is measured against him- or herself. Below we will briefly examine the advantages and disadvantages of these two approaches to grading.

CLASS-CURVE GRADING

Many teachers and school systems grade using a class curve[7]— by comparing the performance of the student being graded with the

[7]The technical term for this is *norm-referenced* grading.

performance of other students in the class. As natural a process as grading on the curve may seem, it is inherently unfair because a student's grade is determined as much by the other students in the class as it is by his or her own ability. A young woman unfortunate enough to have unusually bright classmates—or classmates who have had more previous exposure to English—will probably be permanently consigned to lower grades than she would have had in a duller group (unless of course she can manage to wrest a higher class standing from some other member of the class and knock him or her down the ladder). The sting of curve grading is sharpened if used by a teacher who always reminds students to focus on improvement and constantly urges them not to compare themselves with their classmates.

I would not want to exaggerate the potential of curve grading to create bad feelings in your classes. Despite the manifest unfairness of such an approach, it is used so widely that most students accept it as an inevitable part of life, rather like colds or myopia. Grading on the curve also benefits many students—there are as many winners as losers—so grading in this fashion won't alienate an entire class. But you should not underestimate the potential of this approach to alienate some of the students in a class and to undermine their incentive to learn. When grades are based on comparison with other students, students who learn more slowly—or those whose only sin was less English training before the course began—have to struggle simply to retain their current humble class ranking, and they may choose to give up rather than investing the extra effort needed to improve their class standing. They may resent the overseer of such a system.[8]

Despite the disadvantages of curve grading, I will not suggest that it should be done away with completely. First, it simply isn't possible. Many if not most educational systems have class curve grading built into them, and you cannot change that fact single-handed. Additionally, because curve grading is the norm in many school systems, students not only expect it but may even be confused by or uncomfortable with other approaches to grading.

Another reason that curve grading will not likely disappear soon is that it is too convenient. Grading on the curve is easy, especially for a beginning teacher who is still in the process of figuring out the goals of a course. It takes no preparation or planning to compare the performance of a group of students on a given task because there is a ready-made standard which you can use for each situation—the average performance of the students in that class. As we shall see, other forms of grading require more preparation. Thus, what I will suggest below is that in addition to grading on the curve you should

[8]For programs that allow students to choose the course level at which they study, another problem with curve grading is that it gives students a vested interest in being placed in classes that are too low for them.

also make a genuine effort to award grades on the basis of progress. This will go a long way toward restoring the motivation of weaker members of the class to keep plugging away.

IMPROVEMENT-BASED GRADING

If the goal of a course is to help students improve their English skills, it seems only reasonable that the students be graded on the basis of how much they improve rather than their level at any particular point in time. The motivational advantage of this approach for students who start out at a lower skill level is that they still have a relatively equal chance to get good grades; higher level students also see that in order to get a good grade they have to improve further rather than simply coasting.

To measure improvement, it is necessary at the beginning of a course to first test students and determine their starting level of skill, final grades then being awarded on the basis of how much progress is made during the course. One way in which this progress is commonly measured is through use of a criteria system. Consider the following simple example for measuring interactive speaking skills in an interview setting:[9]

1 —Cannot respond to even the most simple questions.

2 —Can respond to a few simple questions with utterances of a few words.

3 —Can respond to basic information questions about self (yes/no, wh-questions) using short sentences.

4 —Can respond to most questions about self, daily life, and local environment, and can elaborate beyond simple responses.

5 —Can respond to questions about a range of topics, including current affairs and cultural or social issues. Can explain and argue opinions.

[9]Please note that this is only intended to be an example—it is far too simple to be of any actual use. For a more developed scale, see Chapter 7. A very detailed criteria system for measuring langauge skill proficiency, the proficiency guidelines established by the American Council on the Teaching of Foreign Language, is available from ACTFL (6 Execuive Blvd., Upper Level, Yonkers, New York 10701). These guidelines are also found in Omaggio Hadley (1993) and in simplified form in Rubin and Thompson (1994). Marshall (1989) also includes a system based in part on the ACTFL guidelines.

Given the advantages of improvement-based grading, why is it not used more often? One reason is that this approach requires more preparation than curve grading, especially because of the need for pretesting and a criteria system (note that designing an effective criteria system involves both a clear sense of goals and a lot of work). This demands additional work from you at the early stages of the course, a time when you may still be focused more on getting through the next class period than on long-range plans.

Another problem with improvement grading is that it is difficult to see skill improvement over short periods of time, especially in broadly defined skill areas. Improvement in general skills such as reading and speaking takes place relatively slowly, and 1 or 2 months of study may not make enough difference for improvement to be noticeable. This is particularly true at the advanced stages of English study where progress becomes increasingly harder to detect. Considering again the sample criteria system above, it is quite possible that within a 3-month course, students who started at Level 1 might reach 2 or even 3, but a student who started at 4 would probably still be in the 4 range at the end of the course.

Recommendations for Course Grading

1 Base your grades on improvement as well as level of ability. Despite the problems involved in initially setting up an improvement-based grading system, in the long run the effort involved in setting goals and designing a criteria system works to your advantage because it forces you to prepare more carefully and ultimately makes your grading process both simpler and fairer. Improvement-based grading also has better backwash effects on students than curve-based grades because the former focuses attention on skills rather than classmates.

However, as suggested above, it may be neither wise nor possible to grade solely on improvement. Grading on improvement alone is difficult and problematic because the picture of student ability that such grades communicate may well be inaccurate. Grades will often be taken by school authorities and others to indicate how good a student's English ability is, and your grades therefore need to represent ability as well as progress. It is therefore often wise to make the final grade a compromise between progress and ability. When it comes to the question of balancing ability and improvement (or effort) in grading, a good rule of thumb in borderline situations is to put a little extra weight on the side of the balance on which a student is stronger. One could argue that this is the fairest approach, and it is certainly the most politic.

2 Let students know how they will be graded. The most important way to ensure a sense of fairness in grading is to communicate clearly and regularly with students about your goals, your evaluation methods, and how you will grade. This is done not only by explaining your grading system to students, but also being consistent in the way you evaluate. Many students will not fully understand explanations in English, and will rely heavily on their experience in early tests and homework assignments to help them figure out what you are really after. Students who know what is expected of them are far less likely to become hostile over a bad grade than students who feel that they have been misled or caught by surprise.

5 Lesson Planning and Classroom Survival

- In order to be able to concentrate on the educational goals of a lesson, it helps first to have confidence that you have adequate material for each lesson and that students will respond reasonably well.

- Planning a lesson—and putting the plan in writing—is one important way to ensure the success of a lesson. A well-planned lesson enhances student confidence in you and increases the likelihood that they will respond well.

- Creating a warm, friendly class atmosphere makes both teaching and learning easier for all concerned. Fun is a legitimate part of the language classroom.

For all but the most self-confident VTs, the overwhelming priority during the first few months of teaching is getting through as many class periods as possible without disasters such as exercises that take twice as long as planned, instructions that students completely misunderstand, and activities that students respond to with overwhelming apathy. Another form of catastrophe—possibly the worst—is running out of activities when the class period is only half over. During my first year of teaching, my response when caught short was to have the class play Hangman, a harmless little spelling game that could easily dispatch half an hour of class time before everyone began to get restless. It didn't teach much English, but allowed me to survive a class period without running out of material. In many ways, Hangman serves as a symbol of my early teaching days because the primary object of my class planning was to prevent myself from winding up like the hanging man himself, dangling in front of a class to which my inexperience had been suddenly revealed.

As suggested in the introduction, in our EFL Hierarchy of Needs, until you have confidence that you can get through a lesson with your dignity intact it is difficult to focus on higher level issues such as how to use the class hour as effectively as possible. This chapter will address the issue of planning for the class hour, with an eye to getting you as quickly as possible past the survival stage.

The first level of our EFL Hierarchy of Needs was the need to get through class without running out of material. Making careful lesson plans—and writing them down—makes it more likely not only that you will have enough material for each day's class but also that each lesson will have a clear sense of purpose.

It may help to first consider some of the aspects of a good lesson. In a study of one particularly effective reading teacher, Richards (1990) concludes that qualities which made this instructor's lessons effective include the following:

1 Lessons were designed around the goals set for the course.

2 The instructor made his theories of language learning and teaching explicit to the class. In other words, he told the class why they were doing what they were doing.

3 Lessons had a clear structure. There was an order to the activities, and at the beginning of activities students were given an idea of how long the activity was to last.

The net effect of constructing lessons as above is that they have a strong sense of direction. Not only were course goals translated clearly into lesson plans, but the connection was made clear to students. Designing lesson plans in this way increases not only your confidence that you know what you are doing but also students' confidence in you. This, in turn, increases the likelihood that students will

Planning Lessons

be willing to follow where you lead, and that they will respond to activities with at least some enthusiasm.

The most important way to ensure that you have enough material and that your lessons have a clear sense of direction is also the most obvious and most important—you need to make a plan for each lesson. A few gifted individuals can regularly wing it in the classroom and get by reasonably well, but such people are the exception rather than the rule (and many members of this select minority are more skilled at entertaining than educating). Teaching well and establishing a good classroom atmosphere is hard enough if one prepares properly; to skimp on preparation is to beg for a lousy day in class.

Two habits will help ensure that you prepare adequately. One is actually blocking out time in your schedule to be used for preparation. Preparation can seem a rather ephemeral and undefined kind of activity, at least when compared with classroom teaching or composition correcting, and it is therefore sometimes relegated to scraps of time left over from other activities. Reserving prime time specifically for preparation ensures better lesson plans.

Second, plans for a class hour should be written down rather than kept in your head. This not only gives you something to which you can refer in class when you need to jog your memory, but also leaves you with a written record which you can draw on if you want to use that particular lesson again. However, the most important advantage is that it forces you to think through your plan more carefully. Class plans that are dreamed up but not written down have a tendency to seem more thorough than they in fact are, much in the way that a polluted river seen in dim moonlight may appear a lot nicer than it really is. The habit of letting plans first see the light of day by being laid out on paper is generally very helpful in ensuring that details have been worked out.

Another way to give your lessons a sense of continuity and direction is to use a basic set of techniques on a regular basis. Of course, variety is important in preventing a lesson or course from becoming boring, but there is no need for each day's activities to be totally different from those of the day before; the effect of excessive variety may well be to convince students that you are on a never-ending search for something that works. By having a set menu of methods and tasks that you draw on, you not only reduce the amount of time that you spend figuring out each day's activities, but also reduce the amount of time you need to spend explaining activities in class. As Stevick (1988) notes, this regularity also helps students relax in class because they have a sense that you know what you are doing.

A Sample Lesson Plan

The following is a sample of the kind of written lesson plan you might make before going into class. This example is designed for a 50-

Aspects of a Lesson Plan

minute class period in a first-year college English course. Because students will take a standardized English test covering the textbook, one goal of the course is mastery of the grammar and vocabulary presented in the book. The school has also made it clear that they want as much speaking as possible included in the course. Regular activities in this course are question-and-answer between teacher and students, vocabulary quizzes, pair and small-group work for speaking practice as well as practice of vocabulary and grammar structures, and in-class reading. Today's lesson is on minor health problems and advice giving.

Sample Lesson Plan

(5 min.) Warm-up/review: "I feel _____." "I don't feel _____." (Complain about some minor problems and get students to give you advice.)

(10 min.) Vocabulary quiz: *headache, cold, runny nose, delicious* (Say words aloud, have students write each word down and then write a sentence that correctly uses the word and demonstrates knowledge of the word's meaning. *Delicious* is from a previous lesson.)

(15 min.) New structure: "How about _____ + ing." (a) Informally make suggestions like "How about going to a movie," have students try to guess meaning. (b) Put the structure on the board. (c) Have students look at the dialogue in the book, find the target structure, and say what it is used for. (d) Note that "How about _____ + ing" can be used as a suggestion or an invitation.

(10 min.) Pair practice: "Your friend is has nothing to do and is bored. Make some helpful suggestions." (Remind class why they are doing this activity—or better yet have them remind you. Have students change partners several times. Close the activity on a light note by asking students about the best and worst suggestions they heard.)

(10 min.) Reading/skimming practice: (Have students quickly skim the dialog in tomorrow's lesson and then tell you the main point of the lesson.)

Reserve activity. Game: 20 Questions. "I'm thinking about something in the room." (Have students try to figure out what it is using yes/no questions to get clues. You only answer questions if they are properly formed. Also give occasional hints such as "How about asking about where it is.")

Notes on the Sample Lesson Plan

1. **Purpose:** You should often remind students about why they are doing a given activity (as in the Practice above.)

2. **Variety:** Students generally stay more alert if there is some variety in a class period. Note above that the reading/skimming practice provides a break from the heavy diet of speaking and listening prevailing through most of the lesson.

3. **Timing:** Planning an approximate time for activities will help ensure that they don't drag on too long and that you get to everything in a lesson.

4. **Instructions:** In general, you should try to keep instructions short and clear. Lower level students, especially those with poor listening comprehension, are easily thrown by complicated instructions. For the Pair practice above it may help to dramatize the situation with a little story or play-acting—show students what you want them to do. (One advantage of using similar methods repeatedly is that less time needs to be devoted to giving instructions.)

5. **Warm-ups:** The warm-up above serves not only as review but also as a chance to start class off with real— if somewhat whimsical—communication.

6. **Quizzes:** Predictable quizzes prod students to study on a regular basis, a habit that is essential for learning languages. The vocabulary quiz in the lesson above will help ensure that students learn the vocabulary in today's lesson, learn at least one example of how it is used, and review previously studied vocabulary.

7. **Presentation of new material:** The core of this particular lesson, the introduction and practice of the new structure ("How about _____ + ing"), contains three basic elements which Cross (1991) calls the "three P's":

presentation of new material, controlled practice of the material, and relatively free performance (p. 140). Note these three elements need not always occur in the same order. For example, the lesson above starts with controlled practice, allowing students to figure out for themselves how the structure works before the teacher follows up with explanation (presentation).

8. Closure: At the end of the practice activity above note that the closing need not be very long. Having students quickly report what happened during their practice is a fun way to give a sense of closure to the activity. A teacher comment or suggestion can also serve to provide closure.

9. Reserve ("spare tire") activities: It is a good idea to have a "reserve" activity in case the other parts of the lesson go more quickly than planned, leaving you with unexpected time at the end of the class. Games are popular as reserve activities, but almost anything that takes little preparation can fill this role. Note that the game 20 Questions used above reinforces grammar points as well as allowing everyone to have a little fun.

Managing the Classroom

Every teacher has to find a classroom style that he/she is comfortable with, and experience is the only tried-and-true way to do this. Here, however, are a few practical pointers for managing a classroom that may make life a little easier.

Seating

Many Western teachers like a circle or semicircle arrangement for seating because it allows students eye contact with each other. However, in classrooms in many countries this is not possible either because there are too many students or because the desks/chairs can't easily be moved. If a circle is not an option but the chairs are movable, try to arrange seats so that you can get as near as possible to each student when walking around the classroom. If you are fortunate enough to have the opposite problem—a large room with few students—you might gently but firmly seat them together in the front rather than scattered throughout the room.

When having students work in pairs or groups, having them sit as closely together as possible not only helps keep the general noise level down but also tends to make them more willing to talk to each other—physical proximity also creates a stronger sense of emotional closeness.

Eye Contact

Good eye contact is one of the main ways in which you can establish and maintain a sense of student involvement in the lesson, especially when speaking to the whole class.

Your Speech and Voice

When you are attempting to put a point across in class (giving instructions, for example), you want to make sure that it is understood. There is therefore a temptation to make your speech as easy as possible to understand. Within bounds, this is not a bad thing, and it is essential that a VT learn how to communicate as clearly and simply as possible. However, if your speech becomes simplified to the point that it is unnatural—for example, if all your contractions are ironed out into fully pronounced words—it loses its value as listening practice for students. Try to strike a balance, speaking slowly and clearly (though not unnaturally) when necessary, and a little more normally at other times in order to challenge students' ears.

Also remember that students may be straining to understand you, and if you add to their burden by speaking so quietly that they have trouble hearing you, more students will tune out.

Teacher Talk

There is some debate as to how much the teacher should talk in a language classroom; some practitioners feel that teacher talk should be kept to a bare minimum while others point out that teacher talk is one of students' main opportunities for listening practice. My own feeling is that in an EFL setting, particularly one in which there are few other opportunities to hear native English, you should not feel bad about talking often in class. However, you should remember that it may well be quite an effort for students to understand you, and that you need to give them opportunities to speak not only because they need the practice but also because they may need a break from the strain of trying to follow you.

Movement

You don't want your movements around the class to become distracting, but a certain amount of movement helps the class seem more lively. One tip: When a student tends to speak quietly, your natural tendency will be to move closer. However, if you want the rest of the class to listen you need to do the opposite, moving further away so that the student is forced to speak up.

Question and Answer

The effectiveness of a question asked to the whole class is enhanced greatly if you pause before calling on someone to answer; this ensures that everyone has both the time and the motivation to think through an answer.

Using the Blackboard

1 Make sure that your writing is large enough that people in the back can read it.

2 Try not to waste a lot of time writing on the board during class. If you need to write something relatively long, put it on the board before class.

3 Try not to talk to the board. In my experience, there is nothing wrong with allowing students a moment of respite from the sound of your voice while you write a sentence or two on the board as long as the break doesn't become too long.

4 Use the blackboard to entertain. The main attraction of many of my classes is the pathetic attempts at drawing with which I illustrate points. Students laugh at the drawings, I make my point, and the atmosphere in class is a little lighter. If you can draw well, so much the better.

In poorer countries where students do not have access to textbooks you may need to write the necessary material on the board so that students can copy it before or after class.

Establishing a Good Class Atmosphere

The second level on our Hierarchy of Needs was the need for positive response from your class. The success or failure of an English class should not be measured primarily on its popularity—it is, after all, a class rather than a variety show—but the question of how students respond to your lessons is a real and important one, for pedagogical as well as emotional reasons. A class that both you and your students enjoy is not only much easier to face each day, but also more likely to generate positive feelings toward the learning of English. Of course, student response to your class is not entirely within your power to control; some students no doubt hated school or English class long before they ever met you, and you cannot always expect to see a complete reversal in their attitudes. However, by developing a good rapport with your students and by keeping your class as interesting as possible, you can often make a significant difference in students' attitudes and response.

Establishing a Good Rapport

Perhaps the single most important step toward establishing a good rapport with your students is learning their names. In a foreign country where you have large classes and students' names all seem strange to you, learning all the names in a class can require a considerable investment of time and energy. However, it is an investment that will pay significant dividends as the term goes on, and is generally worth the effort (at least for those classes you see more often).

Gower and Walters (1983) list a number of ways to learn student names, including the following:

1 Initially memorize the names using the Name Game. Have Student 1 say her name, Student 2 say his name and the name of Student 1, and so on until the last student has to recite the names of all the students in the class—just before you do it. This requires considerable concentration, and tends to drag in classes with more than 30 students, but is a good way for you to learn a lot of names quickly and to see that your students learn each other's names (if they don't know each other already). The Name Game is, incidentally, an excellent object lesson in the importance of repetition and concentration in memorization of vocabulary.

2 Have students make up name/biography cards (as suggested in Chapter 2). If possible, even have students attach a small photograph.

3 Keep attendance—this forces you to review names.

4 Especially during the first few lessons, make a conscious point of using students' names.

5 While students are doing pair or group work, spend time mentally reviewing their names.

6 Use the returning of homework assignments or papers as an opportunity to review names.

Gower and Walters (1983) also offer several other suggestions for the development and maintenance of good rapport with your students:

1 Show interest in your students, their country and culture. Having students tell you or write about these topics both demonstrates interest on your part and gives them valuable practice in explaining important aspects of their lives to outsiders.

2 Show interest in students' English progress. In large classes it is often difficult to establish a personal relationship with each stu-

dent, but any show of concern that goes beyond correcting mistakes and assigning grades is usually much appreciated.

3 Ask for students' comments on the class from time to time. In many cultures students are not accustomed to giving their teachers feedback, especially if your request is vague and general. (In other cultures students might cheerfully give you an earful.) You will probably get more feedback if you ask a very specific question which seems to relate more to the class and student needs than to your personal performance. A spin-off benefit from such requests on your part is that they demonstrate respect for the students and openness to their opinions.

4 Respond to what students say as well as whether or not they say it correctly. This not only shows that you consider language use to be genuinely communicative, but that you consider your students people whose ideas and feelings deserve to be treated with respect.

Keeping Class Interesting

Several of the most important ways to keep class interesting have been mentioned earlier, but a quick review here may be helpful.

Ensuring that students have a clear sense of direction and progress will go a long way toward maintaining morale. As suggested earlier, setting specific, narrow course goals allows students to more readily perceive progress, and regularly reminding students of why they are doing what they are doing is also helpful.

Regular use of communicative activities also helps keep class more interesting. One of the perennial favorite pastimes of the human race is chatting; most people love to talk about themselves, their activities, other people, world events, and just about everything else, and there is no reason not to take advantage of this interest in the classroom. Language practice activities that allow students to say what they want to say are inherently more interesting than noncommunicative drills.

In the English teaching field, one of the newer buzz-words is the term *information gap*. The idea is that the way to structure a communicative activity is to see that Person 1 knows something that Person 2 doesn't, thus ensuring that Person 1 has something to communicate.[1] One of the best things about teaching English in a foreign country is that when you communicate with your students there is no need to create an information gap—the difference between your culture and theirs provides an incredibly rich fund of interesting topics to

---

[1] This is in contrast to situations in which both partners already know what the other is going to say, a situation common in dialogue practice.

communicate about. They will generally be quite curious about your country and its ways, and also willing to initiate the greenhorn (you) into the mysteries of their own culture. Some of the most memorable compositions I have ever read were stories my students wrote about life in southern China during their childhoods; likewise, one of the speaking class activities I always look forward to is having my Chinese students pick China's top 10 heroes, listening to the reasons they present for their choices, and then responding with a few American heroes of my own. Taking advantage of this information gap whenever possible allows you to raise the interest level of your class while also teaching/learning about something that is important in its own right.

Another way in which interest levels can be enhanced is through giving language learning activities some of the appeal of games. This can be done with many kinds of activities if an element of fun and lighthearted competition is introduced. Consider a few examples:

1 An element of fun can be introduced into many conversation activities by requiring that a choice be made. For example, a mock job interview becomes more interesting if you have each employer interview more than one prospective employee and then announce which candidate he or she decided to hire and why.

2 Content lessons can be livened up by introducing them with a short contest. For example, instead of just launching into a lecture on American holidays, divide students into groups and give them a few minutes to list as many holidays and their dates as possible. The group which compiles the best list gets rewarded with praise or whatever else you have an adequate supply of. The same can be done with vocabulary (e.g., lists of colors, animals, feelings) or even grammar (e.g., lists of mass nouns, ways to describe things in the future).

3 Even subjects as drab as spelling or vocabulary can take on a bit more interest if they become a contest (spelling bees being a case in point). I, for example, liven up my Chinese vocabulary memorization by competing against myself. Each day as I look at my vocabulary list, I check to see if I can quickly and accurately pronounce the Chinese characters and state their meaning. If I can't, I have to review the word but leave it on the list. When I get one right, I allow myself the satisfaction of crossing it off my list with a bright yellow highlighter.

Finally, part of the art of being a good teacher is knowing when to lighten the pressure a little bit by scheduling what I call *candy*: a game, song, or film for class. All of these can have educational as well as recreational value, but we would be kidding ourselves if we didn't admit that we often use such activities more because students like them than because they offer the most efficient road to language proficiency. However, it is good to remember that one of the most important goals of any language program is to help students become more interested in studying the language, and a song that makes up for weakness in grammar teaching efficacy by kindling a student's desire to learn may affect the student long after a grammar point would have been forgotten.

6 Putting It All Together: Sample Course Plans

It seems only right to conclude this first section of the book with a few examples of what a plan for a semester course might look like. Below are considered several teaching situations most commonly confronted by VTs, general course plans and typical lesson plans. These should give you some idea of how the material in previous chapters is integrated to produce a plan for a course; with a few alterations perhaps you could even use one of these as a preliminary plan for your own course.

Course 1: Beginning General English

Situation

A large high school class (50 students) who have had little previous study of English. They have already studied a few basic grammar structures and some vocabulary, and can say a few common phrases, but they understand very little of what you say in class—including most classroom directions. This is a required course that is part of the regular curriculum, so students expect to do some homework most evenings, and there is a textbook for the course consisting of simple dialogues, short readings, vocabulary, and grammar notes. Your school expects you to teach the material in the book.

Goals

To a large degree, the textbook will determine what material you teach and which skills you emphasize because this course is part of a larger program and certain things need to be taught so that students are ready for the following course next year. This, however, does not mean that you cannot add elements of your own agenda. One of these should be building students' listening skills so that they can follow directions in class, and teaching them to ask the questions they need to get further information in class. A second should be to help students see that English is a tool for communication, not just a subject for classroom study.

Methods

1 As much as possible, have students study new vocabulary and grammar structures as homework; the short readings can also be studied at home. This leaves much class time free for practice.

2 Use in-class listening exercises to review vocabulary as well as build listening skills. As noted above, early on you might emphasize classroom directions. Note that until students' listening skills improve, there is little point in trying to explain grammar or anything else.

3 Read the dialogues aloud and have the class repeat after you to work on intonation and pronunciation and to ease the students into more challenging speaking tasks.

4 Use pair practice of the dialogues—perhaps first memorized set pieces and then later freer conversation—to allow for speaking practice and practice using new grammar structures and vocabulary.

5 Due to students' poor listening skills, do not explain the readings, which might serve little purpose. Instead, encourage students to practice asking information questions (e.g., "What does _____ mean?"). Also, use material from the readings to create reading exercises (e.g., write statements on the board to which students are required to respond true or false).

6 Combine listening and elementary writing by asking students to write down short sentences as you say them (dictation). You could also ask students to write short dialogues.

Evaluation

You should try to integrate your testing and evaluation methods with those of the rest of the program, finding out what methods other teachers use and following suit. However, you also need to see that your evaluation process encourages the kinds of practice you want. For example, if your school generally only uses midterm and final examinations you might also want to give occasional quizzes to encourage students not to put all of their study off until the night before the exam. Also, if the testing methods generally used in your school do not create positive backwash for communicative language use, you might give listening quizzes or grades for participation in pair practice.

Typical Lesson Plan

1 Warm-up: Practice understanding classroom directions. Give directions (Open your books. Find a partner) and have students do what you ask.

2 Review homework vocabulary: For example, say (or write on board) simple sentences containing new vocabulary; have students respond *true* or *false*.

3 Review homework reading passage: For example, first encourage students to practice asking questions about the reading; your responses can serve as listening practice. Then check comprehension by dictating simple questions. Have students write down the questions and then answer them.

4 Read the dialogues chorally, then have students practice in pairs.

5 Introduce one or two points from the next lesson by using them in some question and answer with students; see if the students can figure the points out for themselves by guessing from context.

Course 2: Beginning-Intermediate Oral English

Situation

A large class of university students, not English majors, who have already studied English for several years (mostly vocabulary, grammar, and reading) but have weak speaking and listening skills. The students come from a variety of different majors, so it is not clear how they might use English after graduation. The students seem enthusiastic, but this is not a core course, so they will probably not have much time to do English homework. The course was recently added to the university English curriculum because of the presence of a foreign English teacher—you—but is not integrated into the rest of the program and only meets once a week for 2 hours. There are no materials—text or tape—for the course, little is available in local stores or libraries, and there is no photocopier. However, you have a fairly free hand with the course because there is also no standardized test or follow-up course to consider. The only goal given to you by the school is to improve students' spoken English.

Goals

What these students need most is an opportunity to practice conversation using the English they have already studied; you may wish to teach some new vocabulary, phrases, or grammar to facilitate classroom exercises, but teaching new material should be a secondary priority. To the extent that there is a content element in the course, it might best be based on a series of common social situations (e.g., making conversation with a new acquaintance, politely refusing an invitation) and the cultural and language knowledge necessary for dealing with these situations. Another goal might be to get students in the habit of practicing English with each other outside class—2 hours a week of in-class practice won't result in much improvement.

Methods and Materials

1 For materials, come up with a list of situations that you wish to cover in class. If you don't have a book with a ready-made list, look through other English textbooks for ideas. (See also Appendix B: Culture Topics List.)

2 Work vocabulary, phrases, or structures that you need for working with conversation situations into short model dialogues and introduce them through dictation—hence adding an element of listening practice. Pertinent cultural information (e.g., what constitutes an acceptable excuse for refusing an invitation) might be presented as a brief talk, or embedded in the model dialogues.

3 Spend class time in speaking practice based on the situations (e.g., practice dialogues, role plays). Discussion of cultural issues raised by the situation or comparison of Western culture with the host culture could also be a major focus of class practice.

4 If possible, try to get students to do some speaking practice in pairs or groups outside of class. Alternatively, if you can make and reproduce tapes and students have access to recorders, listening homework would be a good use of their time.

Evaluation

For this kind of course you will probably have to give a final grade, but it may not count for very much and hence not be a very potent motivator for students. The best approach to such situations is often to do enough testing to show that you take the course seriously, but be rather generous with your grades. In short, this is a situation for the carrot more than the stick.

Beginning and final interviews—either with individuals or groups—would be a good way to encourage students to practice communicative conversation during the course. Giving grades based on in-class pair and group practice would also reinforce the message that the main goal of the course is to practice and build skills. An additional way to assess mastery of culture and language points would be through quizzes or tests that require students to write out dialogues dealing with the kinds of situations discussed in class.

Typical Lesson Plan

(For a lesson on how to politely borrow something.)

1 Warm-up: Ask to borrow things from several students, using the language you want to introduce. If this is a class that likes to joke around, ask to borrow some more absurd items or offer to return things at ridiculous times—this will test their listening and also introduce the idea that there are rules as to what can be borrowed from whom for how long.

2 Model dialogue dictation containing language and culture points you wish to introduce: (e.g., "Could I borrow_____?" "Would you lend me _____?" "I need this because _____," "Would it be all right if I gave this back tomorrow?").

3 Pair practice based on the model dialogue: Have students politely borrow things from each other. As they get the hang of this, you might introduce ways to politely refuse to loan something out.

4 Contest: Have students try to borrow as many things as possible from as many other students as possible. Insist that in order to borrow, they need to come up with good reasons—and the same for refusing to lend.

5 Small-group discussion: Discuss the "rules" in the host country for borrowing money (e.g., books, notes)—who can you borrow from, how much, and for how long. Compare with Western culture.

6 Homework: Repeat the contest above, but this time have students do it outside class over the coming week and for next class be ready to report what happened.

Situation

Course 3: Intermediate English for a Standardized Test

A large college class of non-English majors who have studied English for several years. They can understand classroom directions and simplified talks as long as you speak slowly and clearly, and can express themselves in basic spoken English; their reading skills are stronger, although they tend to read slowly and use their dictionaries often. This is a required course with a set textbook, and at the end of the year the students will have to take a standardized examination that has reading, vocabulary, and grammar sections, and a recently added listening component. Student interest in the course does not appear very strong, although they are willing to do some homework because they want passing scores on the standardized examination.

Goals

Obviously the main goal of the course should be to prepare students for the examination, but an important secondary goal should to get students to see English as a tool for communication—not just a test subject. If students do not become interested in English, they may cheerfully abandon it as soon as the test is over.

Methods

1 Because of the pressure of the examination, expect that students will probably be willing to study grammar and vocabulary and do listening and reading practice as homework. Class can then be used for communicative forms of language practice.

2 Review and practice grammar and vocabulary in class through speaking exercises.

3 Focus in-class reading practice on skimming and reading for main ideas—useful skills in both test situations and real-life reading.

4 For listening practice use talks based on topics from the texts and using vocabulary introduced there.

Evaluation

Tests modeled on the standardized examination would help students prepare for that examination. Aspects of the course not directly related to student examination performances are probably best not included in the grading process—these will need to be sold on their inherent interest and value.

Typical Lesson Plan

(For a 1-hour lesson introducing conditional sentences and containing a story on a girl who finds a lot of money.)

1 Warm-up: Ask students "What would you do if somebody gave you $100.00?" Follow with pair practice.

2 Have students ask any questions they have about the homework reading text. Check comprehension by orally asking a few questions and having students write short answers.

3 Give a short talk about what you would do if you found a lot of money. Have students take notes. Follow up with comprehension questions.

4 Prepare for the next reading text by quickly skimming it in class.

Situation

A class of students who are going abroad to study for graduate degrees in an English-speaking Western country and are now in a special one-semester preparation course that meets twice a week, 2 hours each time. They can read a broad range of materials in English, although they tend to read slowly, carefully, and with much dictionary use. They can understand much of what you say on general topics as long as you speak slowly and clearly, but they have trouble with natural or quick speech and there are many words they can read but don't understand when they hear them. The students are well motivated, but most also have jobs and sometimes cannot come to class or do homework. The course textbook consists mainly of articles about life abroad, and there is an accompanying tape on which the articles are read aloud.

Goals

For academic work in the West, these students will need to learn to cope with large reading assignments quickly. They will also need to be able to follow lectures, even if those lectures contain unfamiliar vocabulary and are not always delivered in standard teacher English. Third, students need to be able to discuss readings, express their own opinions and critically evaluate readings. If time permits it would also be desirable to introduce the basics of writing an academic paper, although time constraints may make it impossible to make much progress in writing.

Methods

1 Students will need to work independently at home when they have time. They should especially be encouraged to read as much as possible outside class, using whatever materials are available but limiting dictionary use.

Course 4: Preparing for Study Abroad

2 Because students' reading skills are stronger than their listening skills, a good approach to homework might be to have students first listen to the tape, taking as many notes as possible, and then checking their comprehension by reading.

3 You can build students' listening skills by giving talks on subjects such as culture, study skills, university life, and so on and having students practice note-taking. The talks should challenge students' listening skills and force them to guess.

4 Reading practice in class should include practice skimming articles to get the gist as quickly as possible. Discussion of readings could focus on analysis of the author's main ideas, bias, and assumptions, and it would also be beneficial to have students begin critiquing articles.

5 Many of the basic skills of academic writing can be practiced by having students write critiques of the readings.

Evaluation

Students in such a class will probably already be quite motivated to improve as much as they can before departure, so formal evaluation might not even be necessary except in order to help students pinpoint weaknesses. In order to encourage students to work as much outside class as possible, you could offer to go over any work they do independently. For example, encourage students to tell you about any extra reading they do. If they want to practice writing, you might suggest they write and submit short reviews of books they read.

Typical Lesson Plan

1 Give anyone who independently read a book or article the chance to do a quick review and recommendation for the class.

2 In groups have students quickly discuss the homework reading, answering questions like: What were the main ideas of the text? Was the author objective? Was this a good article? Stress that students need to explain and back up their opinions.

3 Have the groups report their decisions and then discuss. During the discussion answer questions about the reading.

4 Give a talk on a topic related to the reading, using some of the new vocabulary introduced in the reading. Students practice taking notes.

5 Have students skim the next article under time pressure.

Situation

A class of advanced students at a private night school, many of whom are preparing to take the TOEFL in hopes of going to study abroad. The class meets two evenings a week. The school has provided a textbook that has dialogues and readings about life in the West. You have also been able to obtain a book with sample TOEFL materials, but the students don't have a copy. This course is not a TOEFL course per se, but you know that in advertisements for the course the school claims it helps people prepare for the TOEFL, and this is the reason why approximately half of the students are in your class. The others are interested in improving their English for a variety of different reasons.

Goals

It is clearly important here that you help students prepare for the TOEFL, but also that you provide a general English course that will benefit those who will not take the TOEFL. TOEFL test items include grammar, vocabulary, listening comprehension, reading comprehension, and writing, so a good strategy would be to strengthen students' skills in these areas in ways that will enhance their test performance yet also improve their ability to use English for other purposes.

Methods

1 It is probably safe to assume that those students who want to take the TOEFL will be willing to invest time doing TOEFL-related homework, so you might organize them at the beginning of the course to copy parts of your TOEFL book for their homework. This will give them a chance to practice TOEFL-specific skills without requiring the whole class to spend a lot of time doing multiple-choice grammar or vocabulary items. Other students in the class can do homework from the course text.

2 Reading exercises that stress rapidly getting the gist of a text would benefit both the test takers and the non-test takers. You can add a speaking component to this kind of exercise by first having students read a passage, then trying to answer comprehension questions on their own, and finally discussing their answers in small groups.

3 Listening exercises modeled roughly on TOEFL test items would also be of use to anyone in the class.

4 The type of written essay used in the TOEFL (as of 1995) requires students to present arguments on two sides of an issue and then present a conclusion. In-class writing exercises that follow this pattern

would allow students to practice basic writing and grammar skills as well as important elements of expository writing.

Evaluation

In a private school it is likely that grades are unimportant or none are given. Because students have presumably paid for the course, they are also likely to be self-motivated. Feedback on performance on exercises would thus be more useful than emphasis on scores. For those interested, you might also organize a practice TOEFL, giving them practice with the general format, rules, and time pressure of a TOEFL.

Typical Lesson Plan

1 Warm up with a short listening comprehension exercise based on the homework reading and using vocabulary from the reading. The format might be modeled on a kind of TOEFL test item.

2 Answer any questions students have about language points in the homework reading.

3 Have students discuss comprehension questions about the reading in groups, covering both content and "reading between the lines" issues such as main idea and author bias. Close with discussion.

4 Have students write a short in-class essay following a TOEFL-type format. Follow this up with class discussion of ways to organize an essay on this topic.

5 If time permits, quickly skim the next reading assignment.

Course 6: The English Club

Situation

An evening class that meets once a week for English conversation practice. Anyone can come, so there is a huge range of different levels and also little consistency in who shows up or how large the group is. Some of the students are very interested in improving their English, and others are mainly interested in getting out of the house and meeting some new friends. There is no textbook and no examination expected. The sponsor's only stated goal is that participants improve their English, but an important implicit goal is that participants enjoy the class.

Goals

With such a range of skill levels and no consistency in attendance, you should not expect to carry out an organized program of study. A more realistic goal is to give students a chance to practice their speaking and listening in a communicative setting, and let them have as much fun as possible in the process.

Materials

A list of cultural topics such as birth, school, marriage, occupations, and so on. (See Appendix B.)

Methods

1 Games can be used for warm-ups, conversation practice, and opportunities for people to meet each other.

2 Heavy use of pair and small-group activities is recommended because these allow students to work at their own level much more than large-group activities do. Interviews and opinion surveys are especially good because they are conceptually simple—hence can be done even by beginners—yet can also result in in-depth conversations.

3 Introduction of Western culture through simple talks would give students a chance to improve their listening and also learn something interesting.

Evaluation

Probably none.

Typical Lesson Plan

(For a lesson on occupations.)

1 Warm up with a game, especially one that gives students a chance to meet and chat briefly with others in the class they don't know. For example: "Find the person in the class whose birthday is closest to yours, and be prepared to introduce him or her." Close by having introductions of anyone you haven't seen before.

2 Briefly introduce the topic and a few key language items. Based on the topic give students one or more questions and then ask then to conduct a quick survey of their classmates. (e.g., "What are

the most difficult kinds of jobs?") Close with survey results from a few volunteers.

3 Give a short talk on the general topic, introducing Western culture and comparing it with the host culture.

4 Small-group discussion task. Allow students to divide themselves into groups (so that they work with others they are comfortable with) and give them a discussion question. For example: "What occupations are more suitable for women and what are more suitable for men."[1] Close the exercise with reports from a few groups and general class discussion.

Course 7: The Last English Course

Situation

A general English course for students who will finish a 2-year training program at the end of this semester and go out to be middle school English teachers. They have a fair command of basic grammar and vocabulary, can understand clear English, and can read newspaper and magazine articles—although only with difficulty and the help of a dictionary. After graduation, they will be working in areas where there are few naturally occurring opportunities to use English outside their classrooms, and when teaching they will only need to use very basic English. (Many of their English teaching colleagues will not use English in class at all.) Under these circumstances it is not unusual for the skills of graduates to gradually deteriorate. There is, however, a locally published weekly newspaper in English, and English language radio broadcasts can be received almost everywhere in the country. A reading text is available for your course, but the school has given you considerable freedom to decide what you will teach and what materials you will use.

Goals and Materials

In this last semester progress toward getting the students to take charge of their own learning by starting a self-study program is probably more important than teaching through one more textbook. Given the availability of the English newspaper and radio broadcasts, it would seem reasonable to focus your course on these in the hope that increased familiarity will increase the likelihood that students will continue to take advantage of these after graduation.

---

[1]Remember that you need to consider the sensitivities of the local culture in choosing your topics. This particular topic works beautifully in some cultures and would be anything from uncomfortable to offensive in others.

Methods

1 A program of reading the English language newspaper, especially skimming through and picking out interesting material rather than slowly working through all of each issue.

2 A program of radio news listening. Have students choose the types of stories they will focus on according to their interests.

Evaluation

You want to encourage students' efforts as much as possible, so you might either give fairly easy quizzes and tests or dispense with testing altogether in favor of having students do some kind of self-reporting of how much they read/listen. If they don't begin evaluating their own progress now, they will be less ready to do it after they graduate.

Typical Lesson Plan

1 Warm up with bulletins of the day. Students report what they heard on the previous night's news. You are available to answer questions about vocabulary, names, or whatever students ask.

2 Discuss one of the articles from this week's newspaper, with one or two students (previously selected or volunteered) as leaders. The discussion leaders assign questions and manage the time. You circulate among the groups to answer questions or join in the discussion until the leaders call a halt. Then, as the groups report, you are available to answer questions and make comments.

3 You might close the class by asking for predictions as to what is likely to happen in a number of the ongoing stories in the news. Students can then check their guesses when listening to the news that night. (See Chapter 7 for more discussion of courses based on radio news.)

PART II

Aspects of Language Teaching

The first six chapters of this book have described how to construct a language course. In this section we will now go back and examine in more detail the basic building blocks used in constructing a language course.

CHAPTERS 7 through 10 will address four basic language skills: listening, speaking, reading, and writing.

CHAPTERS 11 and 12 will consider vocabulary and grammar, and

CHAPTER 13 will discuss the role of culture in language teaching.

CHAPTER 14 concludes the section with a discussion of some of the problems most often faced in EFL classrooms.

7

Listening: Putting the Horse Before the Cart

- ◆ In many settings, listening is the most used language skill and also the channel through which students get much of their language input. Development of listening skills should thus take priority over development of speaking skills.

- ◆ Students need to learn to use both bottom-up and top-down strategies when listening.

- ◆ Even in areas where there are few chances to speak English, there may be more opportunity to listen to English than to speak it. Listening skills are thus a good potential target for breakthrough-type plans.

One of my most frustrating language experiences occurred in 1978 during a summer in Russia. I had recently completed a college minor in Russian, and though I was under no illusion that I was fluent, I assumed that I would at least be able to cope with basic conversation. It was thus disheartening to discover that when confronted with real Russians in conversational situations, I was virtually helpless. The problem was not my speaking skills; I could generally make myself understood, if only imperfectly. The real problem was that I could understand almost nothing that I heard—everything seemed to be a blur of sound that was less clear and much faster than the Russian my teacher had always used in class. My speaking skills were thus virtually useless because I had no idea what to say. Even as simple an act as buying books involved emotional trauma because when I plucked up my courage and asked the price in Russian, I could never understand the response. After several futile attempts to communicate with me verbally, the clerks generally resorted to writing or holding up fingers. This, naturally, was quite humiliating for someone who had spent 3 years in Russian classes, and I was frequently tempted to preserve my pride by pretending I had never studied any Russian at all.

Unfortunately, my experience with Russian is typical of that of many English learners. Bowen et al. (1985) comment: "Students with 10 years of English instruction and even more find that when they arrive [in an English-speaking country] they have major difficulties trying to comprehend even simple sentences of spoken English" (p. 83). This happens in part because many language programs—intentionally or due to oversight—devote more attention to speaking skills than listening skills. Another reason is that to the extent that listening practice is provided, it often consists of the slow, clear classroom speech of the teacher or language tapes on which unrealistically clear and formal voices read aloud materials which students have already read in their textbook. For students whose goal is to listen to native English speakers, listen to the radio, or watch films, such a diet is inadequate.

A student whose listening skills are weak faces problems for several reasons. The first, illustrated by my example above, is that students who have weak listening skills are not very functional in most conversations no matter how well they can speak. In contrast, a student whose listening skills are good but who does not speak well can generally at least keep a conversation going by being a good listener and occasionally responding with simple questions, short answers, or even grunts and nods. A second problem is that much of students' language input normally comes from what they hear, and if this channel is blocked students will learn less new English. Thus emphasis on speaking at the expense of listening puts the cart before the horse, resulting in a learning process that is both slower and more difficult. A third problem arises from the frequency with which listening skills are used; as noted in Chapter 3, listening may well be the most often used language skill. Even in EFL settings where native speakers of English are few and far between, students may have opportunity to listen to English radio programs, television, or films. Students who have not had much listening training will be ill-prepared to take advantage of these opportunities. This is especially unfortunate in that, given the scarcity of other opportunities to use English in many EFL settings, listening opportunities represent one of the few realistic targets for a breakthrough plan of the type described in Chapter 3.

To native speakers, listening is such a natural and easy task that it is easy for us to underestimate how difficult listening in a foreign language is. However, a student trying to understand spoken English is confronted with an impressive range of obstacles, and has to learn to:

Listening Skills: The Problem and the Goal

1 Hear small differences between English sounds; for example, the vowel sounds in *fear, fair, fire, far, and fur.*

2 Comprehend reduced forms of pronunciation, which are very common in normal spoken English; for example, [fer] for *for*, [ta] for *to*; [wanna] for *want to.*

3 Attend to intonation or emphasis cues. For example, it is only intonation and emphasis that distinguish "You want *him* to go?" from "You want him to *go!*"

4 Adjust to regional, class or group accents.

5 Understand a great deal of vocabulary when they hear it. This often presents serious problems for learners in EFL settings because they learn most vocabulary through reading.

6 Understand grammar structures.

7 Understand rapid speech. Even speech in which students know all the vocabulary and grammar may be impossible to understand if it comes faster than students can process it. As Ur (1981) notes, this is especially true when students listen for longer times; listening to an unfamiliar language can be very tiring and as fatigue sets in comprehension drops.

8 Develop a range of cultural background knowledge. Lack of background information can deprive students of vitally important clues for comprehending a message; it also reduces their ability to predict what they might hear (see Chapter 12).

When we consider all of the ways in which a spoken English sentence can trip up students, it may seem miraculous that students ever learn to understand English at all. Fortunately, students do not need to be able to cope with every aspect of every utterance in order to be able to comprehend. As Omaggio Hadley (1993) describes it, the process of comprehension is much like that of completing a puzzle. Learners don't need to have every piece of the picture in place in order to make sense of it; at some point, the pieces of the puzzle that the learners do understand allow them to make a guess about what the whole picture should look like, and this hypothesis guides the process of completing the picture.

Listeners go at the comprehension problem in two ways. One kind of process, known as a *bottom-up process,* means using the smaller pieces of the picture to make a guess at the larger picture. For example, when a student sees her English teacher in passing and hears a muffled sentence starting with "How ... today", the words which a listener does understand provide clues to the whole utterance. The other kind of process, known as a *top-down process*, involves using background knowledge to guess what goes in blank spots in the picture. As Ur (1984) points out, "a real-life listening situation is normally rich in environmental clues as to the content and implications of what was said" (p. 5). In the example above, the context makes it fairly likely that the teacher's murky utterance was some kind of greeting, and this knowledge can help the student fill in the missing words.

The analogy of completing a puzzle, as useful as it is for understanding the comprehension process, goes astray at one point: it implies that the goal is to complete the puzzle—every last piece of it. Unfortunately, many learners set this goals for themselves because it was the goal language teachers set for them in their early years of English study, and learners who have this expectation may have trouble in listening at higher levels because they tend to freeze when they come across words or phrases they don't understand. The real goal in most listening is not to understand every word, but for listeners to comprehend the information that they want or need from a message. In the example above, the key is for the student to realize that the sentence beginning with "How ... today" was probably a greeting— whether it was "How are you today?" or "How're ya doing today?" makes little difference. In some cases, a listener needs a high degree of comprehension (and retention); more often, it is sufficient to get the gist of a message and the rest is ignored or quickly forgotten.

All of this has two important implications for learning and teaching listening skills. The first is that in listening practice exercises it is not necessary to expect 100% comprehension in all cases. The expectations you set for listening exercises, like the goals of listening in real life, should be appropriate to the situation, and you should often ask only that students work to understand the main points of a message.

The second implication concerns teaching methods. In real life, even native speakers do not always understand or hear every word when they are talking with someone or watching television—people mumble, cars pass by, and so forth. In most cases, however, this does not cause serious communication problems because native speakers are skilled at filling in gaps; using situational or linguistic clues, they can guess much of what they did not hear or understand. As students practice listening skills, it is thus important that they practice using top-down strategies as well as bottom-up ones—using all the clues available to help them guess.

Some obstacles to listening comprehension are worthy of special attention and should probably be discussed and practiced in isolation.[1] However, in general the best approach to building listening skills is ample practice listening to the teacher, tapes, or whatever is available. It is to the question of practice that we turn next.

The basic listening comprehension task consists of a few basic elements.

Listening Tasks in Class

I. Text:[2] Something to listen to (e.g., a story told by the teacher, a dialogue on a tape, a TV show).

2. Context: In real life most listening takes place in a context which provides clues for listeners as they try to comprehend a text. For example, understanding a conversation is easier because listeners can see the expressions and gestures of the person they are talking to; understanding a radio news broadcast is made easier by knowing that the text is a news broadcast and that news broadcasts follow certain rules and patterns. Thus, listening exercises are made easier by use of pictures, realia, or anything else that helps students put the listening act in a context. (Note that the major exception to this rule is provided by language tests in which students may be asked to listen to language for which there is no context at all.)

3. Purpose: The most basic purpose should be general comprehension, but often the purpose should be more focused than this. In real life, listeners often have some idea of why they are listening to something, so it is entirely appropriate—and generally a good idea—to let students know before they hear something what they are listening for.

---

[1]Comprehension of reduced forms for intermediate and advanced learners deserves extra attention, and Bowen et al. (1985) argue that the unstressed schwa sound is an especially troublesome problem in understanding natural native English.

[2]At the risk of some confusion, I will use the word *text* to refer to written material as well as oral language such as conversations, lectures, radio programs, and so forth.

4. Task: Most kinds of listening exercises work better if they are made into tasks, that is, if students are expected to respond in some way to the material instead of just listening to it. This keeps students alert as they listen and also helps focus their listening.

The types of listening practice tasks suggested below are arranged roughly according to the level at which they are most likely to be appropriate, starting with tasks for beginners. (It is difficult to assign these tasks to a precise level of skill because they can be made easier or more difficult by adjusting the vocabulary, speed of delivery, clarity of speech, depth of content and so forth.) Though the focus below is on listening practice, many of the tasks also involve practice of other language skills.

Total Physical Response (TPR)

A good task for beginners is having students respond to oral instructions like "Pick up your book" or "Please open it to page five" by doing what you ask rather than speaking, thus allowing them to focus on listening without worrying about how to say anything. TPR exercises are a good way to learn to understand classroom directions, and the physical activity also makes them a good warm-up activity at the beginning of class or a break in the middle. (TPR can also be used for more advanced levels; for example, I have walked students through weddings and baseball games with oral instructions as part of culture lessons.)

True-False Exercises

Using vocabulary and structures from your lessons, make up a list of statements—some true, some ridiculous (e.g., Today is Tuesday. Students love tests.) Then read the statements aloud to students and have students respond "true" or "false"—either verbally or in writing. Good for reviewing new vocabulary, and can also add a touch of fun to class—try and fool your classes with absurd statements and deadpan delivery. (Based on Ur, 1984, pp. 77-78.)

Dictation

Prepare a text that consists of either short sentences or sentences broken into phrases of seven or eight words. Then read the sentences aloud, repeating if necessary, and have students write them down. Good for basic listening comprehension and also for practicing basic written English (e.g., capitalization, spelling). The danger of dictation is that it trains students to listen for every word more than for meaning, so it should not be overused. Attention can be focused more on meaning if you dictate questions and then ask students to answer them.

Dicto-comp

This is similar to dictation but stresses meaning more than word-for-word accuracy. First choose a short passage, then introduce any words that are new to your class. Next read the passage aloud three or four times while students listen carefully and try to remember as much as possible. Students may ask questions after each reading. Finally, have students write down as much as they remember of the content of passage, preserving the meaning, sequence, and even exact wording when possible (Bowen et al., 1985).

Teacher-Focused Question and Answer

Although question-and-answer between teacher and students is often thought of as a speaking activity, it is probably more effective in building listening skills; each student spends much more time listening than speaking. If you ask real questions and expect real answers, this activity is a good way to establish the idea that English use should be communicative.

The major disadvantage of this activity is that students may not be very interested in your interaction with another student, and when it is not their turn they are tempted to tune out. (A teacher who interacts with students in an orderly, predictable pattern is virtually begging students to doze off until a few seconds before their turn comes.) To keep everyone's attention, interact with students in a random pattern, and try to keep conversation communicative and interesting.

Stories

Stories provide a relatively enjoyable form of listening practice. Recommended are those stories widely known in your home country or throughout the West, be they children's stories, stories from film or literature, or true historical accounts. In my experience, students especially like personal stories about you and your country.

The inherent appeal of stories makes them one kind of listening practice for which accountability may not be necessary; many students will strive to understand just because they are interested. If, however, you wish to treat a story as a listening task, you can have students respond in the following ways:

1 For lower level students, have them take notes and then write a summary or retell the story to a classmate.

2 Require students to be ready to ask a question or two about the story after you finish. This might be a comprehension question or one which pursues issues raised by the content of the story.

3 At more advanced levels, have students discuss what they did and did not like about the story, or what they found interesting or surprising.

4 Have students revise the story to improve it or make it fit into their cultural norms better.

5 Leave off the end of the story and have students devise an ending of their own.

Focused Listening

Before having students listen to a text, tell them what to listen for. For example, have students count the number of times certain kinds of items—fruits, furniture—are mentioned in a passage, or listen to a dialogue and count the number of excuses an employee gives his boss for being late. For another form of focused listening, choose a passage and then create an information grid or form for students to fill in as they listen. (See Sophie's Choice example below.) A third and potentially lighthearted form of focused listening is to alter a passage or dialogue, introducing contradictions or absurdities. Students then either have to shout out or take notes when they hear something suspicious. (Above tasks based on Ur, 1984, pp. 75, 81, 116-117.) Good for encouraging students to listen for important information rather than every word; providing a focus also helps make challenging texts more manageable.

Problem Situations

Present students with a problem situation, have them take note of relevant information, and then ask them to discuss the issue. Perhaps the classic in this genre is Sophie's Choice,[3] an exercise in which students hear about a young woman who has to choose one of three appealing-but-flawed men as a marriage partner or ignore them all in

[3]Sophie's Choice and other similar activities can be found in Donald Byrd and Isis Clemente-Cabetas's (1980) *React Interact* (Regents).

favor of a career opportunity. This can be made into a focused listening task by giving students a graph or form to fill out. For example:

	Age	Occupation	Married?
Tom			
Dick			
Harry			

After listening to the information about each suitor, students are encouraged to ask questions to clarify any information they missed. Then they either discuss the issue or respond in writing. Many such problem situations can be found in commercially available texts, but they can also be custom-designed to fit the needs and interests of your students.[4] Good for combining listening with speaking or writing.

Lectures and Note-Taking

This task is distinguished from the focused listening above in that you do not focus students' listening; as in a university classroom, it is up to them to decide what is and is not important to note down. You can check comprehension by having students turn their notes in, answer true/false questions, or write a summary of the main points of the lecture. Another quick and more communicative way to check on student comprehension is to require that they each write down one or more follow-up questions based on the lecture. Good for building higher level listening skills and practicing note-taking.

Culture Talks

Talks on cultural topics are especially useful because of the value of the content to students. Students can be asked to respond to the talks as above. A method more specific to culture topics is to let students know that after the lecture they will be required to compare what you describe to a corresponding aspect of their own culture, either as part of a group discussion exercise or a written assignment.

[4]See Ur (1981) for a variety of such problem situations.

Exercises for Reduced Forms Used in Informal Spoken English

Reduced forms such as [doncha] (*don't you*) and [gonna] (*going to*) are very commonly used in most dialects of natural spoken English, and students will be hard put to follow conversation between native speakers, movie dialogues, and the like if they cannot understand reduced forms. It may therefore be worthwhile to introduce a number of these in class. Tasks for practicing comprehension of reduced forms include:

1 having the class listen to your reduced sentences and then repeating the sentence back in its "proper" form

2 having students try to repeat the reduced forms after you

3 using reduced forms in questions and answers (e.g., Do ya wanna take a test now?)

4 taking dictation

Listening Outside Class: Tapes

It takes a long time and considerable practice to develop listening skills to a high level, and generally the practice that a student gets listening to the teacher in class is not sufficient. An important part of a good listening program therefore involves giving students listening comprehension homework and getting them accustomed to making good use of other kinds of listening practice opportunities available in many EFL settings.

Even in many developing nations, tape recorders and recordings of English are widely enough available that it is possible to assign taped listening homework—and begin breaking the unfortunate tradition of trying to learn speaking and listening skills primarily from books. Tapes can include a wide variety of material spanning the spectrum from simple dialogues to academic lectures, and the methods for using these materials for listening tasks are essentially the same as discussed above. In this section, therefore, my attention will be directed primarily to the advantages and disadvantages of the tape format itself and suggestions for its use.

Tapes offer three major advantages as an avenue for listening practice. The first and most obvious is that they allow students to practice listening to native spoken English even outside class. The second is that when students are listening on their own machines (as opposed to in a group in a language laboratory) the tape format gives students a high degree of control—students can stop the tape and review when they need to. The third is that a tape will not slow itself down the way a softhearted teacher will, and thus it forces students to try to follow along at whatever rate the speaker is speaking. This fact, combined with students' ability to control the number of times they listen, makes tapes a good way to expose students to more rapid, natural speech (assuming the tapes are of natural English).

The great drawback of the tape format is that listening to tapes is often very boring. Students have no visual stimulus other than a slowly rotating tape, and from personal experience I can assure you that the tape keeps rolling without protest if a student nods off to sleep. The problem is often exacerbated by the material on the tape, which was generally not designed with entertainment first in mind. Unfortunately, finding new and more stimulating recorded material is not always an option—particularly if the local bookstore only has three different English tapes—so in order to learn to use taped material effectively students need to learn to stay alert.

Studying With Tapes

Staying alert while listening to a taped dialogue, story, or lecture is easier if students treat it as a puzzle to be unraveled. I suggest teaching students to use an approach something like the following:

1 Students should first listen to the whole taped passage once, trying to get the general outline of the picture. If there is a script available, students should not use it at this time—they will probably read more than listen. It helps students stay on task if they take notes or make an outline; this also gives visible form to the puzzle.

2 Students then listen again to try and fill in the blanks in their outline. This time, they should stop and go back over sections as necessary.

3 Once nothing more can be squeezed from the tape, it is time to look for clues. A glossary of new vocabulary items would be especially helpful because it provides helpful clues without giving away the whole puzzle. Armed with new hints, students can then return to the tape for another assault.

4 Finally, if a script is available, students can turn to it as the answer key to check their comprehension and solve any remaining mysteries. After they have checked, it doesn't hurt to review the tape one or two more times, listening for new vocabulary items. (Incidentally, students who listen to the tape again after a good night's sleep will often be surprised to discover that they can understand things that fatigue caused them to miss the night before.)

If you assign taped listening homework, you should cover it in class to give a sense of closure to the activity and to ensure that students actually did it. In situations where students do not have a script of the tape, you should go over the main points so that students can determine how well they solved the puzzle. When they do have a script, you might provide closure by discussing the content of the tape, or simply by asking students what parts of the tape they found difficult and why.

Choosing Appropriate Taped Material

In choosing taped material for homework assignments, care needs to be given to the level of difficulty of the material. In my experience, teachers and students both frequently err on the side of choosing listening material that is too difficult. Earlier I alluded to the belief that a good stiff dose of hard work, painful though it may be, will do wonders for our language progress. The listening skills version of this hypothesis is that if one listens to an unintelligible news broadcast long enough, the opaque will eventually become clear. This theory may appeal to our ascetic tendencies, but it is not a very effective way to develop listening skills. Listening to overly difficult material is very frustrating, and repeated listenings can only improve students' comprehension to a certain point. If material is too hard, students are frequently forced to give up on their ears and try to find another way to decipher the message (often by reading scripts of the tape, if available). Such material also forces students and teachers to invest large amounts of time in working with small amounts of material, reducing the amount of listening practice and vocabulary reviewed.

If ideal material cannot be found, I feel that it is generally better to err on the side of material that is too easy. Relatively easy material tends to reduce learner anxiety and larger amounts of it can be assigned. Such material also makes it more possible for students to guess the meaning of new words from context, and makes it more likely that they will be able to understand words and phrases which they have previously learned by sight, thus giving students practice in rapidly recalling the meanings of semifamiliar words and improving the speed at which they can process and comprehend what they hear.

In the beginning you may find it quite difficult to predict how easy or difficult your students will find a given listening passage. Experience as a language learner will help sensitize you to the difficulties your students face, but the best way to check the difficulty of material is still usually the traditional trial-and-error approach: Try some material in class and see how much of it students can comprehend. My rule of thumb is that if most of the students can understand some of the material the first time through, and get the highlights on a second try, the material is suitable.

When choosing taped material, another question which should be asked is whether or not the material provides genuine listening comprehension practice. This might seem obvious, but the point is still worth making because many kinds of commercially produced listening material involve little comprehension. For example, some tapes which accompany textbooks consist entirely of a voice reading aloud the material found in the text. Of course, if the student has read the text before listening to the tape, or reads it while listening to the tape, little listening comprehension practice occurs. Many tapes also consist of pattern drills which require students to manipulate sentences or fill in blanks; these also require little comprehension once the student has figured out the pattern of the drill. In order to develop listening comprehension skills, students must listen to material that is new to them and which demands comprehension rather than a mechanical response.

Producing Your Own Taped Material

While making your own taped material requires an extra investment of time, it is often well worth the effort to produce materials tailor-made to the needs of your classes. Producing your own tapes allows you to control the level of difficulty, choose content which you think students will find interesting, and personalize tapes by bringing in local topics or people. It also allows you to give students listening material for which they have no script.

There are several kinds of material you might consider taping:

1 Stories, either from a book or from your own experience. When teaching in China, for example, I taped several stories about my adventures exploring in Taiwan and then placed them in the language laboratory for anyone who was interested. As references to my adventures began cropping up in conversations later in the semester, it was clear that at least quite a few students had chosen to listen to the stories. If you can get other English speakers to tell stories, so much the better—students will be exposed to different voices and accents.

2 Lectures, formal or informal, on topics of interest. Again, this gives you a chance to share ideas from fields you are interested in.

3 Taped interviews. I often choose a topic or issue based on students' reading material and then tape an interview with another English-speaker about the topic. Because these interviews are relatively unplanned and informal, they have the features of natural language (e.g., false starts, fillers, reduced forms) that are too often absent in commercial tapes. The fact that they are based on material which students have read means that students already have some background knowledge and vocabulary for the topic, but the spontaneity of the interview means that students cannot fully predict its contents.

With regard to language, homemade tapes need not be professional; in fact, it is better if they are not. Normal speech is not flawless, and there is no reason why tapes should be. The main result of insisting that tapes have no mistakes in them is that they become more burdensome for you to produce. If you make a mistake while taping, just say "whoops" and go on.

Sound Quality

When making your own tapes—and in working with tapes in general—it is important to pay attention to sound quality. Students already face many obstacles in efforts to understand taped material, and there is no reason to exacerbate the problem with poor sound quality. Thus, several words of advice:

1 Always check tapes for sound quality. Remember that the sound quality on tapes deteriorates as they are used, so you cannot assume that a tape that was good last semester is still good now. Also, each time a tape is copied there is some loss in sound quality, so if a tape is to be copied for students, you need to remember that the copies won't sound quite as clear as the original.

2 If you plan to use a tape repeatedly over more than one semester, make a copy of the master right away and then use the second generation copy to make further copies for students. The sound on the copies will not be as good as that of the master, but if the master is often used for making copies its sound will deteriorate and eventually you will have to make the tape all over again.

3 Learn a little about tape and tape recorder maintenance and pass that knowledge on to your students. Poorly made tapes will quickly foul tape recorder heads (the metal devices which rub against the tape during recording and playback), so it is important to use the best tapes possible and to clean the heads on tape recorders frequently. Dirty tape recorder heads not only result in poor sound quality, but also damage tapes. A bit of cleaning will often make the difference between a tape that is almost unintelligible and one that is reasonably clear.

Language Laboratories

Language laboratories can be divided into two basic categories. The more useful kind consists of individual tape players which students can use for doing tape homework. Such a lab provides a place where students can work at their own pace on tapes of their own (or their teacher's) choosing. The second and more problematic kind is essentially one tape recorder hooked up to sets of headphones which allows a teacher to play a tape for a class. Such a set-up allows a teacher to let an entire class to hear the same tape under favorable listening conditions, but also forces students to all listen to the same material at the same pace in an environment which is often stultifying.

On the whole, a VT can provide clearer and more lively listening practice for a class by speaking in person rather than playing a tape, so teaching in a language lab tends to be a hinderance to a VT more than a help. However, it is not unusual for VTs to be placed in language labs because the school looks at the lab as a status symbol and there is a desire to give the guest teacher the best. If you find yourself in such a situation, the problem is often more cultural than educational, consisting of gently persuading your school to let you teach in a classroom which does not hinder communication by blocking space into little cubicles. It may help to point out to your school that the real value of a language lab is that it replaces a native speaker, allowing any teacher to present students with native-quality speech. You might also plead unfamiliarity with the equipment and suggest that someone more skilled in its use could do a better job, pointing out that your expertise is in direct conversational interaction.

If you do have to teach a language lab course the main battle is generally against boredom, so it is important to turn off the tape from time to time and wake students up with interaction or variety. TPR activities are helpful in labs; having students raise hands in response to questions helps keep them awake and lets you check on whether or not they are paying attention. Language labs are also good settings for letting students listen to songs; music breaks the boredom, and students are much more likely to be able to hear the words to a song over headphones than through a small speaker in a big classroom.

Radio Programs

In many parts of the world, one of the few opportunities to hear English regularly—hence one of the best opportunities for the kind of breakthrough described in Chapter 3—is provided by radio broadcasts. VOA and BBC broadcasts are audible in many countries, and even many non-English-speaking nations (including China, Japan, and Russia) have English language broadcasts, usually news programs.[5] Because of their fresh and timely content, radio news programs tend to be inherently interesting, and the absence of a script forces students to rely on their listening skills. A course of study which involves radio news also has an unusually high degree of validity for students because the ability to understand radio news is a useful skill in and of itself.

The problem with most radio news is that, for a number of reasons, it is quite difficult for learners to follow. First, while the speech

[5]News broadcasts are often propaganda outlets for the governments that sponsor them, so listening to them may be a sensitive issue. Be aware not only of what English broadcasts can be heard in your host country but also of which are politically acceptable for you to use or recommend in class.

of radio announcers is usually both clear and standard, it is sometimes a little rapid (especially when compared to that of the average English teacher). News also contains much low-frequency vocabulary and many names of places and people. Third, frequent and sudden jumps between topics make news programs difficult; often just as the listener has figured out what the announcer is talking about, he or she switches to a new topic. Finally, news items are usually short, so they often include little background explanation or redundancy.

Because the availability of English news broadcasts makes radio news one of the best chances for students to develop an English skill which they can continue to use over the years, a particularly valuable kind of course for advanced students is one designed to prepare them for radio news. Elements of such a course would include:

1 Study of place names and names of prominent people in current affairs. Place names are especially important because they are often placed at the beginning of an item to establish a context for the item.

2 Lots of practice listening to news items, using both bottom-up and top-down comprehension strategies. Students will not only need to be able to rapidly decode words as they hear them, but also to guess effectively to cover the many holes created by words or points of information they lack.

3 Regularly keeping up with the news using any means possible—including newspapers and news reports in the students' native language. The more students know about current news, the more vitally important background information they will bring with them to the task of understanding an English news broadcast.

At the early stages of a course, it is helpful if you record news broadcasts so that students can listen to each more than once. This also allows you to provide students with a vocabulary list, and perhaps even a script if you are feeling magnanimous. In the beginning of such a course you might choose to focus on a few ongoing news stories (e.g., the Arab-Israeli peace process, AIDS research) rather than exposing students to a broad range. This not only simplifies students' task, but also demonstrates an effective strategy for making radio news broadcasts easier to follow—building up background knowledge of a story.

As students improve to the point where they can get the gist of a story even listening to it only once, you can assign them to listen to radio broadcasts as homework and then come to class with notes or summaries for class discussion. Alternatively, you can give each student a "beat," asking him or her to be responsible for a certain kind of story or news from a particular part of the world. Using this approach, students still need to listen to the whole news broadcast to find out if there is any news about the country they were assigned to, but they will have a stronger sense that some part of that broadcast is their responsibility.

The hope of a radio news course is that ultimately students will become comfortable enough listening to radio news—and any other kind of radio program in English—that they will continue to listen long after your class ends. For students who have limited opportunities to use English once they leave school, this might be one of the few lifelines through which they maintain and develop their English skills.

Athough less widely accessible than English language radio programming, another English listening opportunity in some countries is provided by films and even television programs. English-language films are shown widely throughout the world, often with the English soundtrack left intact. English language television programs—both imported and locally produced—are also shown in some countries. (Even China has started showing Chinese-produced English language news programs on television.) Of these listening opportunities, films are probably the most widely available and also the most challenging, so it is on films that I will focus the following.

Films and Videotapes

Films have a number of important virtues as an opportunity for English practice. The picture helps students maintain interest, transmits cultural information, and also gives students an additional set of clues to work with as they try to decipher what they are hearing. Films are also designed to be entertaining, so the content is more compelling than that of textbook dialogues. A final benefit for advanced students is that films often have very natural English and provide a good opportunity to practice listening to material that has a range of accents and styles.

The great curse of movies flows from the final advantage; the natural language in many films tends to make them difficult. A student watching most modern films will encounter rapid, fragmented or unclear speech, unfamiliar vocabulary (especially very informal vocabulary), regional or class accents, and problems arising from gaps in background knowledge. Additionally, the sound in many films is less than crystal clear—some actors try to talk over the sound of screeching brakes or gunshots, others habitually mumble. Thus, it is not unusual for unprepared students to get lost somewhere early in a film and then sit in bewilderment through the next hour and a half.

In recent years, the increased availability of videotape machines and films on videotape format has made teaching film courses a much more realistic option, even in many developing nations. As with radio programs above, one of the best arguments for offering film courses for advanced students is that it can successfully pave the way for them to feel comfortable watching English language films after they graduate. Students who learn to be comfortable sitting back and enjoying a film, being satisfied with comprehending as much of the language as possible and guessing the rest from the picture, can often tolerate enormous quantities of this kind of practice.

One common approach to teaching English with films is showing a film in small segments, allowing students to see each segment several times and supplying them with all the necessary vocabulary. Chopping the film up in this way lessens its appeal but has the virtue of making the film easier to understand and may be a viable approach for classes who are not yet ready to watch films in their entirety. A second approach involves providing students with an introduction to the film (often a plot summary), a vocabulary list, and a list of comprehension questions, and then showing a film in its entirety (preferably twice). This approach maintains the integrity of the film, but is generally not very effective in helping students understand unfamiliar language in the film; a written list of words does little to prepare students to recognize these words aurally when they come darting out of a cloud of barely understood dialogue. This approach is most suitable for students who are already very advanced in their listening skills.

If you have the opportunity to teach a course to advanced students using films, I recommend an alternative method which gives students preparation for using bottom-up strategies by exposing them to some of the language in the film, encourages them to practice top-down strategies, and yet leaves the film intact. This method requires quite a bit of advance preparation on your part, but if used in a sustained way in a film course the results are worth the effort. The approach is as follows:

1 Choose an interesting film which has as much clear dialogue as possible. This is easier said than done; in my experience it is often necessary to sample several films to find one that is suitable.

2 Watch the film and take notes on each segment of dialogue in the film, noting the counter number on the VCR so that you can locate the dialogue later.

3 Select 5-10 key segments of dialogue (hereafter called "scenes") to be recorded onto a cassette tape. Include some but not all of the key turning points of the film, scenes which contain key vocabulary, and scenes which are important to the plot but especially hard to follow. For a normal feature film, the total time of the selected scenes should be about ten minutes.

4 Using the outlet jacks at the back of the VCR and a patch cord, tape these scenes onto a cassette tape, leaving a few seconds of silence between each scene. If you want to be really professional, use a microphone and record scene numbers at the beginning of each scene, or even vocabulary items and explanations.

5 Prepare written material based on the scenes on the tape. I generally include a list of the film's characters, a brief introduction which provides the setting for each scene, and a list of vocabulary items for each scene.

6 Prepare a list of comprehension questions which students will answer later when they view the film. These may be based both on the scenes selected for the cassette tape and on other portions of the film.

When using this approach I normally spend some time going over the tape with students before they see the film—studying the tape is usually very hard work because the scenes appear without much context, so students may need both help and encouragement. Then I show the film at least twice. In my experience, both as a learner and a teacher, the second showing of a film is very valuable because students will hear many things which they miss the first time.

A few general comments about the use of films: First, it is important to let students hear the sound as clearly as possible. The speakers on many TV sets are small and many classrooms echo, conditions which make the soundtrack of a film even harder to understand. If it is possible to run the sound of a VCR through a listening lab and have students listen on headphones, students can understand much more of the film. Another approach is to run the sound through a PA system or stereo.

Second, it is very important to preview films before showing them because your remembered impressions of how hard a film will be to follow may not be very accurate. Ideally you should preview films along with someone who isn't a native speaker of English and can help you determine how difficult the film will be for your students.

Although the discussion above focuses on videotaped films, documentaries and TV shows make equally good—if not better—classroom material. Documentaries are usually narrated in nice clear English, and are thus easier to understand than many films. TV shows are more manageable than films because they are shorter, and the sound recording of studio-taped programs also tends to be clearer. There are now also commercially produced videotape series designed for English teaching, and if you have access to these they can provide an excellent initiation into film and TV viewing.

Evaluation

Many of the tasks listed earlier in this chapter can readily be adapted for quizzes and tests. Below I suggest a few relatively easy evaluation methods which also have positive backwash effects. The tasks are ordered more or less by level of difficulty.

True/False Statements

Make a number of statements, some true, some false. Students simply write down T or F. This type of quiz is good for checking vocabulary as well as listening, and can be used even at beginning levels. Caution 1: Unless you intend to test knowledge as well as listening skills, be sure your test items test listening comprehension, not mastery of trivia. Caution 2: This kind of quiz makes it relatively easy for students to cheat, so keep an eye out.

Dictation

This is an easy kind of test to give, and can be used to check basic writing skills as well as listening. The main problem is that over-use of dictation can focus students too much on listening for words instead of meaning. (One way to ensure that meaning is not totally ignored is by using questions as the dictation items, and then asking students to also answer the question.) For more advanced students, dictation is an easy way to check whether or not they can understand sentences containing reduced forms.

Listening Comprehension Passages

These can consist of stories, dialogues, readings, or lectures presented one or more times. Comprehension can be checked in several ways:

1 Ask a series of true/false questions based on the passage.

2 Ask short-answer questions.

3 Have students fill in a grid, form, or outline.

(Note: For these first three methods, you need to decide whether or not to give students the task/questions before they hear the passage. If you do, it will help focus their listening and make the task easier. If not, you will be testing memory or note-taking as well as listening comprehension.)

4 Have students take notes and turn them in.

5 Ask students to write an outline or summary.

8 Speaking: A Linguistic Juggling Act

- ◆ Speaking in a foreign language involves a variety of operations, and learning to perform all of these quickly requires extensive practice.

- ◆ During class speaking practice, the more students who can talk at any given time, the better. Pair or small-group work allows more students to practice speaking than large-group discussions or teacher-centered activities do.

- ◆ Most adult learners will not achieve native pronunciation in a second language. Clear but accented pronunciation is not only a more realistic goal, but may also be more desirable.

- ◆ Some correction of students' errors may be helpful, but there is little evidence that correction is of much benefit in improving students' accuracy. Overcorrection can make students self-conscious and discourage them from speaking.

Having spent 2 years in a Japanese program that focused almost exclusively on speaking, I should have at least a fair command of spoken Japanese. However, I don't. Part of the fault is no doubt my own—I certainly could have been more persistent in seeking out the many Japanese on our campus for practice. But part of the problem also lay within the program, which consisted mainly of memorizing dialogues and learning to perform them as fluently as possible in class. This approach was successful in teaching me quite a bit of Japanese vocabulary, and even some grammar, but gave me precious little practice in expressing my own ideas in Japanese. Thus, when I could rope a Japanese friend into speaking with me, I was generally trying to construct my own sentences for the first time, much like a piano student who shows up for a recital having practiced only scales. The results were uneven at best—whenever I wanted to say something that fortuitously coincided with a sentence I had memorized, I could rattle it off fluently and flawlessly; but whenever I tried to say anything else I had to hem and haw for an agonizingly long time as I tried to put even basic sentences together. Needless to say, I found these forays into real conversation frustrating and eventually gave them up to go back to memorizing the dialogues and getting a passing grade.

Unfortunately, this kind of problem is not uncommon in EFL settings. In class, genuine speaking practice is often neglected in favor of choral drills or memorization, and other kinds of practice opportunities are hard to come by. Thus students' ability to speak lags far behind their knowledge of grammar and vocabulary. Often, your school has invited you, the native speaker, for exactly this reason, hoping that your presence will improve students' spoken English. In fact, sometimes you may get the feeling that everyone expects your appearance in the classroom to have a miraculous impact on students' speaking skills, even in classes of 30 or more where you can hardly speak to each student once a day. (Some students may get around this problem by visiting you and practicing at all hours of the day and night.)

Even if you can't personally provide each student with extensive practice opportunities, one of your greatest contributions—and most important roles—is often serving to create an environment where for the first time students really speak in English for communicative purposes. Your presence not only forces students to use English, but also does much to enhance their motivation by making English come alive as a real vehicle for communication. However, much of your success as a teacher of spoken skills will also ride on how effective you are in creating vitally important practice opportunities for your students. Thus, as we discuss the teaching of spoken skills below, the emphasis will be on ways in which you can provide students with the kinds of practice they need in order to develop oral skills.

The Process of Speaking: The Problem and the Goal

When we consider the various parts of the speaking process individually, no single one of them presents overwhelming difficulties. For example, neither pronouncing a word correctly nor deciding what verb tense to use is impossibly difficult if you can focus all of your attention on that single problem. The difficulty arises from the fact that, like a juggler who is trying to keep 10 balls in the air at the same time while also tap dancing and playing the harmonica, a speaker has to simultaneously perform an impressive list of operations. Consider, for example, the case of Lan, a student who has overslept and arrived late for English class for the third time this week. He is now standing in front of a stern-looking foreign teacher who wants an explanation. A peek inside his head will give a good illustration of all the things he needs to consider in the process of producing a sentence:

1. **Goals:** ("Should I try to win mercy or sympathy?")

2. **Strategy:** ("How would this foreigner react if I lied and she found out? Should I be honest and play the contrite sinner or lie and play the misunderstood victim?")

3. **Listener's background knowledge:** ("Does she know the local traffic situation? Maybe I can get away with an excuse about the traffic.")

4. **Word choice:** ("Do I say *crowded traffic* or *busy traffic?*)

5. **Grammar:** ("Is it *Excuse me to be late, Excuse me being late,* or *Excuse my being late*"?)

6. **Pronunciation:** ("Pay attention to that consonant cluster at the beginning of 'Excuse.'")

7. **Intonation:** ("Does *Excuse me for being late, but there are always many cars in the morning* end with falling or rising intonation?")

8. **Gestures and facial expressions:** ("Do I look her in the eye or avoid her eyes? Do I smile or look unhappy?")

Finally, poor Lan's problem is compounded by the fact that he doesn't have very much time in which to make all of these decisions—it won't be long before the patience of an annoyed teacher wears dangerously thin.

Of course, not all communication situations involve the kind of immediate pressure Lan faces above, but the steps involved in speaking and the need to perform these operations quickly are normal parts of the speaking process. The time element deserves special attention. The world has some people—mostly English teachers—who will wait indefinitely as a learner of English struggles to construct an utterance, but most people are not so saintly and will sooner or later give up on those who cannot communicate at a reasonable pace. A student who can communicate an idea even faultily without slowing conversation down too much is more likely to be able to sustain conversation when the opportunity arises than is a more accurate but slower comrade. This, in turn, means that the quicker student is likely to have more conversation and practice opportunities and therefore continue to improve. The quicker student will almost certainly also find conversation easier and more enjoyable, and is thus more likely to seek out such opportunities as exist.

Hence, if students are to reach a breakthrough point in spoken English, the primary goal is for them to learn to express their ideas in English with a fair degree of fluency. Accuracy is also desirable, and issues such as correct grammar and proper use of vocabulary should not be neglected. In fact, communicative effectiveness and accuracy cannot be entirely separated; if a student's grammar or vocabulary is too far wide of the mark, the listener may get the wrong message or no message at all. However, it is safe to say that the goal of most speaking situations is communication more than formal accuracy, and a course intended to teach speaking skills should favor the former.

Clearly then, one of the most important roles of a speaking class teacher is seeing that students get the maximum possible amount of practice speaking English, particularly kinds of practice that allow students to express their own ideas. This is especially true for students at intermediate and advanced levels of spoken skill, but even at beginning levels it is desirable to give students choice in what to say so that they have to communicate ideas as well as words.

A second important role is seeing that students get new language input. Actually, in most EFL settings students will get much of their new language input, such as new vocabulary, phrases, and grammar structures, from textbooks. Your role is thus to ensure that they learn material in ways conducive to improving their speaking skills, that is, by stressing that students learn how to use new vocabulary and grammar structures.

Your final role is helping students learn for themselves what kinds of practice are effective for developing spoken skills. It is not uncommon for students in many countries to practice their speaking at home by reading texts aloud or memorizing dialogues. These forms of practice are not useless, but the skills they develop are not the same as those necessary for expressing one's own ideas, and students need to learn how to choose forms of practice that fit the goals they are trying to reach.

Pairs, Small Groups, and Large Groups

If I asked you to describe a good conversation lesson, perhaps the first images that would pop into your head might be of a teacher briskly fielding questions from an enraptured student audience, or perhaps of a lively class debate. Upon a little reflection, the problem with the first option is fairly evident—in this kind of exchange the teacher does most of the talking. The second activity might initially seem to be an improvement because it is more student centered; presumably the teacher need not say very much. However, the large-group focus of the activity means that at any given time only one student has a chance to speak, so in a 50-minute class with 25 students, even if the teacher never says a word each student would only get 2 minutes of speaking practice, and students would spend most of the period listening to their classmates, an activity that is probably less useful than listening to the teacher speak.

So, how should in-class speaking practice be set up? In general students should work in pairs or small groups as often as possible because the division into smaller groups allows more students to practice at the same time. Pairs are the most efficient grouping in that they allow the most students to talk at once, but small groups also have advantages. The presence of at least two other people means that a shy student can sit back and listen, but the small size of the group means that the shy student is still likely to feel included as a participant. As Ur (1981) points out, the physical closeness in small groups also helps improve motivation, so small groups provide a good environment for encouraging reluctant students to make their first attempts at speaking.

However, breaking students into pairs and small groups is not without its problems, the main one being that some students won't practice spoken English with their classmates unless you are watching. Sometimes this is because they are being lazy; in other cases the problem is that they feel the only useful kind of speaking practice is conversation with an English speaker who has native mastery of the language and will correct all their errors—in short, they expect to do their practicing with you! Such students are often reluctant to practice with their peers because they doubt the usefulness of such practice, or because they fear making uncorrected errors, building bad habits, and incurring a vague host of other evil consequences.[1]

Faced with students who resist practicing spoken English with each other, you probably need to resort to a combination of persuasion and persistent pressure. For your campaign of persuasion, you might point out that the main problem in speaking is one of quickly forming thoughts into English sentences and that this kind of practice does not require a native speaker as listener. (In fact, it doesn't require any listener at all, and I quite heartily advocate that students talk to themselves in English if they don't mind occasional quizzical looks from passersby.) A culturally relevant analogy may also help; for exam-

---

[1]Lewis and Hill (1985) also warn that smaller groupings tend to result in more noise and even a touch of chaos in your classroom, but this is generally a price worth paying.

ple, you might ask students who will learn kung fu (or violin or basketball) more rapidly—a student who practices 2 hours every day or one who only practices during his weekly half-hour lesson with the teacher? For pressure, I personally prefer a prescription of light-toned nagging ("Lan, that doesn't sound like English.") and occasional pep talks on the importance of practice.[2] However, it is also important to be realistic about how far from supervision you can reasonably expect that students will actually practice English. A good rule of thumb is: Break students into the smallest groups in which most of them will speak English a significant percentage of the time.

This section will briefly discuss activities often used in speaking classes. As in Chapter 7, the activities are presented roughly according to level of difficulty.

In-Class Methods and Tasks

Memorizing Material

Having above made a rather passionate case against memorization of dialogues, it may seem odd that it appears here. However, for beginning students who need to learn high-frequency phrases and sentences like "How are you?", "What is that?", "My name is _____", and so forth, a case can be made for some memorization of sentences or short dialogues that contain a high percentage of such material. Stevick (1988) argues that the conceptual simplicity of memorization and the strong sense that one has mastered the content makes memorization an emotionally reassuring task for beginning students. It may also provide a good way to ease reluctant classes into speaking.

SUGGESTIONS

1 Memorization assignments should be short and contain a high percentage of material that is valuable in exactly the form in which it is memorized; in other words, commonly used phrases and expressions such as "How are you?" and "What time is it?". Memorizing typical example sentences may also help students learn sentence patterns and grammar.

2 To help students memorize a short dialogue in class, Stevick (1988) recommends that students listen to you repeat the whole dialogue once or twice, and that you teach pronunciation of new words before

---

[2]Some teachers have students monitor each other, levying a minimal fine on those students who speak something other than English in class (the proceeds eventually to go to a class party). I am personally uncomfortable with the idea of demanding money from students and making the speaking of the native tongue a misdemeanor, but it seems to work for some. Ur (1981) suggests that placing a tape recorder near an offending group may increase their amount of English practice.

students try to repeat anything. Then, he suggests that a good trick for helping students memorize is to build each sentence up from the end, an approach that preserves natural sentence intonation. For example:

Teacher: "Today." (Students repeat)

Teacher: "A nice day today." (Students repeat)

Teacher: "It's a nice day today." (Students repeat)

Finally, you might have students role play the dialogue in pairs, perhaps even acting it out.[3]

3 If you require that students memorize dialogues as homework, encourage them to keep as much focus on communication as possible. If you ask a few students to recite their dialogues in class, have them act it out in pairs, accompanying the language with appropriate actions. When students recite dialogues, it is more important that they know what they are saying than that their fluency be flawless.

Teacher-Directed Question and Answer

As noted in Chapter 7, conversation between the teacher and the class is generally more valuable as listening practice than speaking practice because of the limited amount of time each student spends speaking. However, teacher-student interaction can be a good model of genuine communication if you are really interested in what you ask students about, and conversation with a native speaker may have a motivational impact on students that goes beyond the practice it provides, especially if the interaction is fun and nonthreatening.

To prepare for a question/answer activity, take material from whatever texts the class has been working with, and then come up with questions that will generate real communication. The more you and the class are interested in the answers to the questions, the more genuinely communicative the activity will be. For example, if today's lesson in the book is on travel and the present perfect verb tense, a natural way to start class is by asking students "Have you ever been to _____?" To keep the interaction communicative, respond to what students say rather than just passing judgment ("Good!") or making grammar corrections.

[3]See Stevick (1988) for more detailed discussion of techniques for memorizing dialogues.

SUGGESTIONS

1 If you allow a pause after a question before calling on someone to respond, you can ensure that all the students in a class practice formulating responses even if they don't always have a chance to verbalize them. Talking with students in a random order also helps; students who don't know whether they will be called on next are more likely to try and think of a response to every question.

2 The problem of excessive teacher talk can be minimized if you start a line of questioning or a chain of dialogue, but then have the students continue it. For example, after asking Student A "What did you do yesterday?" (for practice in past tense verbs), you can have Student A ask Student B the same question rather than doing it yourself.

3 Students called on to respond in public may get nervous and freeze. One way to help students who panic, suggested by Omaggio Hadley (1993), is to ask a question that involves limited choices. For example: "Do you like reading or watching TV?" A question like this contains a possible answer and thus helps students toward a response. Yes/no questions are also easier to answer than open-ended ones, but generate less speech. Generally there is less tension in class if you rely heavily on volunteers to answer questions, only occasionally calling on those students who rarely volunteer.

Model-Based Dialogues

The whole idea of learning speaking skills from a book is rather odd; the very nature of the format naturally tends to pull students toward reading and away from conversation. (Arguably, a set of tapes might be a better "text" for a speaking course.) However, the reality is that throughout the world books containing dialogues are staple fare for conversation courses, so the question is how one should deal with them.

As suggested above, it is sometimes beneficial for beginners to simply memorize short basic dialogues, but as learners move on and the dialogues get longer this is a less and less useful approach. If dialogues are at all realistic—culturally and linguistically—a more productive approach is to use a dialogue as a model of interaction involving both language and behavior. Consider the following example:

Lan: *Let's* go get some food.

Jan: I *would* really like to, *but* I have a test tomorrow.

Lan: *Can't you* study later?

Jan: Not *really*. This is a *pretty* important test and I haven't prepared much yet.

What is important here is not the dialogue as a whole, but the individual elements. In addition to grammar and vocabulary, students should pay attention to how the participants do things with language (functions), and the cultural patterns of the way they interact. Points that could be taught in the dialogue above include:

1 How to make suggestions. Lan makes two: "Let's + simple present tense verb" is one of the most common and generic ways to suggest doing something. "Can't you _____" introduces another suggestion, but a rather pushy one. Apparently Lan and Jan are close enough that Jan doesn't feel the need to be overly polite.

2 How to politely refuse. "I would like to, but + (specific reason)." Here, students should learn both the language and the fact that to be polite in a Western context an excuse should be believable and specific. Note that the words *really* and *pretty* in Jan's second response serve to make the refusal less abrupt.

You can teach key language and cultural features of a dialogue by simply presenting them; alternatively you might point the features out and asking students to make an educated guess as to what function they serve. After the points have been introduced and explained, have students practice a dialogue that has the same kinds of gambits as the model dialogue, although not necessarily the same content. For example, after studying the dialogue above, you might give student pairs the following instructions:

A: Make a suggestion to B, and be persistent.

B: Keep finding polite excuses for refusing.

This kind of practice allows students freedom to improvise, but also makes it likely that they will practice new material learned from the text.

Treating a dialogue as a model of both language and culture gambits will teach students to pay attention to patterns of behavior, and practicing the moves allows students to rehearse and learn specific material. This kind of practice is also good for classes of mixed levels because it allows students who are unsure of themselves to stay close to the model while those who are more comfortable have freedom to improvise.

SUGGESTIONS

1 You can encourage students to personalize dialogues, using their real names and backgrounds or creating new identities and playing new roles.

2 Pair practice is livelier if you have students move from partner to partner cocktail-party-style rather than only practicing in seated pairs; this also allows them to practice the moves in the dialogue several times instead of just once.

3 Checking dialogues by having all the pairs perform at the end of practice is often boring and consumes a lot of class time. To more quickly give closure to the practice, select a few pairs (either at random or by asking for volunteers) to perform their dialogues. A more fun way to achieve the same end is to ask pairs what happened in their little encounters (e.g., "What excuse did Lan give you for refusing your invitation?"). Closing the activity this way focuses attention on the content of the conversations and helps keep the focus on communication.

4 Being stuck with an uncooperative partner can make pair practice burdensome, so I usually either let students change partners often or choose their own partners. In my experience, partners who choose each other eventually learn to work with each other reasonably well.

Role Plays

Not all students are hams, and some are put off by role playing, but for students who enjoy this kind of activity this can be a very effective kind of language practice activity. As Ur (1981) points out, many students feel freer behind the mask of a role, and the element of creative play involved in role playing can do much to make a lesson livelier.

Rather than trying to create role play situations from whole cloth, you might base them on dialogues or readings from your textbook. When role play situations are based on material from the textbook, the role play gives students a chance to practice using previously studied material in a less controlled type of activity. To set up a role play, give students roles and a problem situation. Often you will want to write each role on a separate piece of paper so that each member of the pair knows something about the situation that the other doesn't—as often happens in real life. Consider the following example:

> **A:** There is a very good movie in town tonight and you want a friend to go see it with you. B often goes to films with you, so you have decided to persuade her to go.

> **B:** You plan to go to a party tonight with some classmates. These classmates don't want to invite A, so have asked you not to tell her about the party.

After giving the members of each pair their roles, you might want to give them a moment to think about how to handle their situation, and then turn them loose to practice. After the pairs complete their role play, you can close the activity by asking a few pairs how their role play turned out. If your students enjoy performing you might also have a few pairs recreate their role play for the rest of the class. Although public performances may run too long if you are not careful, they have the advantage of allowing you a chance to comment on language or the cultural appropriateness of how students handle the situation.

Surveys and Interviews

Surveys and opinion polls provide a relatively easy and lively form of pair practice. Because students presumably need to poll several classmates this is a good chance for them to get out of their chairs and move around a little, and also provides a good opportunity for students to practice a limited range of questions and answers repeatedly. It is also relatively easy to come up with survey questions that involve a real information gap and that are of genuine personal interest to a class. (Appendix B may provide some helpful ideas.)

Interviews allow a pair to converse in greater depth and are a good activity for intermediate and advanced students. These can be handled as role plays in which one student acts as a reporter and the other takes on the role of a famous person, a visitor from an exotic country, or even the man/woman on the street. Alternatively, students can conduct real interviews with each other about their personal histories, interests, and ideas.

For both surveys and interviews, a good form of closure is to have a few students report the results of their investigation.

Small-Group Problem Solving

The key element of a good small-group activity is a clear task. Merely telling students to discuss something is generally not enough; they need to have a clear sense of direction and to know exactly what they are expected to produce. Different types of problem solving tasks include:

1. **Making a decision. For example:** Your foreign teacher has been offered two jobs upon return home, a stable but boring job in a bank and a riskier but more rewarding job putting out oil-well fires. Which should he or she take? (Details can be added at will.)

2. **Prioritizing a list. For example:** On graduation your group will be given a group ticket to visit three places in the world. What are your first three choices and why?

3. Listing steps. For example: Your teacher wants to apply for a driver's license in your country. In order, what are the proper steps?

4. Making plans. For example: Your school system is short of money and needs to raise more. Come up with a plan to improve funding for education (Ur, 1981).

5. Planning campaigns/advertisements. For example: Your group has been given the job of selling a new detergent. Come up with a 30-second advertisement to be presented to the class (Ur, 1981).

Normally, as the group discusses the issue, one person should be selected as the recorder.[4] Then, after the groups have completed their task, have one member give a brief report to the class. Of course, the primary value of small-group discussion lies in the practice rather than in the final reports, so the time devoted to reports should be kept to a minimum. However, as Ur (1981) points out: "It is not fair to students to ask them to put a lot of effort into something, and then to disregard the result. . . . What groups have done must then be displayed and then related to in some way by the teacher and class; assessed, criticized, admired, argued with, or even simply listened to with interest" (pp. 22-23).

SUGGESTIONS

1 In small groups, when discussion gets enthusiastic even well-intended students will often slip into their native language. For some groups, a reminder that discussion in their native tongue doesn't help them learn English is sufficient. For other groups, gentle nagging may be necessary. Remember that the goal is not to ensure that students speak only English, but rather to see that they get substantial practice speaking English.

2 Cross-cultural situations and topics can provide a rich fund of material for small-group discussion. (See Chapter 13 and Appendix B.)

Debates and Large-Group Discussions

In their favor, large-group discussions and debates allow students the opportunity to express real opinions, so these activities have the potential to generate a fairly high level of interest. Large-group discussions can also allow students more autonomy and encourage

---

[4]Cross (1991) makes the interesting suggestion that if you don't let students know who you will call on to report, they all have to pay more attention.

them to take responsibility for their own speaking practice. However, the fact that only one student speaks at a time means that students get only minimally more practice than they do in teacher-focused dialogue. This problem is exacerbated when a few students dominate discussion or when it is difficult to get discussions going.

SUGGESTIONS

1 Discussions get going more rapidly if there is a specific proposal or question to discuss rather than just a general topic. It is much harder to get discussion going on "Divorce" than on "Should parents with children be allowed to divorce at will?"

2 Choice of topic is important. Good topics are those that students know something about and have a variety of opinions on. In my experience, the surest ways to find good topics are to pay attention to what issues people argue about outside class and to ask other teachers what topics have worked well in their classes. You can also ask students to suggest topics, although they may tend to choose topics they find interesting but all agree on or know nothing about.

3 It is generally best to give students some time to think a topic over, discuss it in a small group, or write about it before large-group discussion. Discussion also works better after some kind of input (a reading or film) than if students approach a topic cold. Having students work in small groups to prepare cases for a debate is especially effective with many classes.

The idea of uninhibited and freewheeling discussion is quite appealing in theory, and many VTs consciously or unconsciously take this as the ideal for a good speaking class; in fact, some VTs become quite critical of classes who do not respond well to this method. However, the limited practice that the large-group discussion format allows each student severely diminishes its value as a form of speaking practice. It may be that the primary virtue of large-group discussions is as an occasional treat to break the monotony of class, or as a way for you to arouse class interest in a topic you wish to lecture about or have students write about. As a regular item in the class menu, large-group discussion is best limited to small classes of advanced students.

Having students practice speaking English outside class may not always be possible. They may be too busy with other homework, find it too awkward to talk to their peers in a foreign language, or simply not have enough interest in English to practice when the teacher isn't around to make them do it. However, the limited amount of class time available for speaking practice means that if students are ever to develop their spoken English very far, some practice outside of class is virtually essential, so one of the goals of your courses should be to teach students to take responsibility for their own practice. In order to reach this goal, over time you should try to move students toward

Speaking Practice Outside Class

135

less structured, more voluntary kinds of activities. The menu of activities below is arranged from those that provide the most accountability to those that provide the least. (Most of these activities are very similar to activities discussed for in-class use, so I will confine my comments to points specific to their use as out-of-class assignments.)

Memorization and Recitation

The use of memorization assignments for homework has one great advantage: Students can readily be held accountable because it is so easy to tell who did the homework and who didn't. This may, therefore, be a kind of assignment that would be useful in getting students into the habit of doing spoken work outside of class and is an improvement over assigning no speaking homework at all. However, memorizing a text for recitation in class is quite a different process from expressing one's own ideas in English, and this severely limits the value of this kind of practice. Memorizing texts also tends to be hard, boring work.

Dialogues and Role Plays Prepared Outside Class

Having students create their own dialogues outside class is a type of assignment that provides a fair degree of accountability, yet still allows students to practice expressing their own ideas in English. The main problem is that once students have invested time in preparing the dialogues it becomes necessary to give them a chance to perform, and watching such performances is generally not a very good use of class time. One way around this problem is to spot check by selecting a few pairs/groups to perform and then allowing other groups to volunteer. An alternative is to have students tape their performance or even videotape it in those rare situations where the proper equipment is available.

Small-Group Discussions Outside Class

Small-group discussions out of class can be handled in the same way as in-class small-group discussions and have the same benefits. The absence of direct supervision makes accountability more of a problem, but it can still be provided to some extent by having students turn in notes, tell you what the conclusions of their discussion were, or even just report how long they talked. An alternative way to provide accountability is to have the out-of-class discussion be preparation for an in-class activity such as a debate. Some students will no doubt take advantage of your absence to avoid speaking English, but as long as some groups are speaking English a significant amount of the time, the activity is probably worth continuing.

For advanced students, a useful variation of this activity is an ongoing discussion group focused on a particular kind of topic or material. Examples of this might include a group that gathers to listen to and discuss the news, or a reader's club that meets to discuss books. Another possibility is a group in which members agree to take turns preparing presentations that are then discussed by the group. For example, I once participated in a Chinese study group where each of the three members regularly made a presentation in his or her academic area. We thus rotated between discussions of Chinese history, literature, and linguistics.

SUGGESTIONS

1 Appointing group leaders—or having groups choose their own leaders—ensures that someone in each group is responsible for getting things started and also simplifies the process of holding the group accountable.

2 As in the case of in-class small-group discussions, groups will find it much easier to start their discussion and keep it moving if you provide a specific question (task) and clear instructions as to how the group should report on their discussion.

Free Conversation Activities

For motivated students at any level, the ideal way to practice is to begin bringing English into their daily lives, using it for real communicative purposes. This can be done in a variety of ways.

1 Setting up "English tables" in a cafeteria or "English corners" on campus where students socialize and discuss issues in English (or at least partially in English).

2 Chatting in English in the dormitory or while taking a walk.

3 Talking aloud to oneself or thinking in English.

By breaking away from the idea that English is only used when in class or doing homework, opportunities for practice are greatly increased. Combining English practice with social activity, as the first two methods above do, also has the potential to make English practice more enjoyable.

Heavy-handed attempts to hold students accountable tend to destroy the spontaneity and fun of such activities, turning them into another form of homework. However, indirect approaches such as casually asking students what they talked about at the English table are often sufficient to show that you consider such activities important.

Fishing for Native Speakers

If you are in an area where there are other native speakers of English, an assignment to consider is sending intermediate or advanced students out to find and speak with them. Because the enormous range of situations possible, generalizations are difficult; sending students off to make friends with GIs is not quite the same as having them waylay tourists. However, no matter what kind of native speakers your students talk to, even a small dose of such practice helps reinforce the idea that learning to speak English is mastery of a skill that involves more than grammar and vocabulary. Also, if some students are lucky enough to establish relationships with English speakers, they may have the opportunity for a lot of excellent practice.

SUGGESTIONS

1 If you require students to try to make contact with outside English speakers, it is important that you teach them culturally appropriate ways of approaching and interacting with their quarry. What little practice might be had in an aborted conversation with an annoyed Westerner could be outweighed by negative feelings, so students need to know how to start out on the right foot. For example, they need to be warned of the dangers of seeming too pushy, or giving the impression that their desire to practice resembles the interest of a cat in a scratching pole more than that of one human interested in communicating with another.

2 It also helps if students being sent out to start conversations with strangers are given a clear and culturally appropriate mission. For example, you might have students interview native speakers on their reasons for coming to the host country or their impressions of it. Having a clear rationale for the activity will help students know how to start the conversation and will make it more likely that the interviewees will cooperate.

Pronunciation

No matter how good the English of your host country English teaching colleagues is, unless they learned native pronunciation at an early age they will probably still have a marked foreign accent. It would therefore seem that one of the most valuable contributions you could make to your program is your native pronunciation. Unfortunately, this does not always work out as well in practice as it does in theory. First, many VTs teach students who have already studied English for years and whose pronunciation habits are not easy to change. A second problem is that native speakers of English produce sounds so naturally that we are often not aware of how we do it, so even when you know that your students' pronunciation is wrong, you may not know what the problem is or how to correct it. Finally, many VTs will work in countries where the standard English pronunciation taught is different from their own. This is particularly a problem for non-British teachers working in countries that were once British colonies. Most VTs are American, but in many countries school systems and materials still follow a British pronunciation standard. (Despite my impeccable Minnesota English, a school in China once decided that I should be replaced by a Chinese teacher during the pronunciation segment of my English course lest students pick up bad American pronunciation habits from me.)

The upshot of all this is that teaching pronunciation may not be as easy as it looks. However, by giving students reasonable expectations, drawing their attention to the various aspects of the problem, and being a model of native pronunciation, you can make a valuable contribution to your program.

Goals and Expectations

Many students, even those whose pronunciation is quite clear, are still dissatisfied with their pronunciation and will see the chance to study with a native speaker as the long-awaited opportunity to finally achieve native pronunciation. However, in practice this goal is very rarely achieved no matter how good the teacher or student is because it is inherently very difficult, especially for adult learners, to change pronunciation habits that are already set. Furthermore, it may even be unwise to try. A foreign accent signals the fact that a speaker should not be held to the same level of linguistic and cultural expertise as a native, and thus serves to protect the speaker from misunderstandings. Also, the effort that is necessary to lift a student's pronunciation from the level of "good" to "native" could generally better be invested elsewhere. Thus, a wiser and more realistic pronunciation goal for most students is clear-but-accented pronunciation, not native accuracy (Carruthers, 1987; Scarcella & Oxford, 1992).

This, however, is not to say that improvement in pronunciation is undesirable or impossible. When pronunciation problems affect intelligibility it is vitally important that students try to improve their pronunciation. Moreover, improved pronunciation is possible for most students. Some pronunciation problems occur because students have an incorrect idea of how a word should be pronounced. For example, a problem that often hinders communication is accenting the wrong syllable in an English word, a problem that is relatively easy to correct with instruction. Most students can also make limited improvements in their ability to pronounce sounds. For example, while they may always say [dis] instead of *this*, they may be able to learn to distinguish between long and short vowels (e.g., the difference between *hear* and *her*) in such a way that listeners can hear a difference. Most students can achieve a level of accuracy that makes them easily intelligible, and many can do much better.

Aspects of Pronunciation

Many students tend to think of pronunciation primarily as accurate production of the sounds of English words, but this is neither the only aspect of the problem nor the only important one. Consequently, one way in which you can help students improve is by ensuring that they are aware of all of the important issues.

1. Accurate pronunciation of sounds: As suggested above, this is really two problems, one of ability and one of knowledge. Students first need to learn to pronounce as many of the sounds of English as possible accurately. The particular sounds with which students will have difficulty depend to a large extent on students' first language, but there are some sounds in English, such as the *th* sounds in *think* and *this,* or the short vowels in *head, hit,* and *put,* which are difficult for students from many language backgrounds.

The second problem is making sure that students know what sounds they should pronounce in a given word. Common pronunciation problems include omitting sounds, adding extra ones, or simply pronouncing the wrong sound.

2. Syllable stress: Unlike many other languages, English requires that one syllable in each word be stressed more than others. The importance of putting the stress on the right syllable in English cannot be underestimated; as Bowen et al. (1985) point out putting the stress on the wrong syllable is more likely to make a word unintelligible than is mispronouncing one of its sounds. For many students who are especially hard to understand, misplaced syllable stress is the main problem.

3. Sentence word stress: In English sentences, not all words are given equal emphasis. Key words (usually the words that contain new or important information) are stressed and pronounced more slowly and clearly than other words. Take, for example, the question "Are you going to go to Boston?" If the focus of the question is on *where* the listener will go, the sentence will sound something like "Ya gonna go ta *Boston*"; the word *Boston* would be pronounced clearly and with more emphasis. If, in contrast, the emphasis is on *who* is going, the sentence would sound like "Are *you* gonna go ta Boston?" Students don't necessarily need to learn to reduce the unimportant words in sentence, but they should learn to stress key ones. (Students should also be made aware of English word reductions for listening comprehension.)

4. Sentence intonation: Intonation patterns in English sentences primarily indicate the degree of certainty of an utterance, that is, whether it is a statement, question, or suggestion. Statements rise to a plateau, and then end with falling intonation. Most questions end in rising intonation; however, Wh-questions (who, what, where, when, why and how) end with falling intonation. It is important for students to learn these patterns not only in order to communicate meaning, but also in order to avoid unwittingly sounding rude or indecisive.

5. Enunciation: A final important aspect of pronunciation is clear enunciation. Some students lack confidence in speaking or are unsure of their pronunciation, and therefore speak either very quietly or unclearly. Obviously this makes them more difficult to understand, and students should therefore be reminded that speaking audibly and clearly is an important aspect of pronunciation.

Teaching Pronunciation

The ideal approach to student pronunciation problems is for you to work individually with each student, listening for problems, explaining the proper pronunciation (e.g., intonation), modeling correct pronunciation, and listening to the student practice. However, this is usually not possible because of time limitations and class size, so the discussion below will focus on approaches that can be used with a class. These approaches fall into two categories: The first suggestions deal with teaching students what sounds they should produce; the later suggestions deal with practice.

LISTENING AND PRONUNCIATION

Unless you are fortunate enough to have very small classes, it will be difficult to give much individual attention to students' pronunciation. Students must therefore learn to rely on their ears to tell them whether their pronunciation approximates that of native speaker models. However, many students are not in the habit of listening carefully before attempting to repeat. In fact, they have often been trained for years to immediately repeat whatever the teacher says, no matter how vague their impression of the jumble of sounds they are trying to reproduce. Another problem is that while students are listening to the teacher's spoken model, their attention is often focused more on preparing to repeat than on listening. The teacher's sentence consequently serves less as a model for pronunciation than as a starting shot announcing that students should try to speak.

The first approach to pronunciation is thus helping students develop the habit of listening carefully before they speak. To do this, the first time you say a word or sentence, ask students to listen—just listen. They should not murmur the utterance quietly after you; instead they should concentrate on fixing the sound in their memories. It is helpful if you repeat the model utterance several times before asking students to repeat; this not only allows them more chances to listen but also helps students break the habit of blurting out a response as soon as you finish.

Exercises that require listening but no oral response may also help sharpen student listening skills. Minimal pair drills are particularly good for helping students learn to hear the difference between similar sounds. Minimal pairs are words that are pronounced exactly the same with the exception of one sound (e.g., *pin—pen, bid—bit*). Sample exercise: To help students learn to hear the difference between the short [i] and [e] sounds, ask students to raise their pen when you say the word *pen* and a pin when you say *pin*.

Training students' ability to hear sound distinctions will not necessarily result in good pronunciation. As Bowen et al. (1985) comment: "Practice in recognizing may also result in developing an ability to produce the unfamiliar sounds, but this is not a universally accepted conclusion, and many would dispute the value of carryover from recognition to production" (p. 145). However, students who have not clearly heard a sound obviously have less chance to produce it correctly than those who listen carefully.

MODELING PRONUNCIATION

Most native speakers of English have not formally studied the mechanics of English pronunciation, so this is an area in which it would be helpful to do some homework so that you are prepared to explain how sounds are made if called on to do so.[5] However, you will almost certainly be expected to serve as a model for pronunciation, and for this purpose a limited amount of choral drill can be useful. Steps for such a drill would be as follows:

[5]A detailed introduction to the sounds of English can be found in many ESL and introductory linguistics texts. For example, Bowen et al. (1985) provides an

1 Choose a text that represents normal spoken English (as opposed to more bookish language). A dialogue from your textbook would be a good choice.

2 Read sentences aloud, clearly but at a fairly normal speed. Have students listen to each sentence once or twice before attempting to repeat it. Remind them that they should be listening to and trying to mimic the rhythm, stress, and intonation patterns of your speech as well as your pronunciation.

3 As suggested earlier, build up longer sentences from the end.

One enjoyable way to practice the rhythm of English sentences is by taking a dialogue from a book, preferably one with short sentences, and turning it into a "jazz chant." In essence, this means finding the natural rhythm of each sentence and then chanting it with emphasis on the key words, something like a group cheer at a football game or a chant at a protest rally ("Hell no, we won't go" and so forth). Clapping or pounding desks adds to the festive nature of the activity. This exercise is particularly good for driving home the point that not all words in English sentences get equal stress.

Suggestions

1 If you want students to prepare choral drill of a dialogue before class, it is best if they have a taped model to work with. Without having heard a dialogue before they repeat it, they may wind up polishing an incorrect performance.

2 Choral drill is best in small doses. It generally only takes a short period of drill for students to get the point you wish to make, and drill beyond that point rapidly turns into mindless parroting.

PERFORMANCE OF A TEXT

Once students are able to repeat accurately after a spoken model, the next step is to have them practice speaking from a written text. Keeping pronunciation accurate while reading a text aloud is more difficult than repeating after a teacher, but it is still easier for students than maintaining correct pronunciation in free conversation because they can focus their attention on pronunciation rather than grammar or word choice.

One way to do this is to choose a text and copy it for students. If the goal is to teach daily conversational English, it is best if the text

introduction to the sounds of American English and Cross (1991) to the sounds of standard British English. It is, however, also wise to look at English textbooks in your host country so that you know what standard students have been taught and what phonetic notation system they use.

represents normal spoken English, though an argument can be made for sometimes including texts of literary and cultural merit (e.g., famous orations, poems) that were also intended to be read aloud or recited. Having chosen a text, go over it with students in class and have them take whatever notes they need on pronunciation, syllable stress, sentence intonation and stressed words. Next have students practice reading the text aloud (either in class or at home). Students should become very familiar with the text, though I suggest that you not normally require them to memorize it because the time and effort needed for memorizing the exact words distracts attention from the primary point of the exercise. Finally, either have students perform the text in class or—if the equipment is available—have them tape a reading of the text. The advantages of the latter approach are that students don't all have to listen to each other read the same text and that you can listen at your leisure.

ACCURACY IN FREE CONVERSATION

Students cannot depend on always having someone around who is willing and able to correct their errors in pronunciation and intonation, so the final task—learning to maintain accuracy in pronunciation and intonation as they engage in conversation—is largely up to students. Ultimately, students need to learn to hear serious discrepancies between their own pronunciation and that of the native models to which they are exposed, and then correct their own speech.

Adapting to the Local Standard

As suggested in the introduction, you may have some difficulty if the pronunciation standard used in your host institution is different from your own. My first suggestion in such situations is that you generally use your normal accent in class, whether it is the "proper" one or not. Rather than forcing yourself to unnaturally mimic another accent, remind students that there are a variety of different English accents, and that they should become comfortable listening to as many as possible. On the other hand, when teaching pronunciation lessons, try to minimize any markedly regional features of your accent and conform as much as possible to that standard of English being taught (usually North American or British).

A second suggestion is that you familiarize yourself with the local standard. Look at a copy of a local textbook that teaches pronunciation to find out (a) how students are told to pronounce things; (b) what notation system (if any) is used to transcribe sounds; and (c) what students are and are not taught about pronunciation. Having this information will make it much easier for you to decide how to approach your pronunciation lessons, and it will also help you harmonize your lessons with the local system. Students may be held accountable for pronunciation or phonetics on general tests outside your class, and if what you teach does not conform to the local standard, your students may suffer for it on exam scores. Knowing the local system also enables you to point out ways in which your pronunciation differs from the local standard so that students who choose to model their speech on yours are aware of potential trouble spots.

Correction

It is not clear to what extent error correction helps learners improve their accuracy. In some cases correction may help, but it can also disrupt communication and discourage learners. However, summarizing the research, Hendrickson (1987) suggests that teachers should correct errors at least some of the time—mainly because many learners want and expect this kind of help. The question thus becomes when and how.

Correction is most called for when errors interfere with communication—when you can't understand what a student is trying to say. The disadvantages of interrupting here are minimal because communication has already broken down, and it is particularly important for the student to know that the message is not getting through. According to Omaggio Hadley (1993) and Hendrickson (1987), other kinds of errors that are good candidates for correction include:

1 Errors that are highly stigmatized, that is, those that might result in a student seeming rude, offensive, or ignorant. (I am reminded of a young official at a bicycle registration station in Guangzhou who led me into his office, filled out a form for me, then turned around and with a smile said "Get out!" Sensing miscommunication, I suggested gently in Chinese that *get out* was not entirely polite. He took this news in, pondered a minute, brightened up, and said "Get out, please!")

2 Frequent or patterned errors. For example, it is less important to correct occasional confusion between countable and uncountable nouns than a consistent, patterned failure to use plural forms.

3 Errors that reflect misunderstanding of a point that you have recently taught. For example, the -s added to verbs used in conjunction with the third person singular pronoun (I go/you go/she go*es*) deserves more attention if you taught the point this week than it might at other times.

It should also be noted that some students are put off less by correction and learn more from it than other students, so part of the art of knowing when to correct depends on being sensitive to how much intrusion your students can bear.

One form of correction you can use in class is that used most often by native speakers in natural conversation: a corrected repetition of the learner's faulty utterance. (Student: "I like to listen radio." Teacher: "Ah, you like to listen to *the* radio.") This approach to correction disrupts communication less than does directly pointing out errors, and it trains students to listen for this subtle kind of correction; unless this habit is explicitly pointed out to students as a subtle form of correction, many may miss these repetitions. A more direct approach to correction is to pinpoint the error by interrupting and repeating the few words right before the mistake (e.g., S: "And then I eated the food." T: "And then I _____ . . ."), giving the student a chance to self-correct. This approach is appropriate for errors that are easy to correct quickly.

For either of the approaches mentioned above to work, your feedback needs to come as soon as possible after the erroneous statement. If you restate an utterance or call attention to an error immediately after it has been made, students are more likely to be able to find the problem. Correction that is delayed is often more obtrusive because you first need to remind students of what they said wrong, a process that is often mistaken for the correction itself, thus creating confusion and necessitating further explanation. (Teacher: A minute ago you said "I like to listen radio." Student:"I like to listen radio." Teacher: No, no, you said "I like to listen to radio," but you should say "I like to listen to the radio." Student: "Pardon?") In such cases, it is all too often only after the student has been publicly convicted of error that you can begin the process of correcting it, so it is usually better to let the error go or make a note of it for some later time.

Final note: Many students have the mistaken impression that all native speakers of English should and will correct mistakes; in fact, I have heard students complain quite bitterly about native speakers who fail to live up to this assumed obligation. You should let students know that this is an unreasonable expectation for native speakers of any language. Most people are not language teachers and do not engage in conversation for the purpose of teaching language. Additionally, in most Western cultures, it is rude to correct other people's mistakes. As noted above, native speakers will sometimes repeat corrected versions of flawed utterances, but they generally only correct or teach overtly when asked or when communication breaks down completely.

It is important for students to understand this because many believe that the only real road to success in English lies in being surrounded by native speakers who will overtly correct mistakes, a view that subtly suggests that any other approach is hopeless. Of course, being immersed in an English language environment is very helpful to a learner, but not because of correction. The main advantage of having such an environment is that it provides more opportunities for practice and extensive English language input. However, whether students are in an English-speaking environment or not, they will only benefit from English input if they learn to attend to it and then correct their own mistakes.

Evaluation

When considering evaluation of spoken skills, there are two goals to keep in mind. Obviously one is finding out how well your students can speak. However, I would argue that in many situations an even more important goal is the backwash effect that oral testing creates: Students are most likely to practice speaking if you test oral skills. It is especially important to remember the backwash effect with regard to spoken skills because it is more difficult to test speaking than other language skills and testing of spoken skills is thus often neglected. (Even highly influential English tests such as the TOEFL examination do not test oral skills.)

Interviewing is generally the best way to evaluate spoken skills, so it will dominate discussion below. However, complete reliance on interviewing may be impractical in many situations, so other approaches to evaluation are also briefly discussed.

Interviews

Interviewing is the form of evaluation closest to actual conversation and therefore has an excellent backwash effect on students. It also allows you a rare opportunity to focus on the speaking skills of individual students in a situation where you can make a relatively accurate determination of their level of speaking skill. The main drawback of interviewing is that it is very time consuming, sometimes prohibitively so for large classes. Interviews are often used at the beginning of a course as a pretest (and chance to get to know your students) and as a final examination.

PREPARING FOR THE INTERVIEW

The first step in preparation is deciding what exactly you are looking for. Grammatical accuracy? Use of material taught in your course? Pronunciation? Overall communicative skill? Something else? Your choices should flow naturally from the goals you set for your course and the kinds of practice activities you have asked students to engage in. Needless to say, the backwash effect will be stronger if you let students know well in advance of the final examination how they will be evaluated and how they should prepare.

Secondly, draw up a list of topics or questions, giving yourself an adequate supply so that you need not use exactly the same ones with each student. Questions should range in difficulty so that you have easier ones for students at lower levels and more challenging questions for those with more advanced skills. Open-ended questions are best (e.g., What do you think about. . .? Tell me about. . .?) because they don't result in dead-end yes/no answers; they also allow you to see how much students can elaborate on a point, which is one indication of their level of speaking ability. Natural questions for a pretest interview with students you don't know would be questions about their backgrounds, families, interests, and professions. For a final interview you might discuss issues raised during the course, other courses the student is taking, or future plans.

Many teachers draw up some kind of marking chart to help them grade during the interview. A simple chart consists of a list of the points you are looking for with a point scale for each. Consider the following example for a course in which communicative effectiveness was stressed:

Ability to express ideas	1	2	3	4	5
Range of topics	1	2	3	4	5
Listening comprehension	1	2	3	4	5
Intelligibility	1	2	3	4	5

Bowen et al. (1985) suggests an even simpler kind of scoring system in which each answer a student gives is rated 2 (effective), 1 (adequate), or 0 (communicatively ineffective). The advantage of a simpler system such as this is that decision making is easier for the interviewer; the system, however, is also less discriminating.

As pointed out in Chapter 4, another way to grade is to place students' performance on a proficiency scale. Such a scale is intended to describe different levels a student reaches in progress toward proficiency, and is intended for use in measuring skills at all levels. Consider the following sample scale, designed again for a course that stresses communicative effectiveness:

Sample Scale

Beginning (1-2): For all topics, student able to express self only haltingly and with difficulty; frequently unable to express ideas at all. Often fails to understand slow, clear, simple sentences, even after repetition or clarification. Communication breakdowns are also caused by mistakes (inaccurate pronunciation, intonation, or grammar), or by limited vocabulary.

Functional (3-4): Can discuss limited range of topics (self, immediate environment) with patient interviewer. However, on other topics communication is difficult and often breaks down; interviewer's patience tried on almost all topics. Often misunderstands or fails to understand interviewer unless ideas clarified or repeated. Mistakes sometimes interfere with communication, and lack of vocabulary seriously hinders communication.

Intermediate (5-6): Can discuss familiar topics easily, and deeper or professional topics with difficulty. Can discuss own field much better than other topics of similar complexity. On unfamiliar topics, circumlocutions and breakdowns occur; patience of interviewer may be tried. Still has trouble understanding rapid or informal speech, but has little trouble with clear, moderately slow speech. Range of vocabulary adequate for familiar topics, but still limits communication in some areas. Mistakes still common, but don't often interfere with communication.

Advanced (7-8) Can discuss wide range of topics; discusses own field with ease. Occasionally forced to resort to circumlocutions or explanations by lack of vocabulary, but problem is generally resolved quickly; patience of interviewer almost never tried. Communication virtually never breaks down on any but the most obscure topics. Can understand normal speech without difficulty, and can also follow some informal or rapid speech; interviewer doesn't need to pay any special attention to speech. Mistakes occur, but rarely interfere with communication.

Nativelike (9-10): Easily discusses a broad range of topics, and can understand even informal and rapid speech. Still has foreign accent, but this causes interviewer no difficulty. Mistakes rare, and almost never affect communication.[6]

CONDUCTING THE INTERVIEW

Normally, you should allow an average of at least 5 minutes for an interview, plus a little time between interviews so that you can

[6]A more sophisticated speaking proficiency scale can be found in the ACTFL Proficiency Guidelines mentioned in Chapter 4.

take notes and give scores. For advanced students, longer interviews are necessary to give you an idea of their range of competence. An interview should have three basic phases:

1. Warm-up: Open with a few easy pleasantries to relax students. During this phase, you may also try to determine approximately how good their spoken skills are so as to choose appropriately challenging questions for Phase 2.

2. Body: Try to challenge student's speaking (and usually listening) skills. In this phase you have to be careful not to turn a pleasant chat into an overwhelming ordeal, but at the same time you need to raise topics and ask questions that give students a chance to show what they can do. Hughes (1989) suggests that you not dwell on a question if an interviewee gets into trouble; rather, switch to another topic to give the interviewee a fresh start. In addition to asking questions, you can ask students to perform tasks such as describing a picture, explaining how to do something, or entering into a role play with you.

3. Wind-down: End with a few easy questions so that the students don't leave the interview feeling devastated.

Taping interviews allows you to focus on the conversation during the interview, and also makes it possible for you to listen again after the interview. Listening to the interview again, however, obviously makes the whole process even more time consuming. Taking notes during the interview and then assigning a grade immediately is much more efficient, but can also distract both you and the student during the interview. When possible, getting a second opinion from a colleague who either participates in the interviews or listens to them on tape does much to increase the reliability of your grading. Note that interviewing students is a demanding task and your ability to make good judgments will drop quickly as you become tired. It is therefore best not to plan to do several hours of interviews in one fell swoop.

Other Ways to Evaluate Speaking Skills

EVALUATING PEER INTERACTION

In large classes it may be that you can only afford the time to interview each student once, or possibly not at all. This will make it difficult to test spoken skills in a way that gives a very precise picture of each student's level of proficiency. However, it is still usually a good idea to include some evaluation of oral skills in your course for the positive backwash effect it will create. A less time-consuming evaluation method that still requires students to speak involves evaluating them as they speak to each other in pairs or small groups. This will not allow you to get as clear a picture of each student's spoken skill level as an interview would, but it does encourage students to practice speaking.

One way to conduct this kind of evaluation follows a procedure similar to that of interviewing: students come to you in pairs, are given tasks such as role plays, and are then rated. However, you can also choose to listen to and rate pairs or groups during in-class practice, sitting in on a few pair or group discussions each class period. By evaluating a little each day in class, you can cut down on fatigue and reduce the pressure of a do-or-die final interview. (One side effect of this approach is that students take in-class practice more seriously, though you may also find that students get nervous as you hover around their group.)

LISTENING AND WRITING QUIZZES

For extremely large classes, you may find that any evaluation of oral skills is difficult and can be only be done once or twice, thus resulting in fewer grades and less reinforcement than you would like. In these cases, you may supplement oral skills evaluation with tests, quizzes, or exercises that evaluate listening and writing skills. Listening is a vital part of oral communication, hence testing listening tends to have the positive backwash effect of forcing students not to rely on study of texts alone. Writing does not involve as much time pressure as speaking, but like speaking it is a productive skill that requires students to learn to express their ideas in English.

A simple form of this test involves orally asking students questions and then asking them to write answers. A more complicated approach is to orally present students with a situation and then require them to write dialogues based on your instructions. (Dialogues are more appropriate than essays because the language in dialogues is closer to the language of daily communication.) For example:

(Teacher says) "A and B meet on the bus and greet each other. A then asks why B didn't come to dinner last night. B apologizes and offers an excuse. A then invites B to dinner another time."

Then ask students to write a conversation consisting of six turns (A—B—A—B—A—B). Encourage students to write the shortest dialogue that fulfills the instructions. Then grade the dialogues for linguistic and cultural accuracy and appropriateness.

This type of quiz is not without problems. It often takes students some time to get used to this format, so you should practice with the class a few times before the first real quiz. It also puts students whose speaking skills exceed their listening skills at a real disadvantage; I have seen some flawless dialogues that had nothing to do with the instructions given. However, the stress of this kind of quiz on listening is also its greatest advantage; the backwash effect will encourage students to focus on oral English rather than just studying the book.

Reading and Decoding

- ♦ Effective reading involves use of both bottom-up and top-down strategies.

- ♦ Many students of English learn to read almost exclusively in a slow, careful manner relying almost entirely on bottom-up strategies (intensive reading). Overreliance on this reading approach makes reading a slow and often painful process, and tends to discourage students from doing any more reading than necessary.

- ♦ Students who also learn to read in a more rapid, active way (extensive reading) are more likely to reach a breakthrough point where reading becomes a useful and even enjoyable skill.

Like many students of Chinese (and other languages), I learned to read by slowly carving my way through short but difficult texts with a dictionary, trying to memorize every word and figure out the grammar of every sentence. Not surprisingly, this was not an activity I enjoyed. However, fate intervened in the person of a Chinese history professor who suggested that because I had 3 years of Chinese under my belt it was time for me to start using it in his class. He presented me with a collection of short stories—Chen Ruoxi's *Lao Ren* (Old People)—and told me I had a week to finish the book and write a critique. I was horrified. I had never tried to read anything longer than a short story before—at least not within a 1-week period—and knew that there was no way I could apply my look-up-every-unfamiliar-word strategy to a whole book and still finish on time. So I resigned myself to disaster, calculated how much material I had to cover per day, and scraped through it as best I could. To my great surprise, two things happened. First, despite the large number of words I didn't recognize, I was generally able to catch the drift of the story, and in the end was able to write a critique of which I was even moderately proud. Equally important, for the first time in my foreign language reading life, I actually became interested in what I was reading.

Admittedly, this challenge came to me in the right form at the right time. Chen Ruoxi's clear, straightforward style made her work relatively easy to read, and I found the Cultural Revolution setting of the stories fascinating. I had also been studying Chinese long enough to have a reading vocabulary adequate for making some sense of what I was reading. Yet, I still feel lucky that my history professor intervened when he did because I was well on the way to entrenching the habit of a painfully slow and careful approach to reading Chinese, and had already started to believe that this was the only way an American could ever read Chinese—or any foreign language.

The "intensive reading" approach with which my study of Chinese reading began is natural for beginning students. When almost every word and structure is new, this slow approach makes sense as a way for students to learn new words and grammar. What often happens, however, is that heavy use of intensive reading as a strategy for learning vocabulary and grammar becomes confused with reading itself. For many students, the single greatest problem in learning to read a foreign language is that habits and skills intended for language learning become their only approach to reading, resulting in both poor reading strategies and a miserable experience. As we discuss reading skills in this chapter, much attention will thus be given to intensive reading and extensive reading, and to the importance of teaching students to read extensively as well as intensively.

Even when we learned to read our own language in elementary school, our attention was often focused primarily on the problem of decoding words, so it is not surprising that we often instinctively tend to think of reading as a process of looking at words, one after another, and then adding them up to see what they mean. However, studies of reading show that it is in fact a combination of bottom-up and top-down processes. In reading, bottom-up strategies consist primarily of combining vocabulary and grammar clues to build toward meaning. Top-down strategies, however, are equally important. When good readers begin reading a text, they generally have some knowledge of the topic. This, combined with clues provided by the genre of the text, will enable them to guess much of what they will read before they read it. For example, even before beginning a newspaper article with the headline "Plane Crashes In Alaska," good readers have a rough idea of what kind of material will be contained and even the order in which it will appear. As they read, they do not devote equal attention to every word or sentence. Material that they already know will receive less attention than new material, and material that was expected is skimmed over more quickly than that which was not predicted. The best way to understand reading is thus as a process of active guessing in which readers use a variety of different kinds of clues to understand a text and take what they need or want from it, generally as quickly as possible.[1]

This, of course, is quite different from the way most students of English—or any other language—are first trained to read. Instead of being encouraged to use extralinguistic knowledge, students are expected to carefully decode a text, slowly studying every sentence and word, and constructing meaning almost entirely from the aggregate meaning of the words on the page. In order to ensure that they understand every word and every detail of the text, students are encouraged to make heavy use of reference works and devote large amounts of time to relatively short texts.

Intensive reading is not necessarily bad. It is necessary when material is very difficult or when a high degree of detail comprehension is necessary, and the slow, careful approach to each text also allows students to study vocabulary and grammar. However, if this is the only approach to reading that students learn, the following problems arise:

1 Readers who rely on bottom-up processes to the exclusion of top-down processes often have comprehension problems. Habitual focus on detail means that intensive readers often get the details but miss the general picture. As Bowen et al. (1985) note, the time spent decoding also causes readers to lose the drift—hence the meaning—

Reading: The Problem and the Goal

[1]See Scarcella and Oxford (1992) and Carrell and Eisterhold (1987) for further discussion.

of a text, and may even result in their making more mistakes in comprehension.

2 Intensive readers are slow, and are consequently unable to read very much material. This, in turn, slows other important parts of the language learning process. For example, the limited amount of text that can be read means that less vocabulary is reviewed and consolidated (see Chapter 11). The intake of cultural knowledge through reading is also limited. For students who go abroad to study, slow reading can even limit opportunity for interaction with the host culture; for example, on American college campuses intensive readers are often noted for their absence from any activity other than classes and meals—they must spend most of their time at home or in the library struggling to cope with reading assignments.

3 The general unpleasantness of intensive reading—as both a language learning and reading process—tends to discourage student interest in reading English. Note that in classes that emphasize intensive reading, teachers also tend to assign short but very difficult texts packed with new words, a practice that goes further toward killing any interest students might have had in English reading.

It may be argued that intensive reading is necessary at the early stages of learning English when learning vocabulary and grammar is more important than learning reading skills per se. However, if students come to believe that this slow word-by-word process is the only possible way to read in a foreign language, there is little possibility that they will ever reach a breakthrough point where reading in English becomes an activity that is rewarding and interesting enough that it is self-sustaining. Students who eventually learn to read well enough that they can understand English novels, magazines, or newspapers without intolerable investments of time and effort will tend to maintain or even improve their skills after leaving formal English language programs; those who only read slowly and painfully are more likely to regress. It is for this reason that students should be introduced to and encouraged to use extensive reading approaches from as early a point as possible.

Intensive Reading: Methods

Intensive reading is the core of English programs in many countries, and the methods and assumptions used in intensive reading classes may have significant impact on the ideas and learning strategies that students bring into your class. Traditional approaches to intensive reading tend to focus more on building students' knowledge of English grammar and vocabulary than on reading skills per se, and to implicitly teach an approach to reading that is primarily bottom-up. A typical unit is often taught as follows: First students are expected to carefully read a passage at home, looking up all the new words and making sure they understand the grammar in each sentence. They may even be asked to memorize the passage, or be able to translate it. Then, in class, the teacher lectures on the text (often in the host language rather than English), explaining most of the grammar and words or questioning students on these points. Students are not encouraged to guess, but rather expected to work hard and make sure they know all the right answers.[2]

It is very likely that you will be called on to teach intensive reading lessons at some point in your career, and when you do it is important that you use these lessons to build students' vocabulary and grammar knowledge. However, you should also modify the approach described above so that there is more emphasis on building reading skills and a better balance of bottom-up and top-down strategies. It is to methods for teaching an intensive reading lesson that we turn below.

In-Class Methods for Beginners

If you are teaching true beginners, the first task is to help them see the correspondence between written symbols and spoken words and sentences. A few basic methods:

1 Teaching the alphabet. English spelling is rich with irregularities, but there is enough correspondence between letters and sounds that it will benefit students to know what sounds the letters of the alphabet commonly represent.

2 Reading aloud as students follow along. This will focus student attention on words rather than letters, and will help them begin learning to pronounce words as units instead of as collections of discrete sounds. Bowen et al. (1985) also note that this is a good way for students to learn what punctuation is for.

3 Having students read aloud. You can have the class read a text aloud as a group (resulting in a fair amount of cacophony) or have them read semi-audibly to themselves. Sometimes you might ask individual volunteers to read a passage aloud, but be sensitive to the fact that a process that is almost effortless for you is very difficult for those just learning to read, so practice should provide maximum support and minimum public embarrassment. At very low reading levels for English learners, texts should consist primarily of words that students already know in spoken form. This allows a little thrill of

---

[2]You may well have colleagues who regularly teach in this fashion, so before judging too harshly, remember that many English teachers have had only limited opportunity to use English, and are thus in the difficult position of trying to teach a language they cannot speak fluently. The advantage of an intensive reading approach is that the small amount of material covered means that with limited preparation, teachers can present a credible English lesson. It should be noted that despite its flaws, nations that make heavy use of the intensive reading approach often still produce a large number of students who eventually become proficient in English.

discovery when a new word is successfully decoded and also helps reinforce the link between written and oral language.

In-Class Methods for Intermediate and Advanced Levels

For students who can read simple texts (dialogues, stories, articles) in English, a good basic approach to intensive reading lessons consists of three parts:

1 Prereading activity (in-class) for building use of top-down skills.

2 Reading and studying text (outside class) for building vocabulary and grammar knowledge, and bottom-up reading skills.

3 Questions and comprehension check (in-class) to focus on meaning.

PREREADING ACTIVITIES AND SKIMMING

One way to encourage student use of top-down strategies is through the use of prereading activities that require students to actively make predictions about what they are about to read. Basic prereading activities include:

I. Predicting before reading: Before students read a text, have them consider the title and any other clues available (author, source, general kind of text) in order to try to guess what the text might be about. Even if the predictions are incorrect, getting students to guess will make them more alert when reading than if they are simply moving their eyes purposelessly over a string of words.

2. Skimming: A common prereading activity is skimming; that is, quickly looking over a text and reading a few short bits in order to get an idea of what it contains. Many students are resistant to the idea of skimming in a foreign language (largely because of well-developed intensive reading habits), so in-class exercises play an important role not only in familiarizing students with this skill but also convincing them of its legitimacy and value.

Skimming generally involves reading the following parts of a text:

◆ Titles and subheadings.

◆ A few sentences from the introduction.

◆ The first lines of some paragraphs.

◆ Proper nouns (names) and numbers. These are easy to spot and generally helpful in quickly determining what is being discussed.

◆ A few sentences from the conclusion.

For class exercises, choose a text, set a time limit that makes slow careful reading impossible, remind students to skim rather than read, and turn them loose. It may help if you call out the time as students skim, creating something akin to the atmosphere at a horse race. This not only reminds students to keep moving, but allows a degree of fun and freedom that may help convince them that it is really okay not to be reading carefully. When time is up, ask students what they have discovered about the text and what guesses they have as to the remainder of its contents. You might even list their guesses on the board, and have the class go back to check them out later after they have read the passage more carefully. The ultimate goal is for students to develop the habit of skimming a text on their own, so over time you should encourage students to skim whenever they have occasion to read an English text, especially a long or difficult one.

3. Prereading questions: As with focused listening, you can make a reading task easier by providing questions to try to answer as they read. These questions not only help give reading a focus and purpose, but also provide valuable hints as to what might be coming in the text ahead. For lower level students, these might be simple comprehension questions (e.g., What happened at the end of the story?). For more advanced students reading more sophisticated texts, open-ended opinion questions are generally better (e.g., Was the author of this story biased?).

The goal is for students to begin thinking more actively about what they should be looking for as they read, so you should try to get them involved in coming up with their own questions. One way to do this is to have students take guesses they make after skimming the text and turn those into questions.

READING AND STUDYING THE TEXT

There is nothing inherently wrong with having students read and study the reading passages in class, and it may be a good idea to do this from time to time so that you can see how students read a passage. However, class time limitations will mean that you often ask students to read and study passages at home. Intensive reading textbooks usually come equipped with a supply of reading passages, vocabulary lists, notes on grammar, and comprehension questions. So, when you ask students read the texts and study at home, you should require that students do three things:

1 Study unfamiliar grammar structures and vocabulary. Encourage students to not only learn the meaning of new words but also note how they are used in the passage—this will help build the important vocabulary study habit of learning usage as well as meaning.

2 Try to understand as much of the content of the passage as possible, using both bottom-up and top-down strategies. You should let students know that intelligent guessing will be rewarded rather than condemned. Encourage students to use comprehension questions (yours, the text's or their own) to focus their reading and check their comprehension.

3 Prepare questions about any section of the passage they do not understand. Note that here the emphasis is still on comprehension of the passage. Questions on grammar and vocabulary should also be allowed, but the first priority should be comprehension of content.

INTENSIVE READING LESSONS IN CLASS

The traditional in-class intensive reading lesson consists largely of lecture on the passage. One problem with this approach is that too often the lecture is unnecessary and boring for students who did their homework well, and over the heads of those who didn't prepare or whose listening skills are weak. Another is that a lecture approach encourages students to passively wait for the teacher to solve problems. Below are some alternative uses for class time.[3]

Answering Questions

The goal of an intensive reading lesson is not just to explain what a particular text means, but rather to teach students how to unravel the mystery of a text for themselves. Students should therefore play as active a role as possible figuring out each reading passage, and be encouraged to take the initiative by asking you for whatever explanation they need.

---

[3]Intensive reading lessons are often opportunities for teaching grammar and vocabulary, but in order to maintain a focus on reading, I have rather artificially separated these two aspects of language teaching into independent chapters (11 and 12).

Here is the first paragraph from a typical intensive reading passage:

> Scientists at Sussex University appear to be on the way to discovering how the mosquito, carrier of diseases such as malaria and yellow fever, finds its target. They have found that the best way to avoid being bitten is: stop breathing, stop sweating, and keep down the temperature of your immediate surroundings. Unfortunately the first suggestion is impossible and the others very difficult.[4]

To deal with this text, first let students ask you questions about whatever they don't understand. Then, for at least some of the questions, try to respond by giving clues so that students can arrive at their own answer. Consider a few examples:

a. The word *target* (Line 3) might cause some confusion, particularly if students' dictionaries only list a basic meaning such as "something to shoot at." You might respond by asking whose target is being discussed and then asking students to consider what a reasonable mosquito might be interested in. You could also encourage them to look at the following sentence (where the implication is that the target is "you").

b. Students preoccupied with knowing the exact meanings of words might ask about "Sussex University" (Line 1). This question probably isn't worth the investment of much time, so you might just reassure the class that it is only important to know this is the name of a university.

c. The insertion of the long clause "carrier of diseases such as malaria and yellow fever" in the first sentence (Lines 1-2) might trip up some students, especially those who read slowly. A good tactic for dealing with complex sentences is to have students break them down into smaller simpler sentences. Here the result would be two sentences: (a) Scientists at Sussex University appear to be on their way to discovering how the mosquito finds its target. (b) The mosquito is a carrier of diseases such as malaria and yellow fever.

d. The phrase "keep down the temperature of your immediate surroundings" (Line 5) might cause confusion, especially as it seems to be an absurd suggestion. To respond to this, you probably first need to ask the class whether these suggestions are intended to be serious or not, and have them note Lines 6-7. Having established that the suggestions are not serious—indeed, they may be intended as a

---

[4]From *A Guide to the Revision of College English, Vol. 2* (Guangzhou, China: Guangdong Bureau of Higher Education, 1991), p. 17.

joke—then go back to the phrase in question and piece the meaning together using the meanings of the words.

One problem with relying on student questions is that students in some cultures are too shy to ask questions, or may simply be accustomed to listening to the teacher lecture, so it may take both time and nurture before you can be reasonably sure that students will ask when they don't understand. You can minimize this problem by isolating a number of potential trouble spots in the text and asking specifically whether or not students understand these; it is easier to get students to nod yes or no than to get them to ask questions. Another alternative is to require students to each write one question about the reading passage and give it to you before class. A more punitive strategy is to give a comprehension quiz after your class explanation, perhaps even focusing on those points you suspect students should have asked about but didn't.

For classes that go to the opposite extreme by asking about everything, set limits on the kinds of questions that you will answer. One suggestion is that you make it a rule that you will only answer questions relevant to comprehension of the passage being discussed. For example, you might tell students that you are willing to explain what *target* means in this passage, but refuse to be drawn into an exhaustive explanation of all of its other possible uses. Such a rule will make life easier for you because contextualized questions about vocabulary, grammar, and meaning are easier to deal with, and it will also keep students focused on the primary goal: comprehension of the text.

Focusing on Word Usage

One advantage of intensive reading is that its slow pace allows students to take note of how words are used in a text, thus learning usage along with meaning. However, students often study only the meaning of words unless you remind them to attend to usage as well.

Students will often underline new vocabulary words in a reading passage, so one way to get them to pay more attention to usage is to have them underline not only the new word but the words around it necessary for proper usage. For example, in the passage above, if students underline "on the way" as a new lexical item, they should also note that it is followed by "to + a gerund" ("to discovering"). This is in contrast to "the best way" below, which is followed by an infinitive ("to avoid").

Having had students note the usage of a new lexical item, a time-honored practice method is to have them make a sentence using the new item. This can be done either right after you point out the usage of an item in class, or as a homework assignment. Making sentences is a good way to not only help students remember the usage of a new item but also explore variations. Although this can easily degenerate into a copying exercise if you ask students to create sentences for a long list of words, I would recommend this exercise in limited doses for items that pose usage problems.

Outlining

For intermediate or advanced students who are reading expository passages, a useful exercise is to have them outline the flow of ideas in the passage. This can be done either as an individual reading/writing activity, or a small-group project, and you may choose to require either a proper formal outline or a series of notes that summarizes the main ideas and makes clear the relationship between them.

Interpreting a Passage

In order to fully comprehend a passage, especially at advanced levels, students often need to understand more than the surface meaning of the text. The opportunity for careful scrutiny of a passage created by intensive reading can be profitably used to deal with questions such as:

- Main idea. What is the author most concerned to communicate?
- Bias and stance. Is the author objective or biased? Does the author portray a character in a sympathetic or unfavorable light?
- Tone. Is the author serious? Joking?
- Purpose. Why was this written? Is the author trying to entertain? Persuade? Explain? Some combination of the above?

To use these questions for small-group discussion tasks, ask students to not only propose answers but also search the passage for evidence to support their hypotheses. The exercise can then be closed by having each group present its theory and evidence for class discussion.

Dealing with these issues is often difficult for students; even native speakers of English might debate an author's objectivity or purpose. It is, however, important to consider these issues because they are critical to comprehension of a text, and students who are thinking of these questions as they read are more likely to notice clues that throw light on the issue.

To a much greater extent than intensive reading, the development of extensive reading skills offers the possibility for reading in English to become rewarding and enjoyable enough that it becomes an end in itself. If such a breakthrough occurs and students begin to regularly read English books, newspapers, and magazines, they will naturally to continue to develop their reading skills, vocabulary and

Extensive Reading: Methods In Class

163

cultural knowledge. Unfortunately, this breakthrough point is reached only after considerable study and practice. Two important preconditions for a reading breakthrough, the acquisition of a large recognition vocabulary and a fund of cultural background knowledge, are discussed elsewhere in this book (Chapters 11 and 13). This section will focus on two aspects of building extensive reading skills: increasing reading speed and enhancing ability to guess unfamiliar vocabulary.

Building Reading Speed

One important aspect of helping students develop extensive reading skills involves training them to read more quickly. This can be emotionally difficult for students accustomed to intensive reading because reading at a slower pace is more comfortable. However, as noted earlier, increased reading speed is not only important in enabling students to cover more material, but also in enhancing their comprehension. Reading specialists suggest that the minimum effective reading speed is 200 words per minute, the average is 250, and the optimum is around 400-500 (Bowen et al., 1985). For many students, reaching these speeds will require breaking some deep-rooted habits.

For in-class speed-building practice:

1 Find passages that are short enough to be read within a class period and easy enough that students don't often need to resort to dictionaries. Ideally you would have a textbook containing readings that are somewhat longer than those often used for intensive reading. However, you may have to make do with the reading passages in whatever textbook students have by doing a quick extensive-style reading of a passage in class and then having students read it more intensively for homework.

2 Estimate the number of words in the selected passage.

3 Have students quickly skim longer passages before reading them. Given students' tendency to confuse skimming with quick reading, a time limit of 1 or 2 minutes may help.

4 Have the students quickly read the text as you keep time. In order to remind them that they are working against the clock, mark time elapsed on the blackboard or simply call the time out. When students finish reading, have them note how long it took them to read the text and then divide the number of words read by the time taken, arriving at a word-per-minute figure.

5 Have students record their scores, and try to increase them over time.

6 After the exercise, do a quick comprehension check to remind students that speed is not the only goal. However, ask general questions on main points so that the focus stays on getting the gist of the text quickly rather than on detail comprehension.

Improvement in reading speeds tends to be very gradual, so students should not expect their scores to improve dramatically during a semester course. However, doing exercises like this in class is important in helping students see the importance of working to increase their reading speed. The primary value of this type of exercise lies not in the actual practice in rapid reading that it provides, but rather in its power to break the habit of reading slowly and intensively. The fact that this activity goes on in class with the teacher's approval also helps convince students that it is really acceptable to read in this way.

Guessing Vocabulary

In extensive reading, dictionary use should be kept to a minimum because frequent dictionary stops not only slow reading speed but also tend to break the train of thought, thus hampering comprehension of the broader flow of ideas and making the process of reading less enjoyable. If students are to learn to read extensively, they need to develop the habit of guessing the meanings of unfamiliar words or skipping over them and forging ahead.

A useful exercise for helping students become more comfortable guessing goes as follows:

1 Have students quickly read a passage in class, underlining unfamiliar words but going on without stopping. (This could very well be combined with exercises described above for building reading speed.)

2 Have students report some of the words they underlined, and choose a few for class discussion. (Here you might wish to remind students that this is practice in guessing; the natural tendency of many at this point will be to start thumbing through their dictionaries.)

3 For each word, first have students ask the question: Can I quickly guess enough about the word to keep going? In many cases it is only necessary to get a general idea of the meaning of an unfamiliar word, and this can often be guessed from context. For example, in the sentence "She picked the *chrysanthemum* and smelled it" it is probably sufficient to know that a chrysanthemum is a kind of flower, and a student who guesses this can continue reading without any serious loss of comprehension.[5]

---

[5]Note that although this exercise may enhance students' ability to guess new words from context, this is not the main point of the exercise. The goal is to help students

4 If it is impossible to guess much about an unfamiliar word, then have students ask themselves: Do I need to understand this word? It is often possible to skip over unfamiliar words without serious loss of comprehension, and this is preferable to repeated stops. Of course, when skipping over words results in complete loss of the train of thought, students should stop and look the word up, but for extensive reading they also need to learn to become comfortable not knowing the exact meaning of every word they run across.

Extensive Reading Out of Class

For students to achieve breakthrough in reading, they will almost certainly need more extensive reading practice than is possible in class; thus an important part of a reading program is having students read outside of class. Although English language reading material may not be easy to come by in many countries, often at least some books, newspapers, or magazines will be available in English. When such reading material is available, extensive reading skills are often worth special attention because of the potential for breakthrough.

Choosing Material

In some situations you will find that not much reading material in English of any kind is available, but often the problem is not so much one of finding material as of finding material of an appropriate level of difficulty for your students. In China, for example, there is a wealth of textbooks available, and one can also get a national English newspaper and novels in English. The hard part is finding longer texts—interesting fiction, in particular—for students who are not quite ready for classic English novels.

One option is to develop your own lending library. Although this may take time and ingenuity, it allows you to establish a collection of books that you select to fit your own purposes. Of course if you have a generous expense account you can make trips to a well-stocked bookstore in a provincial capital or order books from home, but if you are working within more limited means you might try some of the following approaches:

1 If friends and relatives at home owe you favors, tell them what kinds and levels of material you need and ask them to haunt rummage sales for inexpensive or free books. As noted earlier, in many countries reduced postal rates for printed material are available, so mailing books is often not outrageously expensive (though it may take a long time).

see that it is often only necessary to get a vague idea of a word's meaning in order to continue reading.

2 Write your embassy or consulate to see what free materials it makes available.

3 Subscribe to a magazine or newspaper so you can both stay in touch with world events and build a collection of current events reading material.

4 Other foreigners who are leaving your host country may often be willing to leave old books, magazines, and such behind, so let other people know about your library-building dreams.

Assuming that some choice is available, the best materials for extensive reading are those which are interesting and not overly difficult.[6] To the extent that students have the choice of whether to read or not, it may help to think of the decision as a form of cost-benefit analysis: Students will be willing to read when the investment of time and effort is outweighed by the benefits gained from reading. The "break-even" point will differ from student to student, and will also depend greatly on the kind of material available, but it is safe to assume that students are more likely to voluntarily read materials that are interesting and easy than those which are neither.

Different rules of thumb have been suggested for determining what level of difficulty is appropriate for an extensive reading text. Scarcella and Oxford (1992) think that if a student has to resort to the dictionary more than once or twice per page because of unfamiliar words that can't be guessed and are important to comprehension, the text is too difficult. Bowen et al. (1985) suggest that if a student gets 85% of the words right when reading a text aloud the text is not too hard. My more rough-hewn approach is to have students open a text they are considering and read a paragraph or so from the middle. If they can more or less follow what is going on, the text is probably easy enough for extensive reading.

Group Reading Assignments

Let us first consider situations in which you have enough copies of a book that you can have all of the students in your class do extensive reading practice with the same book. A suggested basic cycle of activities would go as follows:

1. Prereading activities: (see above for intensive reading).

2. Out-of-class reading assignments: Whether the reading material is a short story, an article, or part of

[6]Bowen et al. (1985) argue that in choosing texts, the level of interest is even more important than the level of difficulty.

a novel, you should not only assign a certain amount of reading but also suggest a target for approximately how much time students should spend reading. This will remind students to work toward increasing their speed. As with intensive reading, providing your students with comprehension questions or broader interpretive questions will also help focus student reading.

3. In-class accountability and closure: Extensive reading assignments can be combined with a variety of writing or discussion activities, thus providing both accountability and a chance for students to process what they have read. Perhaps the best kind of activity is some kind of oral or written evaluation, recommendation, or review. For lower level students this might simply be a brief statement as to why they did or did not like what they read; with more advanced you might ask for a review or critique. (See Chapter 10 for discussion of review writing.)

Individual Reading Assignments

When possible as part of a course, it is good to allow students to choose at least some of their own reading material. Although this may be somewhat more difficult to manage than having them all read the same thing, it is preferable at higher levels because it accustoms students to choosing their own material. It is also often a practical necessity when you can't find enough copies of any single book for everyone in the class. For such situations, the following is a suggested cycle of activities:

1. Book selection and contracts: Tell students roughly how much material you expect them to read, and then have them choose their own reading material. One way to make the system more flexible and enhance accountability is by using "contracts" that specify how much reading students will do, in what books, and by what date. For example, if you have asked everyone to read at least 300 pages during the semester, one student might meet the obligation with one 70-page book and one of 230 pages; another student might have two 150-page books. The first student would then be expected to finish the 70-page book and report on it earlier in the semester than the student whose first book is longer.

2. Prereading activities: Have students skim their books either at home or in class. If you wish to ensure that they actually do this, you might ask for a very brief preliminary report of what kind of book it is and possibly some guesses as to what it contains.

3. Reading: As above, encourage students to set limits on the amount of time they spend reading.

4. Accountability: The most natural way to process each book is to have students write reviews or present recommendations orally in class. Students could also be asked to write summaries, responses, or cultural comparisons.

Having students read different books does present some management problems. One is that quantifying assignments by number of pages tends to push students towards books with small pages and big print, a problem you may wish to account for in your calculating system. Another is that it is a little easier for students to cheat if they are reading books you haven't read, though between your knowledge of what a text is likely to contain and the student's report you can usually get a sufficiently clear idea of how well the student has done the reading. However, the extra trouble of setting up and managing such a system is generally well worth the effort because when students can begin choosing their own material they are likely to begin considering reading in English as an activity that they might choose to make an ongoing part of their lives.

Evaluation

Evaluating reading work through written reviews, oral book reports, and other such measures has the significant advantage of a better backwash effect on students than examinations have, placing more emphasis on daily work and avoiding the unhealthy emphasis on one heroic study effort that often accompanies examinations. For situations in which you also need to use quizzes or tests, here are some suggested methods.

Beginning Reading Tests

For students at very low levels, testing ability to comprehend sentences is appropriate. One form of such a test can be constructed by writing a series of statements and then asking students to mark them true/false. A variation involves making up a list of questions to which students have to answer yes/no. The statements and questions can be based either on general knowledge or on some kind of picture drawn on the board.[7] (A problem with the use of true/false or yes/no questions is that students can be expected to get 50% of the answers

[7]For more discussion, see Madsen (1983).

right through guessing, so in order for the scores to have any validity at all you need to include many items.)

Skimming Quizzes

A simple skimming quiz can be constructed by giving students a passage and then asking them to skim and find out as much as they can in a very limited amount of time. When time is up, have them write down the main ideas of the passage. When grading such quizzes, be careful to give higher scores to those who get a sketchy overview rather than those who do a thorough job on the beginning of the passage but ignore the rest.

Passage and Comprehension Questions

The traditional reading comprehension test consists of several short reading passages (each one no more than a few paragraphs long) and comprehension questions for each. The kinds of questions you ask will depend in part on what you have emphasized in your course. If you have stressed guessing vocabulary from context, you should have some items that test this skill. If your focus has been on content comprehension, questions should emphasize this aspect of the passage. If you have had students work with issues of author bias, tone, and other deeper aspects of comprehension, these are fair game as well.

Intensive reading tests normally evaluate students' comprehension of both main points and details, so students should be given an ample allotment of time to read the passage carefully. You may even allow students to use dictionaries.[8] Passages for extensive reading tests should be longer, time constraints should be tighter, less emphasis should be placed on detail comprehension, and dictionary use should almost certainly not be permitted.

There are a number of kinds of test items you might consider:

1. True/false: True/false (yes/no; good/bad) items are easy to grade, but you need a great many of them in order to have a reasonable level of test validity.

2. Multiple choice: Like true/false items, the various forms of multiple choice items (including matching) are easy to grade. However, as noted in Chapter 4, they are

[8]In real-life intensive reading dictionaries are generally used, and their effective use is an important part of the skill being tested. However, if part of your goal is to prepare students for other reading tests, you need to make sure that the rules of your test conform to those of later tests outside your class.

difficult to construct well. Their backwash effect is also questionable as they encourage students to hone skills in guessing between alternatives. My personal feeling is that you should avoid using this kind of item unless it is widely used in your host country and students need to be prepared for them. In that case, try to learn locally how items are normally constructed.

3. Short answers: There are various forms of short answer items. The most obvious would be a simple question such as: "What are the writer's two main arguments?" However, sentence completion ("The writer feels that smoking _____") and filling in a form or grid are other useful forms of short answer items.

Short answer items can be more difficult to grade than true/false or multiple choice items; some answers will be partly correct, others may not be wrong but appear off the topic, and others may simply be hard to decipher. However, short answer items can more easily go straight to the heart of a passage than can multiple choice or true/false items (which tend to force you into testing details), are easier to construct, and tend to have better backwash effect.

Passage and Outline

Another way to check reading comprehension is to ask students to read a passage and then write an outline. (Outlines work best for expository passages.) This is a more difficult task than answering questions, and should probably only be used with classes who have had practice in this type of exercise. However, it is a good task for requiring students to extract the most important elements from a passage.

It is possible to make this kind of test somewhat easier by the use of short answer questions that are organized around an outline of a passage. In other words, your questions might look something like this:

1 What is the main thing the author is trying to persuade us to believe?

2 What is his or her first reason?

3 What evidence does he or she mention to support this first reason?

4 What is the author's second reason? And so forth.

Hughes (1989) suggests an interesting variation of this kind of item in which students are given an article (in his example, one on migraine headaches) and several randomly ordered statements describing the contents of the passage. For example:

1 She gives some of the history of migraine.

2 She recommends specific drugs.

3 She recommends a herbal cure. And so on.

Students are then required to read the article and place the statements in the order used in the article.

Passage and Summary

A simple form of reading test, especially appropriate for testing extensive reading skills, involves giving students a passage to read within a limited amount of time, then taking the passage away and having students write a summary of what they remember of its contents. This kind of test is easy to administer (though in large classes you may need help in collecting the reading passages back from students promptly) and has good backwash effects, but it also places fairly heavy demands on students' writing skills. This type of test is best used with students who have had this kind of practice in class.

Critique

A very challenging kind of intensive reading examination consists of giving students a passage that presents an argument and then having them write a critique or rebuttal of the argument. This tests critical thinking skills and writing skills as well as reading comprehension, and is only appropriate for classes in which this kind of critical reviewing has been practiced.

Translation

For VTs who can speak the language of the host country, the ultimate detail test is having students translate a passage in English into their own language. This, again, is only recommended for classes that have had practice in translation.

Cloze Tests

Cloze tests are sometimes used to evaluate reading skills, so a brief mention is probably necessary. Cloze tests contain a passage from which words have been deleted (every tenth word or so); students are then required to read the passage and fill in the blanks with appropriate words. Open-ended cloze tests allow students to fill in the blanks with any words they think would be appropriate; multiple choice cloze tests give students options from which to pick.

My rather lukewarm attitude toward cloze tests is due in part to the fact that it is not clear that what they measure is really reading skill (Hughes, 1989). However, my main objection is that their backwash effect may be to encourage students to practice cloze exercises rather than actually read.

10

Writing: Keeping Your Head Above Water

♦ Making writing a communicative activity increases students' interest in writing and your interest in what they write.

♦ Students need to learn to find and correct their own errors, hence it is not necessary or even desirable for you to find and correct every error on each paper.

♦ The ability to write well entails learning to plan and edit as well as write.

♦ Large classes in EFL settings make it important for you to learn to respond to student writing quickly and efficiently, and to find ways to reduce the paper marking load.

I was teaching at Fu Jen University in Taiwan the first time I was offered a chance to teach writing, and I was delighted to accept—writing courses paid time and a half. However, it was not long before I discovered that I had not driven a particularly sharp bargain. The sheer weight of the paper correction load more than justified any extra money I was getting; week after week I slogged through stacks of papers, finding and correcting the same grammar errors each week in papers students had obviously written just to get through the assignment. As the course went on and energy dwindled, I began resorting to tactics such as letting papers pile up on my desk or giving students long assignments so that I could rest for a week or two while they wrote. Of course, the problem with these tactics was that when I finally did get around to grading the accumulated compositions, it was all I could do to get through the papers, let alone make the experience educationally productive.

I no longer find writing courses such a nightmare to teach; in fact, now I rather enjoy them. But some of the problems mentioned above—students' lack of interest in what they write, slow improvement in grammatical accuracy, and the burden of correcting papers—are headaches that never vanish entirely. This chapter will discuss traditional concerns related to the teaching of writing such as various tasks that can be assigned, the steps of the writing process, and the mechanics of paper marking. However, this chapter would not be complete—or even very helpful—if it ignored the practical problems that confront a teacher in the large writing classes that are typical of EFL settings: The grandest writing theories seem irrelevant when you are confronted with a pile of compositions you don't want to read. Let me assure you now, I offer no magic solution to these problems, but I will discuss ways to minimize them, not the least of which is seeing that both you and the students have some interest in what is being written.

Message and Form in Writing

Many ESL writing textbooks approach the issue by teaching students the proper forms of written English (how to write a sentence, a paragraph, and so on), and then coming up with topics to give students an opportunity to practice using the form. Other approaches begin with the message, encouraging students to find something they want to say, and then moving to the question of what form will best help them communicate their message. There is no conclusive evidence that either of these approaches to teaching writing is the "right" one. However, I would suggest that a course that stresses message is generally more interesting than one that stresses form, and that by stressing content, you can use the inherent human desire to communicate as an engine to draw students into writing. Also, as pointed out previously, the tradition in many countries is to overstress the formal aspects of language learning, so it is best if the VT can be corrective to this tendency whenever possible.

Be forewarned that even if you intend to focus on writing as a communicative activity, it is very easy to become overly concerned with issues of formal accuracy. One reason is that written language is generally expected to be more formally correct than spoken language, so flaws seem to cry out for correction. The relative permanence of written language also means that teachers can scrutinize compositions slowly and carefully, devoting far more time to ferreting out grammar errors than would be possible with ephemeral spoken language. Finally, obsession with grammar and form is sometimes fueled by a cult of martyrdom among writing teachers who compete with each other to see who slaves for more hours over each batch of papers. In this competition, well-marked papers are concrete evidence of the teacher's merit.

The thrust of my argument here is not that grammar and form should be ignored; training in grammatical accuracy and the forms of composition should be an important part of any writing course. However, overemphasis on the forms of communication can lead to neglect for the message itself. This, in turn, leads to a situation in which students fabricate artificial messages in order to practice grammar or expository form. Students' tendency to ignore communication is compounded when compositions have no audience other than the teacher, and as Raimes (1983) comments: "Traditionally, the teacher has been not so much the reader as the judge of students' writing" (p. 17). When compositions come back to students covered with grammar corrections and comments on form, the students' belief that writing is a formal exercise is confirmed. Unfortunately, most students aren't very interested in writing formal exercises, and most teachers aren't very interested in reading them.

We would be kidding ourselves if we thought that students write compositions for us primarily because they want to tell us something; students in writing courses are generally all too aware that the primary reason they are writing any given paper is that the teacher requires it. This, however, does not mean that students cannot become interested in conveying a message if they are given the chance. Below are several general principles that will help you ensure that a writing class is as communicative—and interesting—as possible:

1 Make an effort to generate student interest in topics before asking them to write. One way to do this—and get in some good speaking practice—is to discuss a topic before writing about it. If students have not considered or discussed an idea, they are not likely to rapidly become deeply interested in it. An equally important reason for talking over ideas is to demonstrate that you are genuinely interested in the ideas themselves as well as the composition that they lead to.

2 Make use of naturally existing information gaps and opportunities for communication. There is a great deal you don't know about your host country, its history and culture, and about your students,

so this is a natural opportunity for your students to educate you through their compositions. There is also much that your students don't know about each other, stories from childhood and so forth, so this is a second natural information gap. Take advantage of these.

3 Ask students to write their own ideas in their own words as much as possible. Many writing texts are filled with exercises that require students to rearrange sentences or correct flawed compositions. Such exercises can be useful for teaching specific writing skills, but they certainly do not provide students with an opportunity to communicate in writing. A steady diet of such exercises will drill home the impression that writing is simply making sure that words appear in the proper formal patterns.

4 See that writers have a real audience for their ideas. If you have asked students to write about their culture, respond to what they say as well as to how they say it. If you are having them write about themselves, have them share what they write with other members of the class. Students need to experience the interest of others in what they have to say if they are to make an effort to communicate.

Teaching the Steps of the Writing Process

The writing process is often described as having three parts: planning, writing, and revising. You need not insist that students always strictly follow this process in their writing because a strict three-step process is not entirely natural; normally some planning and editing occurs during the writing phase, and new plans often emerge during the editing phase.[1] However, especially as students move toward more advanced levels of writing skill, it is desirable for students to begin learning that good writing begins before the first sentence is written and doesn't end with the last word of the first draft. An important part of writing is thus introducing these steps, stressing their importance, and providing students with practice in each.

Planning

The process of planning a composition can be further broken down into three component parts: generating ideas, organizing them, and noting them down for later reference.

GENERATING IDEAS

Essentially, this is the process of finding something to say. Sometimes this happens naturally, but students are often faced with the problem of being required to write about something they have never thought about or have no opinions on, and if they do not generate

[1]See Omaggio Hadley (1993) and Richards (1990) for further discussion.

ideas before starting to generate text, their papers will be more difficult both to write and to read.

One useful in-class prewriting activity is small-group discussion of the topic, followed by a large-group pooling of ideas. This is, incidentally, also a good way to integrate speaking and writing activities. Brainstorming is another useful prewriting activity: (a) Give students a topic or question and then have them think of as many ideas as they can as quickly as they can; all ideas, no matter how absurd or far fetched, are written down. (b) After a large number of ideas is generated, students go back and begin to choose those that seem worthy of further thought.

Although students may find this a little odd, you might also talk with them about when and how they think best. For example, I tend to think best when walking alone and talking to myself, jotting ideas down in a little notebook as they occur to me. Others may find that they think best sitting in a quiet room, or when talking ideas over with friends. Many students' natural tendency is not to think about what they will write at all until they start writing, so discussing with students where and how they do their best thinking will help underscore the importance of thinking as a part of the composition process.

SELECTING AND ORGANIZING IDEAS

This step is probably the most difficult of all steps to isolate from the others; ideas will continue to be added, subtracted, or moved throughout the whole writing process. However, making an initial effort to select and organize material will give students a good head start.

The first—and sometimes most difficult—decision students have to make is exactly what aspects of a topic to focus on. Most topics are broad enough to allow more than a single approach, so students need to decide what points to emphasize. The second step is determined by the first. Having decided what to focus on, students need to look at their material and decide what ideas and details suit the focus. The problem most often encountered here is that students are reluctant to omit any of the precious material that was so painfully generated and try to find ways to shoehorn almost all of it in, so you will need to stress that part of becoming a good writer is learning to eliminate irrelevant material. Finally, students need to arrange the points in the most effective order and decide what to say about each.

To help students develop these skills, in-class exercises like the following are often beneficial: (a) Choose a topic and have the class brainstorm to generate a list of ideas while you write the ideas down on the board. (b) Break the class into small groups to choose a focus, select and reject material, arrange ideas, and write a group outline. (c) If time permits, either have each small group write an outline of their plan on the board or work together as a whole class to produce a group plan.

NOTING IDEAS DOWN

Perhaps the most important aspect of teaching students to plan what they write is ensuring that they actually do it. Students are often tempted to cut corners in their work, and the preparation step for writing is one of the corners most often cut. Many students don't see it as important, or simply don't do it because they are busy and it is easier to get away with not preparing a composition than not writing it. If you require that students produce some kind of written plan before they write—anything from a scribbled list to a neat outline—it is not only easier to hold students accountable for the planning phase of writing but also more likely that they will produce a good paper.

Writing

This is the stage of the writing process that is most familiar to students—in fact, it may be the only stage that many students practice—so less need be said about it than the other two stages. Two comments are, however, in order.

WRITING AND TRAIN OF THOUGHT

Helping students develop smoothness in their writing can be quite difficult if they see grammar and spelling errors as unforgivable crimes and always break their train of thought to look up words in a dictionary or check a grammar rule. Such students tend to write slowly and painfully, and it is not unusual for the progression of their ideas to seem choppy.

One solution to this problem is teaching students to focus on putting their ideas down on paper in as uninterrupted a manner as possible, leaving correction for later. A helpful in-class exercise for this, speed-writing, goes as follows: (a) Give students a topic, and then tell them to write as much about it as they can within a limited amount of time. (b) Then have them count and record the number of words they have produced, and try to increase the number over time. Award praise only on the basis of how much text is produced. Like brainstorming, this can be an enjoyable activity once students get used to the freedom of it, and it can help them break the habit of slow writing. Students may also discover that when they write in this way they are not much less accurate than they are when writing more slowly and carefully.

IN-CLASS WRITING PRACTICE

Even if you prefer to have students do most of their writing at home, it is generally a good idea to occasionally have students write in class. One of the advantages of this is that you can actually watch students write so you can get an idea of how quickly or slowly they produce text, how much they use reference tools, and so forth. This will help you determine what problems students face in their writing, and what kinds of practice they need.

Editing and Rewriting

Editing can be divided into two processes: revising and proof-reading.

REVISING

One problem with revision is that most students are not very motivated to do it. All too often, students see little reason to polish presentation of ideas they never had any real interest in. A second problem is that even when students do try to revise, they often do so the same night as they write, and simply have neither the energy nor the freshness of perspective to see flaws of organization and logic that they might notice were they to look over the composition in the morning.

The best way to convince students of the benefits of revision is to ensure that they actually revise papers so that they can see for themselves how much better a revised paper can be. This may mean having them revise in class so that you can ensure that they attempt revising some time other than the same night the paper was written. You might also occasionally have students hand in drafts that you then hold for a period of time before handing them back—unedited—for student revision. This allows students a rare opportunity to look back on their own work with fresher minds and higher energy levels than they normally bring to the task of revision. A final way to ensure that students actually write a second draft of a paper is to have them turn in both the old and new draft to you. You then grade the new draft partially on the basis of improvement.

Another approach to revising is to have students exchange papers and give each other feedback on content. Initially this may not work very well because students often go to extremes of either being too polite to their classmates or too zealous in the role of critic, so you may need to remind students that the role of the reader is to offer helpful suggestions rather than final judgments, and that the role of the writer is to listen to and take note of the suggestions rather than defending him/herself from them. Of course, the writer may ultimately choose to reject suggestions, but it is best to listen carefully first; even if an unwise suggestion may alert the writer to a point that needs improvement.

Peer editing can be enhanced by giving students a checklist to guide their revision efforts. A simple list of such questions might include:

Is there anything that I don't understand?
Is there any place where I want to know more?
Is there any place where I wanted an example?
Is there anything that seems out of place?
Is there anything that seems unnecessary?

Ultimately, the most important thing you can do to help students develop editing skills is to make writing a communicative activity that they take a genuine interest. The more interested students are in their message and the response of their audience, the more likely they are to master revision skills. Without that interest, no amount of theory will help.

PROOFREADING

This is a difficult skill for many students to develop, not so much because they cannot correct mistakes as because they cannot find them. It is impossible to proofread quickly by mechanically applying grammar rules to every sentence in a composition, so the ability to proofread depends heavily on language sense, an instinctive knowledge of what is definitely correct and what is dubious. Students who have been exposed to a great deal of correct English will often be able to tell that something "looks funny," and students who don't have this sense generally can't proofread very well.

Perhaps the most common exercise for developing proofreading skills is one in which students are given a flawed composition and then asked to find and correct the errors. This same kind of exercise can be done if students exchange compositions with each other to proofread, or if you occasionally have students proofread their own papers in class. (This last exercise should be used sparingly as once students get the idea that they can proofread in class, they aren't likely to do it at home. However, it can be effective if done occasionally because it may drive home the point that if students proofread when their minds are fresh—instead of at midnight—they may find mistakes they would otherwise have missed.)

One way for students to improve their ability to find mistakes is by learning to focus on personal problem areas. By paying attention to compositions that you edit and then keeping a record of the kinds of errors that appear most often, students can learn what they personally need to pay special attention to so that they can narrow the field of their proofreading efforts.

Teaching students how to use reference tools is another important aspect of helping them develop proofreading skills. Bi- or monolingual dictionaries that have plenty of examples are especially valuable tools for writing because the examples provide students with models of grammar and usage as well as word meaning.

The Writing and Feedback Cycle

If you ask students to go through each of the steps above for a paper, and if you provide feedback after each step, the process would look something like this:

1 Prewriting activities (in class) before the writing assignment is given.

2 Planning (in class or at home).

3 Feedback. Students show you their notes or outline. Alternatively, you can have students share and discuss their plans with other classmates in pairs or small groups, or put example outlines of student papers on the board for class discussion.

4 Writing the first draft (in class or at home).

5 Feedback. Either from you or from other students.

6 Revision and second draft.

7 Feedback. Final marking and grading. Class discussion and student paper sharing can also be part of the final feedback.

This is obviously a lot of work to put into one paper, and it is not necessary to ensure that students go through all of the steps above for each and every writing assignment; at times you may wish to have them do an exercise that only involves planning a paper, or you may practice the editing stage alone by having students edit a composition written by someone else. However, it is worth the effort to go through all of the steps for at least some of the writing tasks you assign so that students become used to the idea that all of these steps are an important part of writing.

Types of Writing Assignments

Often, the types of writing you have students do will be determined in part by the materials you work with, by a school curriculum, or by specific needs of your students. However, usually you will have some leeway in determining what kinds of compositions you will ask students to write. This section will discuss various types of writing that could be included in a program.

Writing Tasks for Beginning Students

The focus at beginning stages of writing necessarily tends to be on mechanics of writing, and the virtue of the tasks below (as well as their weakness) is that they don't demand much of students in the way of organizing and presenting ideas, thus allowing students to concentrate on basic formal features of written English—spelling, capitalization, and punctuation—as well as on grammar and vocabulary. Most, however, have the advantage of involving skills other than writing.

1. Copying: For students who are completely unfamiliar with the Roman alphabet, copying sentences, or even short texts from the textbook or blackboard is a way to learn English handwriting.

2. Dictation (See Chapter 7): Dictation exercises provide opportunity for students to focus on capitalization, punctuation, and spelling without needing to worry about grammar at the same time, and can be used even at very elementary levels.

3. Dicto-comp (See Chapter 7): As a writing exercise this is somewhat more challenging than dictation, and is a better way to practice basic grammar points.

4. Dialogues: Having students write dialogues is a good way to allow some creative freedom in writing while still keeping the task conceptually simple. The dialogues can be performed in class as well as handed in as written work.

5. Personal paragraphs: When students are first learning a language, the easiest topics to talk about are those that are most immediate. Having students write about themselves is a good way to learn more about your students and also to establish the role of writing as a communicative activity. A variation on this activity is to have students interview each other and then write about the person they interviewed.

6. Filling out forms: One of the world's great preoccupations is the producing of forms, so practice reading and filling out forms is often of practical benefit. The formal language of most forms (e.g., *marital status, occupation, length of intended stay*) is worthy of special attention.

7. Note-taking (See also Chapter 7): Note-taking is a valuable skill to develop in and of itself, and it is also a good exercise for developing listening and writing skills. The writing component can be strengthened if you ask students to use their notes as a basis for writing a summary or response to what they heard.

Some of the activities above can also be used for students at intermediate and advanced levels, but at higher levels these kinds of exercises should be de-emphasized in favor of more communicative tasks.

Stories

Conceptually, narrative writing is relatively easy because chronological order provides a natural and simple organizational pattern, and most students have ready-made material in the form of their own experiences. A final bonus is that many people enjoy telling stories about themselves, and these stories are often fun to read. (Narrative writing can also be practiced if students retell or summarize a story that they have heard or read, though this tends to be less interesting for both the writer and reader.)

A story writing activity can be conducted as follows: (a) Introduce a topic by telling a story of a dangerous experience (e.g., remarkable coincidence, particularly stupid mistake) of your own. You can either write the story out for your class or present it orally. (b) Then ask students to respond with a similar story from their own experience. (c) Once stories are written, they may be shared with other class members, either by reading them aloud (in small classes) or by passing them around to be read by other students. Public sharing is probably best when stories have already been edited and polished, thus allowing students more confidence and pride in the quality of their work, but sharing of rough drafts for peer response can also be useful.

Story writing assignments present a good opportunity to encourage writers to begin thinking about their audience and about how to structure what they write for maximum effectiveness with a given audience.

Letters

As Raimes (1983) points out: "If a language student will ever need to write anything in the second language, it will probably be a letter" (p. 85). Letters thus have the advantage of high surface validity; students who assume they will never write an academic paper in English might well consider the possibility of writing a letter in English much more realistic, and hence have more motivation to learn this skill. Most students also have experience writing letters in their own language, so it is not as abstract and foreign a genre as some other forms of writing.

PERSONAL LETTERS

Though a great deal of freedom is permitted in the forms of personal letter writing, there are conventions for the proper placement of openings, closings, and date. Otherwise, however, this is an easy genre in which students can write about a broad range of topics ranging from the very simple to the profound. Tasks might include having students write you letters about a topic your are interested in, having a pen-pal in class to whom they write, or finding a real pen-pal in another country.

Personal letter writing assignments can also be generated by situations—either serious or fun. As an example of the former, you might ask students to write a letter of apology for some misdeed; an example of the latter might be a love letter to a famous movie star. Ur (1981) suggests an exercise in which you present students with a "provocative" letter that is "insulting, appealing, complaining, threatening" (pp. 98-105), and then ask them to produce a response. (Ur suggests that this be combined with class discussion.) This exercise can be made more immediate and realistic by using problem situations which you have actually encountered in your host country and then asking students for advice.

BUSINESS LETTERS

A variety of forms is currently in use for English business letters, and although students do not need to learn them all, they need to know at least one well—business letter conventions are stricter than those of personal letters. Business letters are also more demanding than personal letters in that the writer is expected to make points clearly in a well-organized way.

In many countries, the kind of business letter students are most likely to write is a letter of application, so this is often a good assignment for teaching students to carefully choose the points they wish to make, and then supporting the points with explanation and detail. Application letters also provide a good opportunity to discuss cultural aspects of how one presents oneself. For example, a student writing a business letter needs to learn to get to the point quickly without indulging in a long flowery prelude that a Western reader might find superfluous and annoying. Also, students writing application letters need to learn the fine art of presenting their strong points in an objective quantifiable way so that they do not seem subjective and overly boastful to a Western reader. It isn't as good to say "I was the best student in my school" (subjective judgment) as to say "I had the highest grade point average" (objectively demonstrable fact).

In many ways, business letters are short expository compositions, so the basic organizational patterns of expository writing can be taught in the context of business letters. Like any other form of expository writing, the business letter is composed primarily of paragraphs that consist of the following components: point(s), explanation, and specific details or evidence. The importance of accuracy in business letter writing also provides a natural context for the introduction of proofreading and editing skills. Students may see the importance of making a good impression in an application letter—hence not making too many grammar mistakes—more readily than in other kinds of writing assignments, so this may be an opportunity to motivate them to invest the time and effort necessary for developing editing skills.

Expository and Argumentation Writing

Not all students need to have highly developed academic writing skills or the ability to produce a professional report in English. However, most can benefit from practice in learning how to state and support an opinion or point, if only for writing letters.

One can divide expository writing roughly into two kinds: writing that explains and writing that persuades. However, the distinction between these is somewhat artificial; argument almost always requires explanation, and most expository writing has at least some element of persuasion. Both also have the same basic point-explanation-detail organizational pattern: An idea is usually presented at the beginning of a section of discourse (which may range in length from part of a paragraph to several pages), developed through explanation, and supported through the use of examples, concrete details, and evidence that make the ideas clearer, more memorable, and more convincing.

The most basic expository writing assignment is a paragraph or short composition which presents an opinion and reasons for it. Start with an opinion question such as "What is the best place to visit in your country?" or "What do you find most difficult about learning

English?"[2] Then have students state an opinion and then develop it. For example, if a student suggests that the national capital is the best place to visit, she should develop her answer by explaining why, and also providing specific details and examples. Naturally writing longer papers and reports is more complex than expressing an opinion in a paragraph, but the basic organizational pattern for all of these is the same as the point-explanation-detail pattern described above.

The question of whether or not students in a given host country really need training in expository writing is a question that should be raised more often than it is. The common assumption that expository writing should be the focus of EFL writing courses may arise more from the fact that English teachers are trained in academic environments where expository writing is stressed than from the actual needs of students. However, for a number of reasons, training in expository writing may benefit even students who will not function in an academic world:

1 Familiarity with norms of Western expository and argument writing will help students in their English reading. Many kinds of texts—including journal articles, editorials, and many magazine articles, newspaper articles, and books—follow these norms, so familiarity with how this kind of writing is put together will give students a sharper idea of what to expect as they read.

2 Knowledge of the norms of expository writing is also a window on the culture of the West. For example, the preference of most English-speaking Westerners for a simple, direct form of business communication rather than a more ornate or flowery style is a reflection of the way business is done in the West; the impatience of Westerners with communication that is indirect, unexplained, or unsupported by specific factual information carries over into spoken as well as written communication.

3 Expository writing skills require ability to analyze issues and problems as well as to write about them, so the teaching of expository writing almost inevitably moves from the realm of language into the Western approach to critical thinking skills. In the process of learning expository writing, students have intense, sustained exposure to different modes of organizing and presenting ideas, and this provides a rare and precious opportunity to wrestle with an important aspect of another culture.

Critiques

A critique/review is a special kind of opinion paper that evaluates a book, film, article, or even an idea. Most critiques contain the

[2]See Appendix B for a list of possible topics.

following parts: (a) summary; (b) discussion of the strong and weak points of the subject of the review; (c) a final judgment and recommendation to the potential audience. It is critical to the success of the critique that it appear fair, so it is particularly important that both good and bad points be discussed.

Critical reviews are among the most demanding forms of writing to teach, particularly if the text (book, movie, article) being reviewed is from another culture. Critique writing demands a high level of comprehension of the text being reviewed, and also places heavy demands on students' critical thinking skills, especially if the text being reviewed has been produced by a competent professional; flaws are often not immediately obvious, and the student is thus at a loss as to how to do anything more than humbly praise. However, the greatest problem is often deciding on a standard by which to judge the book. A reviewer can certainly start with the question: "Did I like it?", but ultimately needs to answer the more difficult question: "Was it a good book?" The former question is one of personal taste; the latter question implies a standard which is more universal, and finding such a standard can be a real problem.[3]

However, the problems in teaching critique writing are counterbalanced by the significant benefits:

1 After seeing a film or reading a book, the first topic of discussion is inevitably: Was it good? Critique writing can be a good way to get students interested in writing because it draws on one of the most natural of human instincts—the desire to evaluate.

2 Critique writing helps students learn to think critically about what they read or see rather than taking the printed or recorded word as sacred. In cultures where very high respect is accorded to the written word, it may be a helpful for students to consider more carefully the question of whether something is true or good simply because it is written in a book. If nothing else, critique writing drives home the point that Western cultures do not accord the written word quite the respect that it has in some other cultures.

3 The effectiveness of a critique depends to a large extent on its appearance of objectivity; the main difference between a critique and an argument is that the former purports to examine two sides of an issue fairly. Critique writing thus provides good practice in the examining of an issue from a variety of different viewpoints.

[3]When having students write critiques, I ask that they first try and determine the purpose(s) of a work, and then judge it on whether or not it achieves its purpose. The problem with this approach is that it can be very difficult for students from non-Western backgrounds to decide what the purpose of a Western text might be, and I thus need to devote considerable time to discussion of the genres of Western writing and media and what range of purposes is normally found within each genre.

4 Finally, critique writing is a good way to respond to books, articles, tapes, or audiovisual material, and is thus an effective way to combine writing with reading or listening.

Responding to Student Writing

Responding to Content

You should not be the only audience students write for, but you will often be the audience they are most influenced by. Thus, if you want students to take writing seriously as communication, you must respond to the message of papers as well as to their grammar. You may agree, disagree, ask questions, add information, comment on what you find interesting or confusing; sometimes you need to tell a student that you suspect he or she was just filling paper. The point is that your response should convince students that you are paying attention to what they have to say.

Comments in the margin are the best way to give feedback about specific aspects of a composition because the proximity of the comments to the portion of the text you are talking about makes them easier to understand. Questions in the margin are an especially effective way to help students know how to revise and improve their papers while still encouraging them to think for themselves. Unlike comments like "awkward" or "confusing," questions don't seem like a slap on the wrist, and they also establish a sense of conversation rather than judgment. (Students are generally more willing to look over and learn from your feedback if there is an occasional "good" or at least "OK" amidst your margin comments.)

Comments at the end of the composition can be used to provide a general summing up of the strengths and weaknesses of a composition, and perhaps a few personal responses to the ideas. A few suggestions:

1 The longer comments are, the less likely they are to be absorbed and digested, so it is better to make one or two points clearly than to discuss every flaw in the paper. (Remember, it may be quite an effort for students to decipher your handwritten comments, especially if they are scrunched in at the bottom with lines leading all over the page.)

2 Students are more likely to read the comments if you include some good news with the bad. Generally you can find at least one nice thing to say about a paper, and this takes some of the sting out of other comments. It also helps if you phrase bad news as suggestions for improvement rather than criticisms.

There is no reason why your response need be confined to written comments. Assuming that you have students write about something you are genuinely interested in, there is no better way to convince students of your interest than to talk with them about the papers. If, for example, you had students write about the best place to go for a holiday, you might spend a bit of class time asking follow-up questions such as how to get there, where to stay, and what to see—you might even try the place out and come back to report. (When teaching in Guangzhou, my partner and I had students report on the merits and problems of various brands of bicycles. Part of our response was then to use the advice to guide us as we bought bikes!)

Responding to Form

There is no single surefire approach to composition marking that will ensure rapid student progress in formal accuracy (Bowen et al., 1985; Omaggio Hadley, 1993). In fact, one of the most frustrating aspects of teaching writing is that no matter how carefully you mark their papers, students' formal accuracy often improves only slowly. This is especially true in EFL settings where students are only able to devote a limited amount of time to English study, and an even smaller portion of that time to writing. However, marking grammar, spelling, vocabulary, and cultural errors is still an important part of responding to student compositions. Feedback can help students improve accuracy, particularly if you ensure that students pay adequate attention to the feedback; they will not be able to correct every error pointed out to them, nor will they learn from every correction, but they will learn some of the time. Another important reason to provide feedback is that students expect it (Omaggio Hadley, 1993), and if you don't provide it students may assume that you are derelict in your duty. The question is thus not whether to mark errors, but how to mark effectively.

Raimes (1983) suggests that the goal of your marking strategy is to help students improve their own editing skills. Thus, marking a paper well usually does not mean finding and correcting every mistake in it; it means giving students the minimum possible clues that still enable them to locate and correct a substantial number of their errors. If all goes well in your class, over time you should be able to give fewer and vaguer clues, thus forcing students to rely more on their own skills.

For students who have little ability to find and correct their own errors, the best marking system is one that helps students locate errors and gives them clues as to what is wrong. This is normally done by underlining errors and marking them with proofreading symbols that indicate what kind of error was made (e.g., *S* for spelling mistakes,

T for verb tense errors).[4] The advantage of such a system—once students learn the symbols—is that dramatically simplifies the editing process but still requires students to correct their own mistakes, hence increasing the likelihood that they will learn from them.

For problems that students should be able to diagnose and cure by themselves, you may choose to simply point out the problem by underlining it. Another method, appropriate for students with more advanced editing skills, is to mark lines or paragraphs in which there are errors, indicating only the number of mistakes and then leave the students to both find and correct the problems. This approach has the advantage of training students to locate errors by themselves, albeit with some help. As students become even more skilled proofreaders, you may choose not to mark errors in student compositions at all, instead making a comment at the end of the paper as to the kinds of problems students should look for as they edit. These last approaches assume considerable editing skills on the part of students, and may initially prove impractical for many classes. However, the goal should be to move in this direction because these approaches reinforce the idea that students ultimately need to be able to both find and correct their own errors.

When you notice problems students probably can't correct on their own, you might occasionally just correct the error for them. However, such corrections often deal with points far enough above students' current skill level that they won't learn much from the correction, and are also easily be ignored by students, so they should be kept to a minimum.

Having invested effort in marking a paper, you should ensure that students pay attention to the feedback. This may sound obvious, but what often happens is that after several hours correcting and grading, you will be tired of this batch of papers and more than happy just to hand it back and move onto something else. Likewise students often look at the grade, glance at the errors, and file the paper away as an unpleasant memory. Even with the best intentions in the world, busy students will generally not pore over mistakes and failures unless there is a good reason to do so. The tragedy of this situation is that maximum pain results in minimum learning.

One way to ensure that students learn from your feedback is to not consistently let overwork drive you into omitting the editing stage of the composition process. Even if you do not feel that there is

---

[4]You can easily design such a system for yourself, and it may be best if your system reflects the grammar points you have emphasized in class. However, many ESL, grammar, and writing books also contain examples of marking systems. See, for example, Azar (1989) for a relatively comprehensive number system; Bowen et al. (1985) for a very simple system; and Raimes (1983) for a basic list of widely used symbols.

time to have students write a completely new draft of a paper you have marked, ask them to correct the errors you have marked and then turn the original draft back in so that you can check the corrections. (Note: If you mark the corrections in a different color of ink from your original marks, the new corrections will be easier for students to find.) Another way to encourage students to learn from their mistakes is by having them keep a personal grammar notebook in which they make note of their errors and corrections. The keeping of such a notebook is one of those good intentions that is more honored in theory than practice, so you might want to collect it occasionally to show students that you are serious.

Grading Compositions

Skilled professionals are often able to grade compositions reliably and consistently by relying on overall impressions. However, the ability to grade reliably in this way takes considerable experience to develop, and is often difficult to maintain as the grader becomes tired. Thus, this is not an approach I would recommend to VTs who are grading large numbers of compositions.

An approach that is more consistently reliable is to establish a set of criteria before beginning to grade compositions. It is possible to use a ready-made scale like the ACTFL Proficiency Guidelines (see note in Chapter 4), but often it is best to design your own system based on the points that you have emphasized in your course. Designing a criteria scale forces you to carefully think through what you are looking for as you grade, and will both speed the grading process and help you remain more consistent and fair even as your eyelids droop and your mind begins to cloud. In order to avoid writing a new scale for each assignment, you may want to design a basic system based on the goals of the course and then modify it to handle the special features and emphases of specific assignments.[5]

One way to make grading a little more precise—and to give students clearer feedback—is to give two grades to a composition, one for form and one for content. Perhaps the greatest advantage of this is that you are reminded to respond to the content of papers as well as their formal accuracy. It is easy for grammar errors to loom disproportionately large in the mind of a tired grader, and this can create problems if you tell students in class that content is most important, but wind up letting grammar determine most of your grade.

[5]The Goals Menu in Appendix A may help you decide what to look for when setting up a criteria system for grading compositions.

Managing the Load

One of the unpleasant realities of teaching a writing course is that it often turns into a slugging match between you and piles of student compositions, a match that turns especially frustrating when you spend long hours trying to salvage poorly written papers only to find that the next round is little better. To a certain extent this is inevitable. As Raimes (1983) points out, even many adult native speakers of a language find writing difficult, and there is consensus that writing is the most difficult language skill for nonnatives to master (Bowen et al., 1985; Nunan, 1989). Also, no matter how well a writing teacher manages homework assignments, teaching writing generally requires more out-of-class effort per hour of class time than the teaching of other kinds of English skills, especially when teaching the large classes that are not uncommon in EFL settings.

The analogy I use for writing classes is going hiking with a heavy backpack—no matter how you arrange the pack, it will be an effort to carry. However, the hike offers rewards as well as work, and by arranging the pack well you can make the trip much more pleasant. As promised in the introduction to this chapter, I offer no ultimate remedy for the paper correction problem, but will suggest ways in which you can minimize your burden and maximize your effectiveness through choice of writing assignments and through effective editing and marking strategies.

Assignments

The bane of the writing teacher's life is the raw sewage paper—the unplanned, unedited paper written by a student who believes it will get a decent grade if only it is long enough. There may well be a place for free writing in a program, but no teacher should be forced to read all of it any more than a piano teacher should be required to listen to hours of a student playing scales. Careful structuring of assignments can do much to prevent this situation.

1 Guarantee that students plan and edit a paper before you have to read it. As suggested above, you can ensure planning by giving students time in class to plan—under your watchful eye—and you can also ask to see written evidence of planning. To increase the chances of a serious attempt at revision, have students write a draft of a paper and bring it to class. Once you check to see that a draft was written, either give students time in class to revise, or make revision a homework assignment. Alternatively, you can collect the papers and hold on to them for several days before giving them back for revision.

2 Make the goals of a writing assignment very clear and specific. This not only helps students know what they are supposed to focus on, but also makes your work easier by giving a clearer focus to

your response. Consequently, when you sit down to read student papers, you will already know what limited set of points you are looking for. A variation on this is to have students submit a list of points on which they want feedback, thus requiring students to focus your editing. This method has the added advantage of involving students more actively in the feedback process.

3 Put upper limits as well as lower limits on the length of compositions. As long as students believe that long compositions will get higher grades than short ones, there is the temptation to skimp on planning and editing in order to save as much time as possible for generating text. Even students who have good intentions about editing their massive creations are often so exhausted by the process of giving birth that in the end they just cut the umbilical cord and go to bed. Putting upper limits on the length of a composition helps students take seriously your pleading assertions that long is not necessarily good, and can help ensure that students reserve some time for planning and editing.

4 Choose topics you are genuinely interested in. Like most writing teachers, I am guilty of having asked students to write on topics of dubious appeal such as "Describe a room" or "My summer vacation" because these are examples of a particular form of writing (description and narration, respectively), but after years of suffering through stale piles of essays I have finally learned not to ask students to write about things I don't want to read about. Having students write about things you want to read about not only helps student motivation by making writing more genuinely communicative, but also makes the process of reading papers much less draining for you.

Response and Correction

For responding to the ideas in a paper, short comments or questions in the margins of a paper often take less time to write than comments at the end, and—as noted above—may be more effective.

When dealing with error marking, the keys to efficiency are focus and selectivity; marking a paper is much easier if you know exactly what you are looking for, and if you are not looking for everything. This approach to marking is also generally better for students than marking every error in a paper because students are most likely to benefit from correction if there are a only limited number of lessons to be learned from it; a paper covered with corrections tends to overwhelm more than teach. Selective marking is also less likely to drive weaker writers into a state of despair every time they get a paper back.

One way to focus your marking is to look primarily for errors related to points you have taught in class, and let most other errors go. A second approach is to look for patterns in a student's mistakes. This tends to be more time consuming, but such tailoring of feedback can be very helpful to students. Other criteria for deciding what errors to mark include the seriousness of the error (those that interfere with communication being most important) or the difficulty that students will have correcting the problem.

Low Teacher Investment Writing Assignments

Generally in order for students to get enough writing practice, they will need to write more than you can reasonably expect to read and respond to, so you will need to give some kinds of writing assignments that you can either process very quickly or not read at all. When giving any of these assignments, it is important to spend some time selling students on the idea that writing practice is still valuable even when there is no teacher to carefully mark every error. As with the development of any other language skill, writing practice is useful in and of itself, especially if students are using it actively as an opportunity to rehearse application of points learned in class or through reference materials. Kinds of assignments that do not necessitate lengthy teacher response include the following:

1. **Journals:** Journals can be used to give students an opportunity to write about daily events, past experiences, thoughts, or almost anything else in a format where you only need to read over entries occasionally and comment briefly, generally responding to the ideas more than the language.

2. **Material to be shared with other students:** As suggested above, another approach to the problem of overload is to have students write for each other instead of you. Material written to be read by other students can include personal stories, position papers on issues (as a prelude to discussion or debate), or newsletters on personal or local events.

3. **Pen-pal writing:** Find people, presumably from your home area, who are willing to correspond with your students by letter. Retirees or students might be good potential correspondents. The advantage of a pen-pal program is that it not only provides a form of writing practice that you do not need to edit, but also reinforces the idea that writing is a real communication skill rather than a lifeless class exercise.
    One problem with pen-pal programs is that they can take a significant amount of effort to set up, and

student enthusiasm may die quickly after the introductory letter if students don't know what to say next. Students may also become discouraged if their correspondents (who may also not know what to write about) stop responding. This is a good opportunity for you to stress the importance of thinking about audience and trying to make writing interesting. One specific suggestion you could make is that students introduce interesting aspects of their country and culture, and ask their pen-pals questions on similar topics. A letter full of specific questions is easier for a foreign pen-pal to respond to than one that only makes statements.

Evaluation

I will say little about the testing of writing because writing is a skill area where it is especially important that testing should be de-emphasized in favor of grades from other kinds of writing assignments. Timed writing under testlike conditions is rare in real life, and it also has the undesirable effect of discouraging students from planning, editing, and using reference tools. In-class testing does, however, have the advantage of ensuring that you see student compositions that you know were not copied or written by someone else, and for which you have a reliable idea of how much time was invested. Therefore, although the majority of a writing course grade should generally be based on the regular assignments, it may also be wise to include a few in-class writing assignments.

An in-class writing test is essentially the same as an in-class composition. Give students a topic and a time limit within which to complete an essay. The topic(s) should be within students' range of knowledge, and should include an indication of type of writing expected (e.g., letter, argument). It is best if the topic presents a clearly defined task rather than only a general topic. "Explain why you do/don't. . ." is much better than "Write about. . ." because students have a better idea of what is expected of them. If the topic is clear, 30 minutes is generally more than adequate time for the production of a writing sample. Students should be encouraged, perhaps even required to spend some time taking notes and organizing before they begin to write; in fact, it may be desirable to ask students to hand in their preparation notes along with the paper (though students may find it faster to write their notes in their native language than in English). Students should also be encouraged to save a few minutes at the end to check for mistakes, though they will probably only catch a few of the more obvious errors at best. There is no good reason not to allow students to use dictionaries unless your test is intended to prepare them for some kind of standardized test in which dictionaries are not allowed.

Plagiarism

Over years of teaching writing to students from non-Western cultures, I have been struck by the extent to which their problems in the content aspects of writing (e.g., organization, use of detail, placement of main idea) are similar to those faced by Western students. I have seen problems such as rambling paragraphs, unsupported assertions, new arguments in conclusions, or misplaced main idea statements in compositions written by American students in Indiana as well as Chinese students in Guangzhou. There is, however, one problem area in which cultural differences regularly cause non-Western students special problems in English writing classes—plagiarism. Different cultures have rather different notions of what is and is not fair use of the work of others, and Western culture tends to be stricter in this area than many others. This is not to say that plagiarism is not found in the West (it is), or to say that a knowledge of what is and is not plagiarism is inherent in Western students (it is not). However, teachers coming out of a Western system may have rather different assumptions about what is considered plagiarism than students in a host country will, so the issue deserves special attention.

Teachers from Western cultures need to recognize the high degree of stigma our culture attaches to plagiarism, and we should remind ourselves that rules that govern borrowing the work of others are cultural norms rather than moral imperatives. The West tends to see unmarked use of others' work as stealing—*plagiarism* is after all the name of a crime. But this is not the only possible interpretation of copying. For example, borrowing the words of others could also be seen as a sign of respect (imitation is the sincerest form of flattery?); absence of citation could also indicate that any literate person would be expected to know what was being quoted. Thus, we should not expect that people from all other cultures will look at copying exactly the same way we have learned to.

A second problem concerns the question of what exactly plagiarism is. Westerners, particularly Americans, have been brought up in an educational system that places high value on individual creativity and expression, and that does not place much faith in imitation of the work of others as a legitimate or helpful way to learn. Of course, the exact opposite is true in many other cultures, particularly Asian, where imitation of models is the dominant form of learning. In such a context, the difference between original and borrowed work is not as clear as it would be in the U.S. system, and the stigma attached to copying is not nearly as comprehensible. In a writing class in China, for example, the admonition "Don't copy!" does not mean the same thing as it meant in Michigan. My Chinese students understand that they should not copy other students' compositions lock, stock, and barrel, and would expect a reduced grade if they did so. However, they are sometimes genuinely surprised to be accused of plagiarism because they modeled a composition on something from a textbook and included sentences and phrases (perhaps slightly rewritten) from that text. An unexplained command not to "copy" does not necessarily communicate the message that Westerners consider using a model in such a way out of bounds.

My point is not that you should turn a tolerant eye to student copying, but rather that one of the cultural lessons students need to learn as a part of their English education is what exactly constitutes plagiarism in the culture of English and what does not. This is not simply a process of learning how to use quotation marks or citations, but also of learning to discern the boundary between appropriate use of a model and inappropriate use. In most cases, a single lecture will not dispose of the problem; it will have to be worked out gradually over a period of time. During this process, there are three important points to remember:

1 Find out what the local norms are for use of the work of others, not only what is and is not acceptable according to the stated rules but also what the unwritten norms are. Remember that teachers and staff who teach English in your school are presumably more influenced by Western norms than most people in the host country, and they may present a Westernized picture of the situation to you in order to meet your perceived expectations, so you may need to do a little digging among other people as well to find out how seriously the rules are taken. It may also be enlightening to find out how borrowing is handled traditionally in the host culture.

2 Spell out your expectations very specifically for students. For example, with regard to the problem of using vocabulary and sentence structures from other books, I generally tell my students that anytime they use the same three words in the same order as another text, they must use quotation marks and citations. (I often find that before students hear this guideline, they assume that it is acceptable to use long phrases or even sentences.)

3 Because students may well have a rather different idea of what is and is not a crime than you have, in dealing with violations of Western fair-use norms try to keep moral indignation under control, at least until you are sure the student was cognizant of the seriousness of the offense. Of course, some students cheat and need to be dealt with accordingly. However, not all students who run afoul of Western plagiarism norms do so with malice aforethought, and you need to remind yourself that genuine misunderstanding may also be part of the problem.

11 Vocabulary: Students in Charge

♦ Mastery of a foreign language involves learning thousands of words, and it is difficult to teach more than a fraction of them in class. In vocabulary study it is therefore especially important for students to learn to rely primarily on their own efforts.

♦ Students do not need to learn to use every new word to the same degree. For reading and listening, students need a large receptive vocabulary of words that they can understand though not necessarily use productively.

♦ The teacher's main role in vocabulary teaching is facilitating student study and providing accountability.

The very idea of teaching vocabulary strikes me as somewhat problematic. Not that vocabulary can't be taught—it can be, and teaching it is not terribly difficult. But when I look back on my language learning experience I note that not very many of the foreign language words I know were taught to me in a language class by a teacher, or by anyone at all. Most of them I learned through studying textbooks, using vocabulary lists and flash cards, guessing from context as I read or listened, or through looking them up in my trusty old dictionary. In short, I did most of my vocabulary learning on my own. More to the point, I don't see how I could have developed an adequately large vocabulary had I learned only new words taught in class.

On a moment's reflection, it is not hard to see why a student needs to be self-reliant in vocabulary acquisition. First, learning a word often involves much more than memorizing its basic meaning; it also involves learning how it is used, what other meanings it has, what connotations it has, what other words it is used with, how formal it is, and even how frequently it is used. Obviously, it would take far too much class time for a teacher to attempt such a thorough introduction to a few words, let alone the huge number a student eventually needs to master. Second, a student needs to learn thousands of words, more than even the most zealous teacher is likely to be able to explain in class.

In this chapter, we will examine what students need to achieve in vocabulary study and how they can pursue these goals. Throughout, I will argue that vocabulary study provides an especially clear case for why it is so important for learners to take command of their own study.

Vocabulary Acquisition: The Goal

It is helpful to think of command of vocabulary as falling into two categories: productive and receptive. Productive command of a word involves being able to use it appropriately in speech or writing. As suggested above, learning to do this can require knowing quite a lot about a word. Let us take the everyday word *dog* as an example:

1. Basic meaning: A four legged creature that can be trained to chase sticks.

2. Other meanings: *To dog* = to follow persistently. *Dog-tired* = very tired. *A dog* = something worthless or useless. *Dogs* = slang for feet. *You dog!* = You scoundrel!

3. Usage: *Dog* is a noun. When it is countable (*a dog, dogs*) it usually refers to an animal. When used as a mass noun (*I like dog*), it probably refers to a controversial dinner option.

4. Connotation: Even though we think of the dog as "man's best friend," the word generally has bad or insulting connotations. However, "dogs = feet" has a rural flavor (or is associated with old Hush Puppies commercials). "You (swarthy) dog!" has a slightly antique sound to it, conjuring up visions of a swashbuckler in an old pirate movie.

5. Collocation:[1] *Dog* is often paired with *cat* (e.g., *It's raining cats and dogs*).

6. Level of formality: When referring to the animal, *dog* is not markedly formal or informal. *Dog-tired* is somewhat informal, and *dogs* = feet is very informal.

7. Frequency of appearance: The word *dog* is much more common than the synonym *canine*.

Students do not need all of this information about the word *dog* in order to begin using it in speech or writing, but they do need to know that these other aspects of vocabulary exist and that learning them is an important part of learning how to use words properly. A word needs to fit in its sentence and context in terms of meaning, usage, connotation, collocation, formality, and frequency, and may be amusing, unintelligible, or even offensive if it is not appropriate in these ways.

Receptive command of a word involves being able to comprehend it, generally in context. The good news is that receptive command does not involve as thorough a knowledge of usage, collocation, and the other issues mentioned above as does productive command. In fact, even with only a weak grasp of a word's meaning a student can often still understand it when it appears in context (as most words do). The bad news is that students need receptive command of a very large number of words if they are ever to be able to read or listen to native English. According to Fox (1987), a productive vocabulary of between 1,000 and 2,000 words is generally adequate to allow people to express themselves in English; however, a vocabulary of between 7,000 and 10,000 words is necessary to make most average texts accessible.[2]

What these figures make clear is that a good working vocabulary has a particular shape. To be functional, students need a relatively small fund of words that they know well and can use productively in speech and writing, and a much larger receptive vocabulary of words that they understand in context. This point is worth emphasizing because many English programs do not make a distinction between productive and receptive vocabulary. From the beginning, students are expected to be able to use all the words they learn. The problem this

---

[1]*Collocation* refers to the question of which words often appear together, which words are good friends, so to speak.

[2]An educated native speaker of English may have a receptive vocabulary of between 45,000 and 60,000 words (Gairns & Redman, 1986).

can create is that teachers or curriculum designers, realizing that it is impossible for students to gain full productive control over many words very quickly, cut down on the amount of vocabulary.[3] This, quite predictably, lengthens the amount of time it takes students to reach a breakthrough point in reading or listening.

Learning and Teaching Vocabulary

Some English teachers argue that an important part of a teacher's job is to carefully select the words students should learn and then devote class time to teaching those words.[4] However, this approach can be problematic for VTs because you aren't always in a position to carefully select what words students will learn. You may not know what words a student should and shouldn't learn, and even if you did, choices are often determined primarily by what words appear in textbooks. The larger problem, however, is one of practicality. Time devoted to vocabulary explanation is too often time taken away from other class activities, and as Lewis (1993) notes, it would take literally hundreds of hours for a teacher to teach a passable vocabulary. We should also ask ourselves why students can't be expected to study vocabulary on their own. My own experience has been that where I have structured and carried out my own vocabulary learning programs, I have made far more progress than when I have relied more on a language class to determine my rate and method of vocabulary acquisition.

Given the importance of students' taking charge of their own vocabulary acquisition, discussion in this chapter will center more on how students learn vocabulary than on how you teach it. You will no doubt teach some vocabulary in class, but your primary roles in this process are:

1 to help students set appropriate goals for their vocabulary learning efforts.

2 to integrate the teaching of vocabulary into the practice of other language skills.

3 to encourage students' efforts and fortify their resolve by checking up on them.

How these roles work themselves out in the classroom will vary somewhat according to the level of the students more or less as follows:

---

[3]Lewis (1993) points out that for many years an influential view in the language teaching field was that the vocabulary load should be minimized for students while grammar was stressed. In contrast, he argues persuasively that "the first thing students need to do is to learn to understand quite a lot of words" (p. 9).

[4]Gairns and Redman (1986) argue that "In organizing school learning, we have to select vocabulary carefully to ensure that high priority items are included, and provide varied opportunities for practice to compensate for the lack of repeated exposure available to the 'the street learner'" (p. 1).

1. Beginning levels: At this level you may not need to devote as much attention to helping students set vocabulary acquisition goals because choice of what words to learn will be determined largely by their textbooks, and much of the vocabulary presented will be high frequency vocabulary over which students need productive as well as receptive command. The smaller amounts of vocabulary introduced—and the relatively great importance of each item—mean that at this level you can and should try to find ways to introduce and practice new words in class. On quizzes and tests, you should hold students accountable for both receptive and productive command of all or most of the vocabulary introduced in the materials.

2. Intermediate levels: At this level students' reading and listening skills should begin to move ahead of their writing and speaking, so they must begin taking responsibility for deciding which vocabulary they need for productive use and which for receptive use (Bowen et al., 1985). You will thus want to begin discussing the issue of goals with students. At this level text materials may also introduce larger amounts of new vocabulary, so you will not have time to introduce and practice every new word in class; your focus should thus turn more toward helping students understand what kinds of things they need to learn about new words. In many kinds of lessons as new vocabulary appears, you should raise questions of formality, connotation, and so forth (see below) in order to increase students' attention to these issues. To motivate students to work on vocabulary acquisition, it should be stressed as a part of your evaluation program, regular short quizzes being an especially effective way to get students in the habit of studying vocabulary daily rather than relying on pretest cramming. On quizzes and tests you should begin making a distinction between vocabulary you expect students to have productive command over and vocabulary that you only expect them to understand in context.

3. Advanced levels: At this level, students need to move toward the ability to read and understand native English, hence the need for a large receptive vocabulary is pressing. They should also be doing more work with real English materials and less with textbooks, so will naturally be encountering a wide range of new words, many of them relatively low frequency. At this level students need to make most of their own decisions about which words to add to their vocabularies, and although you might still hold students accountable for limited sets of new words encountered in your class materials, much vocabulary testing should occur indirectly through reading and listening comprehension tests.

Your task then, especially when teaching intermediate and advanced students, is less to teach vocabulary than to help students learn how to go about the task themselves. To this end the following sections will consider what students are up against as they build their vocabularies so that you may guide them more effectively. I find it helpful to think of the problem of learning a new word as having three parts:

1 Discovering what the word means

2 Memorizing the meaning(s) of the word

3 Learning other features of the word (e.g., usage, connotation).

It is around these three problems that the following discussion is organized. Note: The discussion below assumes that in EFL settings learners acquire most of their new vocabulary from books. It would be better if students were also able to learn new words through listening, and it is desirable to give students a chance to hear new words in class, on tape, or in any other way possible. However, books are more widely available and generally easier to use than any aural source of new vocabulary, so for the foreseeable future this is likely to be how most new words are learned.

Strategies for Learning Vocabulary: The Discovery Phase

The first step in learning a new word is discovering what it means. As noted above, this would not be a problem if a student only needed to learn a few words. However, for building a large receptive vocabulary students need to discover the meanings of literally thousands of words, so as we consider the various strategies that students can use for finding out the meanings of unfamiliar words, efficiency becomes a primary concern.

Dictionaries

Good dictionaries provide a wide range of information on connotation, usage, and other issues as well as on meaning, making them very useful for students who want to gain productive control of a word. However, an equally great advantage of dictionary use is that they make students self-sufficient in their ability to discover meanings of new words. It is thus worthwhile to invest class time in teaching students what kinds of dictionaries to use and how to use them.

In many countries you will find that students rely heavily on small, inexpensive glossary-type dictionaries that do little more than list words in English along with a translation into the host language. Such dictionaries often only list one or two possible translations of each English word, hence promoting the false belief that there is a neat one-to-one correspondence between all English and host language words, and the absence of examples or information on usage subtly encourages students to ignore usage when memorizing words. On the other hand, these dictionaries are usually adequate for helping students discover meanings of new words they encounter when reading. Moreover, the availability, convenient size, and reasonable cost of these dictionaries are advantages that should not be overlooked.

Dictionaries that have more information are better, especially those that have an ample supply of examples so that students can learn usage as well as meaning. Examples reinforce the notion that ideas are expressed differently in different languages, and that a host language word that would be translated one way in one English sentence will often have to be translated differently in another context. There is nothing wrong with bilingual dictionaries (despite the prejudice of many English teachers against them) if they include adequate examples in English.[5]

As students attempt to learn to use dictionaries with English entries, the initial problem is learning how to locate the desired word. This involves learning alphabetical order and practicing so that looking up a word does not take too long. The greater problem is teaching students what to look for in an entry. Many will be satisfied as soon as they locate a host language equivalent, so you need to teach them to pay attention to other important information. Of course, students cannot stop and engage in a major learning effort every time they look up a word, but once they have invested the time in locating the word, there is no good reason not to invest a few extra seconds in glancing at the entry to learn a little more than the word's basic meaning. Questions you should teach students to ask themselves include:

1 Does this word have a host language equivalent or not? Some English words do have close host language equivalents; others don't. In a good dictionary this should be obvious from the entry; if a lot of explanation and examples are necessary for the word, it probably

---

[5]Several companies, including Longman and Oxford, publish learner's or advanced learner's dictionaries that are specially designed for students of English and include many examples. If your luggage allowance is adequate for a large reference dictionary, the *Collins Cobuild Dictionary* is particularly good for language teachers because of its examples and careful description of how words are actually used.

has no single host language equivalent, and the student should remember to pay special attention to this word.

2 How is this word used? Encourage students to examine at least one example of how the word is used, and remember the example as a model for usage.

3 Does the word have a strong connotation? Are strong negative or positive feelings associated with it? Is it associated strongly with a certain context? The pattern of examples will provide important clues.

4 Is this word markedly formal or informal? Again, look at the examples.

5 How is it spelled? Unfortunately, English spelling is not as logical as that of many other languages, so this requires special attention.

The major disadvantage of heavy reliance on dictionaries is that they are slow. When students are first learning how to use dictionaries, time spent looking up words is time well spent in developing a useful skill. However, once students know how to use dictionaries, each minute spent looking for a word is essentially a minute wasted. When there are only a few words to look up, this is not a serious problem, but if you ask students to read a passage that is loaded with unfamiliar words, they may spend the lion's share of their study time simply thumbing through pages (a fact that you should consider before giving students assignments that will involve extensive dictionary use).

Guessing Words From Context

Guessing from context, discussed in Chapter 9 as a reading strategy, can also be a way to learn the meanings of new words. For example, instead of having students look up the word *petunia* in the sentence "Harry paused in the garden to smell a petunia", students should have a fighting chance to guess that a petunia is a kind of flower. One advantage of this approach is that students do not need to stop reading and break their train of thought in order to look a word up. Another is that students learn the word in a context, which helps them learn more about the word than its basic meaning.

The main problem with guessing as a strategy for discovering the meaning of new words is that it doesn't work very well unless the context is very clear or the student knows a lot about the topic; in other words, this strategy works best when students are reading very easy texts. (Even a few new words or unfamiliar cultural assumptions on a page may muddy the context enough that effective guessing becomes very difficult.) Unfortunately, many students spend little time reading easy texts. Beginning and intermediate students often have to study textbook passages that are intentionally packed with new vocabulary, and the inherent difficulty of native texts for even advanced students can make guessing hard at that level as well. Therefore, guessing new words often becomes most efficient as a strategy for learners at very advanced stages of English study who already have much lexical and cultural knowledge.

One way you can make guessing vocabulary words a more effective strategy is by having students memorize common English word roots and affixes. Many English words are constructed out of a finite stock of prefixes (e.g., *bi-, sub-, de-*), suffixes (e.g., *-ation, -ed, -er*), and word roots (e.g., *-scrib-, -graph-, -vis-*) and students who memorize the more common of these have a much better chance of correctly guessing meanings of new words constructed from these elements. Knowledge of these roots and affixes is particularly helpful in dealing with many of the low-frequency technical words of English—words that are otherwise hard to learn because they appear infrequently and are easily confused with each other.

Texts With Glossaries

Glossaries are vocabulary lists with host language translations or explanations in English, and often accompany reading or listening texts. When such text/glossary combinations are available, there are considerable advantages to a strategy of relying heavily on them for discovering meanings of new words:

1 Learning a word from a glossary is faster than looking it up in a dictionary. The time saved on each word may seem insignificant, but when multiplied by hundreds the savings is substantial.

2 Getting the meaning of a word from a glossary is easier and often more accurate than guessing. This advantage is especially important for students at lower or intermediate levels for whom guessing is often not an option.

3 When the glossary accompanies a text, each new word appears in a context that provides an example of its use.

In many cases, the textbooks you use in class will already have glossaries. However, in most countries more than one series of English textbooks is available, so as a strategy for building receptive vocabulary you might also encourage students to seek out and study other materials with glossaries.

Of course, the best glossaries are often those students make for themselves. Once students have taken the time to look a word up in a dictionary, it takes only a little additional investment of time to write down the new word, a gloss, and a brief example of usage in a notebook. This is a particularly useful study method not only because it increases the chance that students will actually learn the words they look up (words looked up but not reviewed are generally soon forgotten), but also because over time the vocabulary notebook becomes a glossary tailor-made to the student's interests and needs.

Vocabulary Lists

Many English textbooks, especially those published in England and the U.S., contain lists of the vocabulary to be learned in each lesson. Such lists facilitate assigning vocabulary homework, but they are totally useless to a student who is trying to figure out what a word means. If you are using a text with such lists, it would be a great help to your students if you were to write easy English explanations of the words on the board or a printed page, or get a colleague to write down appropriate host language translations. This is extra work for you, but it will save your students from hours of paging through dictionaries.

Having located an explanation of what a new word means, the learners' next task is to get that meaning into their memory. Unfortunately, word meanings can be slippery little creatures. Often even after several attempts to learn a word, the only thing about it you can remember when you run into it again is that you have looked it up before.

Research suggests that people have at least two kinds of memory: short term and long term. In short-term memory we can hold a limited amount of information (about seven items) for brief periods of time. After that, the information is quickly forgotten. Long-term memory can hold an apparently unlimited amount of information, but it takes more work to get information into long-term memory.[6]

We have probably encountered memory experts on daytime TV shows, individuals who can memorize pages from phonebooks within minutes using powerful memory techniques such as associating words with mental images. (I still remember how to say the words *fried* and *elephant* in Russian because of a particularly vivid mental image associating these two words.) One elaborate scheme, popular in Europe in the 1600s, involved mentally placing words of one category (fruits, for example) all in different positions in an imaginary room, and then constructing an entire memory house or palace as a system for vocabulary recall.[7]

Strategies for Learning Vocabulary: The Memorization Phase

[6]See Gairns and Redman (1986) and Stevick (1988) for further discussion.

[7]For a fascinating discussion of this process as used by Matteo Ricci, a missionary and language learner in Ming Dynasty China, see Jonathan Spence's (1984) *The Memory Palace of Matteo Ricci*. New York: Viking. For a general discussion of mnemonic techniques, see Rubin and Thompson (1994).

The principles suggested in this section will not promise anything quite so dramatic. However, there is much students can do to improve their vocabulary memorization approaches by paying attention to three basic factors: concentration, repetition, and meaningful manipulation.

Concentration

The most basic principle is that learners need to remain alert and pay attention as they try to memorize, and it helps if they seriously intend to remember what they are studying. This is certainly not a novel idea, but neither is it a point that should be neglected. Anyone who has spent much time studying a foreign language knows how easy it is for the eyes to keep moving over a glossary or text long after the brain has ceased to function.

One way for students to stay alert as they work is to use memorization methods that involve physical activity. The combination of mental with physical activity appears to enhance memory, and as long as students are moving it is less likely that their minds will switch off. Some methods include:

- Shuffling flash cards
- Walking around while memorizing
- Mouthing words out loud
- Copying words
- Moving pen and cover over a glossary.

Another way to improve concentration is using memorization methods that involve performance or response; for example, constructing a sentence using the new word. Vocabulary memorization strategies that call for response from learners tend to keep them focused on the activity and help prevent their minds from wandering. For example, when I study words on a vocabulary list, I find it more effective to test myself on each word rather than simply looking at it. Usually I cover the gloss and then check to see if I can get the word right. If so, I allow myself the gratification of slashing it with a highlighter; if not, I have to do it again the next day. The point of this self-testing is not just that it helps check progress; equally as important, it helps students stay alert and keeps them moving.

Repetition

Repetition does not guarantee that a word will find its way into long-term memory, but it certainly helps; a word that you see 10 times is more likely to stick in your memory than a word you see only once, much in the same way that you are likely to more quickly learn the name of someone you see every day than someone you meet only rarely.

Sometimes a combination of sheer concentration and repetition is enough to allow a student to memorize words. The Name Game, described in Chapter 5, is a case in point. Through concentration and frequent repetition, it is possible to learn dozens of names in one class period—albeit at the price of some hard work—and I often use this exercise with classes to show what is possible.

However, research indicates that a more efficient route to memorization lies in introducing a word in a meaningful context or relatively memorable way, and then reviewing it some weeks later. In a well-structured curriculum, this kind of delayed vocabulary review can be built into the program. However, it can also happen more naturally through extensive reading. A student who reads frequently and widely naturally reviews huge amounts of vocabulary—and is much more likely to come across low-frequency vocabulary soon enough after it is learned that it has not yet been forgotten. This is one reason why extensive reading should be a part of vocabulary acquisition programs. The same beneficial effects for memorization can derive from repeated hearing, speaking, and writing of words.

Meaningful Manipulation

Apparently, there is something about the process of using a word in a meaningful way that helps it sink into the long-term memory and stay there. Many language learners have had the experience of finding that a word really sticks in their memories for the first time once they have found an opportunity to use it. As Gairns and Redman (1986) note, "more meaningful tasks require learners to analyse and process language more deeply, which helps them to commit information to long-term memory" (p. 90). Using words in communicative ways is therefore one of the best ways to memorize them.

The implication of this for language study is again that communicative language practice of all kinds is a necessary part of a good vocabulary-learning strategy. Using words productively in meaningful speaking and writing may have a special power to aid memory, but seeing or hearing words as part of meaningful communication is also an effective way to facilitate memorization. Thus, vocabulary acquisition should not be undertaken as a program unto itself (hence the problems students have when they attempt to memorize dictionaries—as some students actually do!), but rather as part of programs of reading, listening, speaking, and writing.

Strategies for Learning Vocabulary: The Familiarization Phase

We have already seen that for productive command of a word students need to know much more than just a word's meaning—knowledge of its usage, connotation, collocation, level of formality, and level of frequency are also important. Even for receptive use knowing the denotation of a word may not be enough; understanding the impact of a sentence may hang on knowing the connotation of a word, or even its level of formality. How then are students to become familiar with all of these facets of a word?

Although it is not practical to introduce each new word fully in class, it is generally a good idea to point out some of these features of words in order to sensitize students to the issues they need to consider in their own vocabulary acquisition. Although this can be done in any kind of lesson as the occasion arises, intensive reading lessons provide a natural opportunity for examining selected words in more depth. Consider, for example, the following reading passages:

> The world's coldest continent, and the most difficult to reach, is Antarctica. For centuries, people have wondered what this continent is really like, since it is covered with solid thick ice and deep snow.

You might want to quickly call students' attention to the issue of collocation by pointing out the phrases "thick ice" and "deep snow." From a purely semantic level, it isn't at all obvious why one couldn't use the word *deep* for both *ice* and *snow*. The fastest—and probably most accurate—explanation for why *thick* goes with *ice* and *deep* goes with *snow* is that in English this collocation is habitual.

From the same textbook:

> A TV reporter wanted to find out what people thought of a new film, so she decided to interview people as they came out of the theatre. She asked one woman what she thought of the film. "It was excellent," the woman replied. "I thought it was the best film I've seen in years." Then she stopped a young man and asked him the same question. "It was dynamite!" he said.[8]

This provides a good opportunity to make a point about formality—note the switch between the proper woman respondent ("It was excellent") and the colloquial young man ("It was dynamite!"). Usage points could also be made about the words *think* (What did you think of the film?), and the phrase *came out* (came out of the theatre).

Ultimately, however, it is impossible to treat every new word in this way, so students must learn to seek this kind of information

[8]Both excerpts from *English: Senior I* (China: People's Publishing House, 1984), pages 267 and 263, respectively.

213

out for themselves. This is another reason why it is important that students have an adequate extensive reading and listening diet; it is only by seeing new words repeatedly in a variety of contexts that patterns of usage, formality, and connotation emerge. I remember learning a Chinese term that my textbook translated as "teaching" (*jiao xun*). Being diligent, I tried my new word out on my teacher at the end of class with the Chinese equivalent of "Thank you for your teaching" but her response was to chuckle and head off to the lounge to announce what I had just said. It was only some years later when reading a novel that I finally figured out what had gone wrong: I noticed that every time this particular word appeared, it was in the context of an elder admonishing a penitent youth. The pattern showed me what the textbook had not.

Evaluation

Vocabulary can and should be tested as an integral part of the evaluation of all language skills. To some extent this happens naturally; when you test reading comprehension or ability to discuss an issue, you are also indirectly testing vocabulary. However, it is often also desirable to have some evaluation of vocabulary acquisition per se, the major justification for this being the positive backwash effect it has on students' interest in learning words (Hughes, 1989).

The process of learning vocabulary requires steady work over a long period of time. Students who cram words into their memories before a final examination often lose much of what they learn soon after the examination. According to Gairns and Redman (1986), about 80% of what is learned is lost within the first 24 hours in the absence of review, so short periods of intense study followed by long slack periods do not do much for vocabulary building. A testing pattern that helps build better habits in students would consist of frequent cumulative quizzes. This would both require students to work on a regular basis, and to review what they learn rather than forgetting it once the pressure is off. So a strategy of frequent vocabulary quizzing and testing may be desirable in order to ensure that students work on vocabulary on a regular basis.

The simple types of vocabulary quiz items suggested below are not ideal in terms of their backwash effect—better backwash results from testing of listening, speaking, reading, and writing skills. Many of these items only require students to memorize a translation or explanation of the target word. However, this low-level command of new words is a good start toward receptive control, and what these quiz items lack in depth they make up for in ease, thus making it possible for you to give short-but-frequent quizzes.

1. English word—definition: Give students the word you wish to check and have them define it by providing a synonym, explanation, or even translation into the host language. This kind of item is very straightforward conceptually, hence easy to explain to students, but it is problematic in that students may know the meaning of the test word, but not know a synonym or a good way to explain it. Translation is simplest for students, but may be hard for you. Since many words have more than one meaning, it is a good idea to provide an example sentence with each test word.

2. Host country equivalent—target word: For this simple quiz, get a colleague to write the host language equivalents of the words you wish to test. Then present these to the class and ask them to produce the English words. This kind of item checks spelling as well as meaning.

3. Filling in blanks: Find a reading passage that contains words you wish to test for, then delete the target words from the passage and list them at the bottom of the page. Students then need to choose the proper word to fill in each blank. In order to make this kind of quiz/ test at least somewhat communicative, you need to make sure that for most of the deleted words the context makes one of the words a particularly good choice; otherwise completing the test turns into a language puzzle.

4. Sentence with target word—response: Write questions that contain the word you want to test, underlining the target word. Make sure comprehension of the word is important to understanding the question. Then have students write an appropriate answer that demonstrates that they understand the test word. An alternative to this is to compose true-false statements using the test word, and then have students respond appropriately.

5. Matching: Present two groups of words and have students match them on the basis of some kind of relationship (e.g., antonyms, synonyms, same kind of thing, same part of speech).

6. Writing sentences: For testing of productive command of vocabulary items, have students use the test word in a sentence that demonstrates that they know the meaning of the word. (Sentences like "*Pragmatic* is an English word" don't count.) This kind of item encourages students to memorize example sentences along with new words, and is most appropriate for high-frequency words that students need in their productive vocabulary.

12 Grammar: Finding a Balance

- In many countries study of grammar is emphasized to the point that it almost becomes synonymous with language study, and this is one of the main reasons why many students dislike language study. One of your tasks is helping students gain a balanced view of grammar study, recognizing the importance of accuracy in language use, but restoring a focus on communication that makes language study both more meaningful and enjoyable.

- Mastery of grammar involves both knowledge of grammatical forms and skill in using those forms. For building the latter, adequate practice is necessary.

- Students' grammar systems normally develop through gradual elaboration from simple to complex. As with vocabulary, there are different levels of control. Students may first gain receptive control of a structure and only later learn to produce it. In the case of low frequency structures, they may never need to gain productive command.

One thing that most students of English would agree on is that they don't particularly like studying grammar. As Stevick (1988) notes: "Difficulties with grammar cause more discouragement and drive away more students than anything else in our profession" (p. 82). What makes this worse is that many EFL classes place special emphasis on grammar, analyzing sentences and drilling structures to the almost complete exclusion of other activities, so by the time students reach your class many of them are thoroughly fed up with both grammar and English.[1] Others will have become firmly convinced that the road to English success lies through the grammar book and will lie in wait for you with questions that would confound a sage.

On the whole, VTs are also not a population known for love of grammar. Most native speakers of English have unpleasant memories of grammar drills in Spanish, French, or German classes, so have no inherent affection for the subject. Matters are worsened by the fact that the average native speaker of English has little explicit knowledge of English grammar rules, so grammar is not a particularly easy subject to teach. The instinctive response of many VTs is to try and avoid grammar teaching as much as possible.

I am not going to try and convince you that grammar is really fun to teach and learn (though it need not be as bad as it is often made out to be). Grammar, however, cannot and should not be ignored, so in this chapter we will examine the questions of what role is appropriate for grammar in language teaching, and of how it should be taught.

Grammar: Some Basic Points

What Is Grammar?

One source of problems in the EFL grammar classroom lies in misunderstandings about what grammar is. Some students view grammar rules as an unimportant set of conventions useful for passing tests but of dubious value in actual English conversation. However, the more common tendency is to go overboard in the other direction, viewing grammar rules as something close to the language learner's version of the Ten Commandments.[2] In this view, grammar rules prescribe correct and unequivocal answers to all language problems, and are all vitally important.

---

[1] See Faber (1991) for a vivid account of how Latin grammar lessons almost destroyed his love of language learning. Discussing grammar-obsessed teachers, he concludes: "They're right in insisting on the importance of grammar, but who says you've got to have it first, as some kind of brutal initiation?" (p. 43).

[2] This analogy is only partly meant in fun. Remember that many of the cultures in which VTs teach give the written word a much higher level of respect than is common now in the West, and the grammar book often inherits some of this almost sacred authority.

An accurate understanding of grammar would fall somewhere between these two extremes. Like most human behavior, language behavior tends to be patterned, and one way to remove some of students' excessive awe of grammar is to point out grammar rules are actually less like regulations than they are descriptions of patterns in the way English-speakers construct sentences. Some of these patterns are stronger than others. For example, a great number English nouns form their plural by adding an -s at the end, so knowing this rule enables students to both comprehend and accurately produce many utterances.[3] Knowledge of common patterns is especially helpful to students as they attempt to construct sentences. Other patterns are weaker, and the rules that describe them thus cover fewer situations. For example, there is no single easy rule that can enable a student to predict whether an infinitive (*to* + verb) or a gerund (verb + *-ing*) should be used following another verb, so mastery of this problem requires a lot of memorization of individual words and situations. For the student who wants a rule for everything, one could always create rules to explain even the most idiomatic expressions, but the more complex the set of rules becomes and the fewer situations it covers, the more it hinders attempts to learn language rather than facilitating them.

If you want to deflate your students' views of grammar even further, there are two more facts you could point out. First, because a grammar is simply a description of language patterns, there is no single definitive grammar of English. Instead, there are a variety of grammar systems and terminology used in the description of English. (Fortunately, the commonly used systems tend to be quite similar, but there are some differences, and it is therefore important that you learn the system and terms used in the country where you will be teaching.[4]) In other words, to argue over whether the word *eating* in the sentence "I like eating hamburgers" is a verb or a noun misses the point—once students understand what the sentence means and how it works, the proper categorization of each word is of marginal usefulness (unless students will face a test that demands such analysis).

The second bombshell you could drop is that because language changes over time, grammar rules change too. Examples of changes in English over the last few centuries can be seen in even casual perusal of Shakespeare or the King James Bible. For example, most of us are

---

[3]This rule is actually a little more complex than it seems, especially in speech. The -s ending is sometimes pronounced /-s/, sometimes /-z/, and sometimes /-əz/.

[4]The one system you may run into that is quite different from traditional grammars is Transformational Grammar (TG). TG is intended more for linguists than language teachers, and using it for teaching would probably confuse your students more than help them. There are, however, ESL reference books that use this system, so before you buy a grammar reference book, make sure it uses more widely used traditional grammar systems.

probably familiar with the sixth commandment in its King James word-ing—*Thou shalt not kill*—a command that uses vocabulary and gram-mar that has long since disappeared in normal English usage. Changes are still in the process of occurring, and students may hear or read English that does not conform to the rules they have memorized. For example, one change now taking place in American English involves the growing tendency to use *their* rather than *he* or *she* in sentences such as "I hope no one forgot their book." (In this case, the change is probably due to a growing unwillingness to use *his* and *her* when speaking of a group that includes both men and women.) Thus, occa-sionally in answer to the question of what is right, you will have to answer that two alternatives are both correct, although for different set-tings.

The point of all this is that students will have a better perspec-tive on language learning if they take a more descriptive and utilitarian view of grammar. Their purpose in studying grammar should be to find out how speakers of English construct sentences, not to master a divine canon of grammar rules per se. A rule that enables a student to construct many correct sentences is worth learning; a rule that is impossible to understand or only covers one or two situations is a hindrance rather than a help. Grammar rules are helpful to students if and only if they make the mastery of English easier.

How Is Grammar Learned?

It may be instructive to briefly consider how children learn a language. A baby learning English usually begins speaking with single-word sentences like "Cookie!", often accompanied by much waving of arms and feet. Later, she progresses to "Sally cookie!", an utterance that is generally perfectly intelligible in context as a request rather than a statement of identity. She then moves on to "Sally cookies now!", and then over time slowly but surely continues experimenting and elaborating on her sentence constructions from there. No matter how diligently parents teach or correct, Sally is not likely to jump in a week from "Sally cookie!" to "Mother, may I please have a cookie?"

Adults may not learn language exactly the same way as children, but current wisdom in the field suggests that there are similarities. Adults also tend to start by learning simple basic rules, and then slowly elaborate their system through experimentation. If we were to use the analogy of drawing a picture, adults will naturally tend to sketch an outline first and then go back to fill in ever finer levels of detail later, rather than completing one corner of the picture in full detail first before moving on to another. In other words, adults are not likely to master all of the verb system before going on to nouns; they are more likely to gain a rudimentary control of both and then—through trial and error, aided by whatever input is available—to elaborate that control. As Bowen et al. (1985) describe the process: "Students usually learn their grammar one small piece at a time; they do not need (and indeed could not immediately assimilate) an entire system" (p. 166).

The first implication of this for teaching is that it is normal for students to go through an interlanguage period during which they have incomplete control of structures they are trying to learn—a "Give Sally cookie" stage. It is not normal for them to rapidly master the verb system of English down to a fine level of control, no matter how clearly you explain it to them. A second is that students need an opportunity to digest grammar input by trying out modifications in their interlanguage grammar system in language practice. Again, to improve their control of grammar, they need to practice using it, not just listen to you talk about it.

How Well Should Grammar Be Learned?

One way in which grammar is similar to vocabulary is that it can be used in two basic ways: receptively for comprehension in reading or listening, and productively in speech and writing. This suggests that, as in the case of vocabulary, it is normal for a student to have complete productive control over some grammar rules and only receptive control of others. Of course this is what normally happens whether we want it or not; usually students gain receptive control over a structure before they learn to use it productively. However, we need not assume that students must ultimately master all grammar rules for productive control. Some grammatical structures in English are not used very much, and it is by no means essential that students be able to produce every one of them. Even "basic" verb tenses such as the past perfect (e.g., *By 8:00 he had slept for 10 hours*) or the past perfect progressive (e.g., *By 8:00 he had been sleeping for 10 hours*) are not often used, and can usually be replaced with a rough equivalent that is more straightforward (e.g., *He slept 10 hours before 8:00*).

One implication of this is that some grammar points are more important than others, and that there is no need for students to gain total productive control over every structure they encounter—certainly not right away. The goal is rather for students to first learn rules that are relatively useful and easy to grasp, and to then fill in the details as time and need dictate (Scarcella & Oxford, 1992). The teacher who insists on complete productive control of every fine point of detail runs the risk of overloading students' circuits and burning them out. Again, students and teachers need to remember that the goal is not mastery of an abstract system of theory, it is practical mastery of a communication skill, and the goal in learning grammar is to learn that which is of use in communicating.

Teaching Grammar

Usually when you are teaching grammar, you will be working with a textbook that determines what grammar structures are to be introduced and provides exercises.[5] As you prepare for your class, the issue is thus usually not deciding what to teach but rather how to approach the material in your text.

The steps I suggest below for a grammar lesson follow more or less those described in Ur (1988): (a) presenting a structure; (b) explaining it; and (c) practicing it.[6] This is basically an inductive approach, that is, it allows students a chance to figure out the structure before you explain it to them. In general I favor this approach because problem solving makes students more active as participants in the learning process; I also suggest it for VTs because you may not yet have a clear sense of what students need to have explained to them—and what they don't need or can't handle—and a deductive approach (explanation first, examples and practice later) may lead you into overly long and elaborate grammar lectures. An inductive approach allows students to try a structure out before you explain it, thus giving you a chance to assess what problems they have with it and what needs to be explained. However, for reasons of culture or learning styles some students are more comfortable with a deductive approach,[7] so you should experiment with the ordering of steps below to find out what works best with your students.

Presentation

Often students will have begun this process before class either as part of their homework, as a result of previous lessons, or simply because they chose to look ahead in the book, so another goal of this part of the in-class lesson is to find out how well they already know the structure.

The most basic way to present a structure in class is to use it communicatively in conversation with students. For example, if the structure for this lesson is the future verb tense, you might begin the lesson by asking a few students: "What are you doing this weekend?" At this first stage, the goal is to let students hear or see the new structure and give them an opportunity to figure out for themselves

---

[5]If there is no text for your course, you can probably find a locally produced text that has grammar lessons—of all the kinds of English teaching materials, texts that center on grammar are the most widely produced. Appendix C also suggests grammar books that could serve as the outline of a grammar course.

[6]Cross (1991) and Eisenstein (1987) suggest a very similar approach.

[7]Eisenstein (1987) suggests that an inductive approach may work less well with older students, with students who are used to grammar explanations, or in cultures where guessing—especially public guessing—isn't favored.

first what it means and then how it works, so you need not demand that in responding to your questions students immediately use the structure. Of course they may well have already studied the structure in their books and have some idea how it works, but reading about a structure in a book and using it in conversation are two very different things, so it is still nice to give them a breathing space before requiring production.

Presentation may also be more focused through use of games or drills specifically chosen to illustrate the structure. For example, when introducing a new structure such as the plural ending, you might use an exercise such as holding up first one book and saying "One book," then holding up and saying "Two books." Here, once students seem to understand you could encourage them to start experimenting with production, responding to what you hold up. However, as above, your main goal is receptive comprehension, so you should only involve production as students seem willing and ready.

Explanation

There are good reasons not to expect that lectures will make dramatic impact on your students' progress toward grammatical accuracy. One problem is that even in the same class students will often have different levels of grammar knowledge, so when you lecture on a grammar point some of the students will already know it, others will lack the foundation to comprehend your explanation, and some others will probably be bored and not pay attention; only a percentage—all too often a small one—will actually learn much from your lecture. A greater problem is that conscious knowledge of grammar rules does not guarantee the ability to produce accurate English. In fact, conscious knowledge of grammar rules is not a necessary precondition to the ability to produce English accurately, a fact demonstrated daily by most native speakers (who have little explicit knowledge of grammar rules), and by many students who do well on grammar tests but still make frequent errors in communication situations. Understanding a grammar point may be the first step toward mastering it, but it is only the first step.

Then why explain grammar structures at all? There is still disagreement within the language teaching profession as to the usefulness of explicit explanation of grammar rules, but consensus seems to be that explanation can be of some value to some students if it is not too far over students' heads. A second and very different reason for explicit explanation of grammar is that in many countries lectures on grammar are an expected staple of the language classroom diet, and if this familiar part of the routine suddenly vanishes, students may be disoriented or dissatisfied. (Another argument for explanation of grammar is that it is in the process of explaining grammar that many language teachers learn it themselves!)

Often the text materials you are working from will have explanation of the new structure and some examples, so you will have some guidance as to how to explain a structure. If you have allowed students to play with the structure during the presentation stage, you should also have some idea of how well students already understand the structure. The goal of the explanation is thus generally to clarify one or two major problem areas, advancing students' understanding of the structure by one or two steps. A few pointers on explanations:

1 Try to start explaining at the right level so that you are not wasting time telling students what they already know or talking over their heads. It is more important to be to the point than comprehensive.

2 Keep explanations short and simple as possible, with a limited number of variations and details that will tend to confuse and overload students. Avoid the temptation to prepare overly thorough explanations of grammar points in order to impress your class.

3 Remember that some points are better memorized than explained. For example, there is little that need be said about irregular past tense verb forms (*eat-ate, write-wrote, read-read*)—students just need to learn them.

4 Examples are often much easier to understand than explanations, so be sure to include several. Given the tendency of students in many countries to read better than they listen, it is also a good idea to write examples on the board.

5 Use pictures, diagrams, and graphs to communicate a point. For example, many grammar teachers explain English verb tenses with time line drawings.

Practice

Obviously, understanding a grammar rule is not the same thing as being able to apply it to communication problems, so a third important step in the study of grammar is practice. Grammar practice ranges on a continuum from highly controlled practice in which learners need to make very few choices to free communicative practice in which learners need to apply grammar rules to real language use situations. It is in productive use of grammar—speaking and writing—that the challenge is greatest, so we will focus on this below.

HIGHLY CONTROLLED PRACTICE

One problem usually not faced by a VT is having to design controlled grammar exercises (e.g., fill-in-the-blank, find and correct the error in the sentence, restate the passive sentence in the active voice)—many English textbooks have an adequate supply of these. Such exercises can be of value as the first step in mastery of a grammar structure because they allow the learner to concentrate on applying a structure in a controlled situation where other problems are eliminated. These exercises are also useful for checking to see if students have a basic understanding of whatever grammar point is being taught.

The simplicity of these exercises is, however, also their major drawback. Exercises such as choosing the right verb tense to fill in a blank or restating a passive sentence in the active voice are unlike actual language production exactly because the learner can focus on one problem to the exclusion of all others. They are thus very unlike real-world grammar application problems, and should not constitute the major part of a student's grammar practice diet. You certainly should not feel that your duty consists primarily of seeing that students do every exercise in the book.

MODERATELY CONTROLLED PRACTICE

An intermediate step between highly controlled exercises like those mentioned above and natural practice activities would be controlled communicative activities in which students must construct their own sentences and express their own ideas, but in which their attention is still clearly focused on the target structure you want them to learn. For example, consider the following pair activity for practicing relative clauses. Divide students into pairs and have them practice a short conversation as follows:

A: (Pointing into a crowd) Who is that woman?

B: Which one?

A: The one _____.
(e.g., who is wearing a hat, who looks like an angel)

B: Oh, that is _____. (e.g., Angie, Kim)

This exercise is communicative in that it can involve real conversation about real people (other students in the class, or people in a picture, for example), and students have some freedom to express their own ideas, but students still know exactly what grammar structure they need to produce, and can focus their attention on it. Many textbooks will contain such exercises, and if not they can generally be readily adapted from dialogues in the textbook.

FREE PRACTICE

In order for grammar practice to be realistic, it needs to involve the solving of multiple language problems at the same time. To this end it is best that the practice take place in a communicative context where the students need to pay attention to what they are saying as well as getting verb tenses right. It is often possible to find topics of conversation that will naturally require that the target structure appears frequently, thus providing good practice in the use of that structure. Examples:

1 For the present continuous tense, have students talk about something—perhaps the actions of a classmate or action on a videotape—as it happens. This will elicit many sentences such as "Sally *is smiling*" or "The man *is eating* dinner."

2 For relative clauses, have students discuss what kind of friends (e.g., movies, food, weather) they like. Of course, different kinds of things can be distinguished with adjectives as well as relative clauses ("I like rich friends"), but many other ideas virtually demand relative clauses ("I like friends who do my homework for me").

3 For practice of use of plural nouns as topics, have students discuss what kinds of animals they like or don't like and why ("I don't like dogs because they are stupid").

Writing is an especially good skill to combine with grammar lessons because it serves as an intermediate step between the level where students can only apply a grammar rule in discrete-point exercises and the level where they must quickly apply a rule in speaking. Like speaking, the process of writing requires students to apply grammar rules while in the midst of a host of other decisions, but unlike speaking it allows students time to think about how a grammar structure should be applied, and even allows students to consult reference tools. Writing also makes it possible for students to go back and check the language they have produced, and thus learn from their own mistakes.

Evaluating Grammar

There are two issues to address in evaluation of student grammar competence. One question is whether or not students know the target structure; in other words, whether or not they can manipulate it under ideal circumstances. The second question is whether or not they can apply their knowledge under normal language use conditions.

Evaluating Grammar Knowledge

Discrete-point grammar test or quiz items focus the attention of students on a particular grammar problem. The main value of such items is that they allow you to determine whether or not students have a basic understanding of the target structure. Basic types include:

1. Multiple choice. E.g.: Tommy _____ the apple.

      A. eat
      B. eaten
      C. eated
      D. ate

2. Fill in the blank. E.g.: Tommy _____ (eat) the apple.

3. Correct the error. E.g.: The apple falled on Newton's head.

4. Rewriting. E.g.: Rewrite the following in passive voice: Tommy ate the apple.

As pointed out in Chapter 4, creating good discrete-point test items is a complicated science, but there are two rules of thumb that will help you ensure that a discrete-point test is reasonably good:

1 Always have someone else check your test items to ensure that there are no ambiguities that you overlooked in the process of test construction.

2 Use a large number of test items. If there are only a few items, a few poorly designed questions or lucky guesses by students can make a big difference in the final grade.

Discrete-point grammar tests have a number of advantages. They are easy to grade, let you check whether or not students have studied specific grammar points, and prepare students for other discrete-point tests (such as the TOEFL) that they may face in the future. The disadvantages are, however, quite serious. Although such tests tell you whether or not students have grasped the basic concept of a grammar structure, they do not tell you how well students can apply this knowledge. Worse, the backwash effects of heavy use of such test items are generally negative because they reinforce the belief that a knowledge of grammar theory is more important than the ability to apply grammar knowledge to real-life situations.

Evaluating Grammar Skills

There are two major advantages of evaluating grammar in the context of language use rather than through discrete-point tests. The first is that evaluating grammar in use, usually writing or speaking, allows you to assess not only how well students know grammar rules, but whether or not students are able to apply them. The second is that the backwash effect of this kind of testing encourages students to learn how to apply their knowledge rather than being satisfied with an understanding of grammar theory.

Written work is a particularly natural context within which to assess grammar because it is a context within which grammatical accuracy is especially important; it also allows you to assess grammar at your leisure. In the same way that practice activities can be designed to call for certain grammatical constructions, you can plan a writing task so that it naturally elicits target structures. For example, a written dialogue about favorite kinds of fruits should elicit use of plural nouns as general subjects (*I like pears but I hate grapes*); a composition about childhood experiences should elicit past tense verbs (*I wore diapers for several years*). If you wish to ensure that students produce certain target structures, list those structures and tell students to be sure to use them. Writing tasks that are explicitly designed to test grammar are, of course, less natural than normal writing tasks because they focus the attention of students on grammar rather than communication, but the loss in naturalness may be made up for by the certainty that you will get the material you need for your evaluation.

Grammar can also be evaluated as a part of general speaking skills. When checking for specific grammar points, however, you will need to make use of tasks that ensure that students produce the target structures. In other words, in your interviews, pair work, or whatever format you use for evaluation, you will need to include some tasks that are at least somewhat controlled. These might be exercises like the moderately controlled exercises mentioned above, or topics that naturally elicit certain structures. (Note: In the latter case, you also need to let students know that you are looking for certain target structures.)

A general suggestion is that you use exercises similar to those you use in class for practice of grammar points (that have the added advantage of being familiar), and then grade using a criteria system. Consider the following task for a class in which you do lots of pair work: Assign students to talk about their early school experiences in pairs, practicing the past tense. Let students know you will be evaluating them for use of the target structure as well as general communication. As you move from pair to pair, listening in, you could rank students on a scale like the one on the following page:

4: Produced the target structure frequently and was usually correct.

3: Produced the target structure a number of times; may have hesitated or self-corrected but was ultimately correct at least half of the time.

2: Tried to produce the target structure several times, but was generally slow or inaccurate.

1: Rarely produced the target structure; slow and inaccurate.

0: Never produced the target structure.

Of course, an approach like this will produce conversation that is rather unnatural, but it has the advantage of encouraging students to use the target structure. It is also simple enough that it can be used quickly, though its simplicity would make it more appropriate for a minor class grade than for a major examination.

One additional possibility to consider, where possible, is having students record their speech. Having a taped record allows you to evaluate student grammar more carefully than is possible in situations where you have to attend to many things at once.

It seems fitting to conclude this discussion of grammar with a few comments on the art of coping with knotty grammar questions in class. It seems that almost every English class has at least one student who is obsessed with grammar and loves to ask questions like "Should I use an infinitive or a gerund after a verb?" The problem VTs often face is not only that they don't know the answer to a question like this (at least not when couched in this terminology) but that they don't really understand the question itself.

The first and most important rule for survival is to never attempt to answer a grammar question—particularly one presented in theoretical terms—unless an example is also provided. By demanding an example, you move the issue onto more familiar ground; even if you don't understand the grammar terminology, you will generally be able to determine whether a specific example is correct or not, and the example will help you understand the question. Another reason to insist on examples is that they serve as a check on the accuracy of the question. Over the years, I have found that a great many impressive-sounding grammar questions, once understood, turn out to border on gibberish. Student grammar questions often begin as specific examples, but are then recast incorrectly by the student in half-understood theoretical language. Once you make the student present the original example, it is much easier to get to the heart of the matter. A final reason to require examples is that it reminds students that the study of gram-

Answering Grammar Questions

mar is intended to lead to application, and that application of grammar rules is often highly situational, a fact that tends to get lost when discussion of a rule remains theoretical.

A second tactic you can use when you aren't sure how to answer a question is to take the students' example, think of several more, and try to work out the rule along with the students. The pedagogical advantage of this approach is that it encourages the development of inductive skills and active learning; the practical advantage is that it gives you time to think.

When you have looked at a few examples and are still puzzled, there is always the temptation to try and bluff your way through the situation with a long answer containing lots of obscure grammarlike terms. However, a better choice is probably to confess your ignorance and promise to find out. This may be somewhat embarrassing at first (though most language teachers get used to it rather quickly), but if you actually carry through, you will both demonstrate diligence and learn something at the same time.

13 Teaching Culture

- ◆ Culture should be included in language courses because study of culture enhances students' ability to understand what they read, hear, and see, and more effectively express themselves to foreign audiences. Inclusion of culture will also make your language courses more interesting.

- ◆ The culture of a group consists of their shared ideas, particularly their shared knowledge, views, and patterns.

- ◆ "Western culture," "U.S. culture," "British culture," and so forth are not monolithic entities; there is also considerable cultural variety even within any nation.

- ◆ In many countries, students may have mixed feelings about Western culture. It is therefore important to present your culture in a way that is as objective and sensitive as possible.

English has become a world language, used far beyond the confines of U.S. and British soil, so it can no longer be assumed that all English-speakers come from Western cultural backgrounds. Many nations in which English is not indigenous, especially ex-British colonies, recognize English as one of their national languages, and English has taken on a life of its own in countries such as India, Nigeria, and Singapore which have cultural backgrounds decidedly different from those of the U.S. and Britain.[1] In fact, in some non-Western nations that have adopted English, there is a conscious attempt to divorce the English language from British and U.S. culture so that the language will be identified more closely with its new national culture. It could thus be argued that in some situations an English teacher should avoid associating English with the teaching of British or U.S. culture.

It is more often the case, however, that sensitive incorporation of Western culture into your English courses will benefit both your students and you. One reason is that many of the situations in which learners use English will involve some kind of cross-cultural communication. This might take the form of an African student reading magazines from Britain, or a Latin American businessman chatting with a North American client. It could mean an Asian watching TV programs or films from Australia, or listening to the BBC radio news. It could mean a Middle Eastern student writing an application letter to a U.S. university or a secretary in Hong Kong writing a business letter to a Canadian company. In all of these cases, the learner of English not only needs to cope with the problems of using a foreign language, but is also trying to understand and communicate with a very different culture. (Even when students use English primarily to interact with non-Western people—say, for example, with Malaysian businessmen or Indian academics—these may well be people who have been heavily influenced by Western culture.)

Bringing culture into your courses will also make them more interesting and genuinely communicative, in large part because of the genuine "information gap" that exists between your cultural knowledge and that of your students. As a native of a Western culture, one of your greatest strengths is your intimate knowledge of a culture that is fresh and new to your students, and your students also possess a great fund of knowledge about their culture that they would probably be pleased to share with you. By drawing on culture topics, you create opportunities for meaningful sharing of important and interesting information, and this helps raise students' interest in communication.

What Is Culture?

The term *culture* is nothing if not broad, and an exhaustive listing of all that it includes would require a book in itself. In review of various attempts to define the term, Seelye (1993) concludes: "The

[1]A highly readable treatment of this issue can be found in Robert McCrum, William Cran, and Robert MacNeil (1987), *The Story of English* (Faber & Faber).

most widely accepted usage now regards culture as a broad concept that embraces all aspects of human life, from folktales to carved whales. What is culture? It is everything humans have learned" (p. 22).[2] Unfortunately, such a broad definition of culture—correct as it no doubt is—does not provide much direction for teachers who are trying to set an agenda for the teaching of culture. Thus, at the risk of being less than fully comprehensive, I will suggest a definition that is more narrow but more helpful to the language teacher.

The essence of a culture lies more in the minds of a group of people than in their physical surroundings, and consists primarily of ideas that members of the group share. I find it convenient to think of the mental constructs making up a culture as falling into three basic categories:

1. **Shared knowledge:** information known in common by members of a group

2. **Shared views:** beliefs and values shared by members of a group

3. **Shared patterns:** shared habits and norms in the ways members of a group organize their behavior, interaction, and communication.

Granted, these three categories overlap to some degree, and most cultural phenomena can and must be analyzed in view of more than one of them. However, this system is fairly simple and manageable, yet has enough explanatory force that it is helpful in setting an agenda for the teaching of culture. We will examine each of these categories briefly below.

Shared Knowledge

Within a culture group, there is a great deal of information that members share in common, much of which is not familiar to outsiders. Compare, for example, the following two identification tests:

TEST 1:
(a) Dec. 7, 1941; (b) home plate; (c) Benedict Arnold; (d) Bill Cosby; and (e) Niagara Falls.

TEST 2:
(a) May 4, 1919; (b) dragon boat; (c) Yue Fei; (d) Deng Lijun; (e) Dun Huang.

[2]See Brown (1991) and Damen (1987) for further discussion.

233

Americans with a high school education would no doubt come close to a perfect score on Test 1, and even an American with no education would probably get several right answers. However, even the average college-educated American would be lucky to get more than one correct answer on Test 2. In contrast, the average Chinese schoolchild would score a clean sweep on Test 2, but probably miss most of the items on Test 1.[3]

These seemingly isolated bits of information are important in communication because they facilitate use of top-down comprehension strategies. Consider the following sentences, the opening lines of a (fictitious) novel: "There was a warm gentle breeze blowing on the morning of December 7, 1941. Bob let his thoughts linger on the slim figure and dark eyes of the woman he had met the night before." By the time they finished reading these two sentences, many U.S. readers would already be able to guess a great deal about the story that is to follow. The story is probably set in Pearl Harbor and revolves around the attack. Even the time of day can be guessed with considerable accuracy—it is probably early in the morning, before the attack. Of course, these are only guesses, but they enable a reader to skim forward much faster in the story, checking guesses rather than trying to piece the story together from scratch. In contrast, students of English who didn't know the significance of "December 7, 1941" would find little more in these sentences than the aggregate meaning of the words and would thus be at a disadvantage in comprehending the story.

The other pieces of information included in Test 1 could also set the scene for a story, convey an emotion, symbolically suggest values, or simply function as vocabulary. For example, the mention of "Niagara Falls" conjures up images of honeymooners and people going over a waterfall in a barrel. "Bill Cosby" is seen by many Americans as more than a successful comedian; he also serves as a role model of the family-oriented father and the successful black professional. Finally, "Benedict Arnold" is synonymous with "traitor" in the U.S.

Another reason why attention to background information is important in language courses is that students need to learn to be aware of assumptions they make about what an audience from another culture does and does not know. Take, for example, a Chinese tour guide who begins his introduction to a temple by saying "This fine structure was built during the Qin Dynasty." Such an introduction

---

[3] Answer key for Test 1: (a) Japanese attack on Pearl Harbor; (b) place where batter stands in baseball; (c) traitor in Revolutionary War; (d) family-oriented comedian; (e) scenic spot for honeymooners. Answer key for Test 2: (a) protests against Japan that mark the begining of modern Chinese history; (b) used in yearly races on Dragon Boat Festival to commemorate the poet Qu Yuan; (c) ancient hero who resisted foreign invaders until betrayed by his own government; (d) contemporary pop singer; (e) site where ancient Buddhist manuscripts and cave paintings were found.

would help a Chinese audience place the temple in a historical context, but would probably be of no use at all to a group of foreign tourists who don't know what or when the Qin Dynasty was. If the tour guide has some idea what he can and cannot expect his audience to know, he has a better idea of what needs to be explained and what doesn't. This enables him to provide appropriate clarification when necessary and avoid boring an audience with superfluous explanation when none is needed.

Much of the material that makes up the shared knowledge of a culture is passed intentionally from one generation to the next, often through the educational system or in the home. In modern societies another very important source of shared cultural knowledge is the electronic media (the performing media may have a similar role in more traditional societies). A final source of cultural knowledge is widely shared experiences such as little league baseball for boys in the U.S. or the turmoil of the Cultural Revolution for the urban population of China.

Shared Views

Within a group, people not only know many of the same things, they also believe many of the same things and share many opinions on a huge spectrum of issues. To some extent, a culture is composed of widely held opinions on such mundane questions as: What is the best treatment for a cold? Is *ain't* an acceptable word? Who is the world's greatest soccer player? However, a culture is shaped much more by a shared world view consisting of the beliefs and values of a culture, its shared answers to basic questions inherent in human existence such as:

> Are there supernatural forces?
> Are humans basically good or evil?
> Who am I/who are we?
> What is my proper relationship to other people?
> How should other people treat me?
> Is my life more defined by what I am like or what I do?
> Should I look more to the future of the past?[4]

Answers to questions such as these are often found in the dominant religious or philosophical thought of a culture, but are also embedded in its stories and its models of excellence (e.g., heroes, art, achieve-

---

[4]Students of cultural anthropology will recognize the influence of Clyde and Florence Kluckhohn's cultural models in my choice of questions. For an easy introduction to their model, see Kohls (1984).

ments). These beliefs and deeply rooted cultural orientations tend to change slowly, if at all, and play a major role in shaping a culture.

A very practical advantage of understanding the beliefs and values of a given culture is that it improves ability to accurately interpret what people from that culture do and say. This is of major importance in cross-cultural communication, where misunderstandings are common and can have serious consequences. Consider the simple example of an Asian student who meets a North American tourist who is obviously floundering in her attempts to shop in an Asian city. The student—partly out of altruism and partly to get English practice—offers to translate, but is surprised when the tourist firmly insists that she wants to do things for herself. A student who has some idea of the importance North Americans place on self-reliance is not so likely to be puzzled or offended by this rebuff; a student who understands little of North American culture has no recourse but to interpret this refusal in terms of his or her own culture and may mistakenly assume that the refusal implies a lack of trust or perhaps even sheer prejudice.

A second reason that students should have some knowledge of Western beliefs and values is that it will enhance their ability to express their own ideas, especially in situations where they need to persuade. Take, for example, the problem of application letters. In many countries, students study English in part because they hope to study or work abroad, and they must thus write application letters for jobs, scholarships and admission to schools. A problem that often crops up in such letters is that students do not understand the fine art of making themselves look good while not seeming boastful. In Asia, one problem I have often seen is that students make broad assertions about their merits ("I was the best student in my school") and do not support their claims with quantifiable objective evidence. Also, it is difficult for them to gauge what kind of arguments will appeal to a Western employer or admissions officer, and they thus sometimes sound too idealistic ("I wish to devote myself to the construction of my Motherland") or too mercenary ("I hope to get a degree in business and then be successful in the construction industry").

Knowing something of the beliefs and values of a culture is especially important in helping students understand why its members act and speak as they do, a level of comprehension that goes beyond the surface meaning of words. An additional benefit of studying this level of culture is that as students look at the assumptions underlying another culture, the contrast may enable them for the first time to clearly see the assumptions that underlie their own.

Shared Patterns

Not all human activity falls into neat patterns, but a great deal of it follows at least a general pattern and much of it is rather strictly ordered.[5] More or less clear cultural patterns can be found in a huge range of things, including daily schedules, events of the year, ordering of events in a meeting, dating and mating, or even the way a story or article is organized. Sometimes these patterns are cultural habits that have no particular values attached to them, such as the U.S. tendency to shower in the morning rather than the evening, or the custom of starting a fairy tale with "Once upon a time. . . ." Often, however, these patterns are evaluative norms, deviation from which is at best odd or impolite and at worst criminal.

Of particular concern to the language learner are the patterns in how a culture deals with communication situations. Although conversations don't always closely follow a preordained script, neither is each one improvised entirely anew. Many common functions of language use, such as polite refusals, responses to compliments, introductions, and so forth, are fairly conventional. For example, in mainstream U.S. culture a polite refusal to an invitation generally involves an expression of thanks or regret followed by a specific reason why the invitation cannot be accepted ("I would love to, but I won't be in town on that day"); note that a vague excuse like "I will be busy" is not as polite. When responding to compliments, Americans will often say "Thank you," but follow that by either passing the credit on to someone/something else ("Thank you, my mother taught me how to cook this") or using the compliment as a springboard into a conversation topic, hence rapidly deflecting attention from the praise given ("Thank you. I bought this shirt on a business trip to Nigeria last year. . .").

Obviously, one reason why students have a vested interest in study of these aspects of culture is that knowing them will help students communicate more politely and appropriately—or at least avoid unintentionally giving offense. A second and less obvious advantage of knowing these patterns is that it enhances students' ability to predict what they might hear or read. This, in turn, makes comprehension easier. For example, if students can narrow the probable range of responses to a compliment, they are more likely to be able to catch key words even when listening to somebody who talks too fast.

A second set of conventions that are especially important to language students are the genre conventions that shape so much printed and audiovisual communication. Many kinds of books, articles, TV shows, films, and other structured forms of discourse tend to follow a formula. For example, romances generally consist of a boy, a girl, and a problem that has to be overcome if the couple is to find happiness. Westerns usually have one or more good guys, a bunch of bad guys, a pretty girl, and a final shootout from which the hero generally rides away more or less intact. Even newspaper news features are laid out in a predictable pattern, starting with location and date, followed first

[5]See Damen (1987) for discussion of this aspect of culture.

by the main points of the story and then by details in order of decreasing importance. The significance of this for readers and viewers is that once they know which formula is being followed, their ability to predict and guess—hence to comprehend—is greatly enhanced. (In the Pearl Harbor example above, even the first two sentences hint strongly that the story is a drama and romance. In fact, I would be willing to bet a week's pay that Bob is a white American soldier, the woman is young, beautiful and of Japanese ancestry, and that the story is about how they will cope with the impact of the attack on their romance.)

A final set of conventions of special importance to language students are those surrounding written language. Most kinds of writing, especially more formal types such as business letters and academic writing, follow rather strict rules as to how ideas are to be organized and presented. Even the layout of the components of a business letter— where to place the date, where to place addresses—is governed by conventions. (These conventions are probably more familiar to most VTs than the genre or behavior patterns mentioned above because the conventions of writing are usually explicitly taught to native speakers in school.)

The main reason I have gone into such detail above describing different types of culture and their roles in communication is that this is information that is useful to pass on to students so that they see why study of culture is an inherently important aspect of language study. This does not mean you need to burden students with a series of lectures on the importance of culture in language learning (although this might not be a bad idea if the listening skills of your students can handle it), but when discussing any given point of culture with students it is helpful to mention why knowing such a point may be beneficial and how it relates to communication. For example, cultural background knowledge is especially important for its ability to enhance top-down comprehension strategies, knowledge of a culture's beliefs and values improves one's ability to interpret behavior and communication more accurately, and knowledge of genre patterns enables learners to better predict—and hence more easily understand—what they will read. Knowing how different kinds of culture affect communication will help students see more clearly both the connection between language and culture, and the importance of studying culture as well as language.

English— Whose Culture?

As we consider the issue of culture in English courses, we may tend to think first and foremost of "U.S. culture" and "British culture," but with a little reflection it is clear that neither of these terms is fully satisfactory as a label for the kind of culture we should teach. Even if we only consider those countries in which English is used as the first (and usually only) language, there are several large nations and quite a few more smaller ones. We must also recognize that even within any given English-speaking nation the culture is hardly uniform; lumping the culture of an ethic neighborhood in New York City under the same label as that of a rural community in Texas or a retirement community in Florida would be problematic at best. Thus, as we consider the issue of incorporating culture in English courses, we need to consider the question of exactly whose culture we are going to teach.

Perhaps the best way to approach this problem is by recognizing at least three general levels of culture that need to be considered in the case of English-speaking nations.

Level 1: Western Culture

Many important aspects of culture are shared not only by the U.S., Britain, and other English-speaking nations, but also by other European nations and nations in which there has been substantial European influence. For example, all of these countries share a considerable portion of their philosophical and religious traditions, a similar approach to law and government, and even much of their literary heritage.

Level 2: National Culture

The stratum of culture that we tend to think of most readily is the national level: U.S. culture, Canadian culture, British culture, and so forth. Although we cannot assume that all Americans (Canadians, Australians, etc.) are exactly alike, it is certainly true that there are cultural characteristics that are shared widely within a nation and that distinguish that nation from others. For example, even despite the immediate geographic proximity of Canada and the U.S., people of the two nations tend to have rather different views of government, Canadians assuming that it is proper for government to play a greater role in provision of medical care and other social services than Americans would expect.

Level 3: Group Culture

In casual discussion of culture, it is easier to work with broad terms like "Western culture" and "U.S. culture" than to be more precise about exactly what stream of Western or U.S. culture we are referring to. The danger of overuse of such terms, particularly in a teaching situation, is that we may obscure the importance of regional, class, religious, ethnic, gender, and occupational cultures. For example, no picture of U.S. culture would be fully complete if only represented the culture presented most often in TV situation comedies—a suburban, middle-class, white family living in a generic community. To complete the picture we also need to recognize strong subcultures such as those of the deep South, the urban poor, evangelical Christians, blacks and Hispanics, women, gays and lesbians, and perhaps even truck drivers.

The question of whose culture to teach is complicated even further by the issue of how much relative weight should be given to dominant cultural norms as opposed to minority cultures. In North America, controversy on this point was sparked by the 1987 book *Cultural Literacy: What Every American Needs to Know* by E. D. Hirsch (Vintage Books), which argues that there is a core of cultural knowledge that all U.S. schoolchildren need to know, and then presents a list of names, dates, and terms that he feels represents this cultural core. Most of the controversy arises from Hirsch's list, which has been criticized as representing only a dominant white, educated culture and ignoring the existence and importance of a diverse range of minority traditions.[6] Although this debate primarily concerns the question of what culture should be taught to students in the U.S., the larger issue of how much to include regional, ethnic, or other subnational cultures has implications for culture teaching in EFL classes as well.

As you consider how to approach culture in your English classes, perhaps your first goal should be to help students see that there are different levels of culture associated with English, in short, that not every point of culture taught in an English class can be neatly labelled "U.S. culture" or "British culture." By being careful to distinguish between aspects of culture that are shared all over the West, those distinct to a particular nation, and those particular only to a smaller group, you will be helping students learn an important lesson about the complexity of culture.

With regard to the question of dominant vs. minority cultures, I suggest a pragmatic approach. In most of the countries in which you might teach, students will often encounter the dominant streams of U.S. and British culture through books, magazines and the media, so it is especially important that students learn about this level of culture. However, you do not want to go so far in this direction that students get the impression of the West or your country as a culturally homogeneous entity. You might even make a special point of drawing on your own experience to introduce aspects of group cultures with which you have had experience.

Teaching Culture: Methods

As often as possible in language courses you should be trying to kill two birds with one stone: having students learn about culture at the same time as they develop their language skills. For example, there is no reason for students to read a story about "Harold the Lazy Badger" created by a textbook writer when they could just as well read "The Tortoise and the Hare." By reading the former, students only

[6]For critiques of Hirsch, see Seelye (1993) and Walters (1992).

develop reading skills; by reading the latter, students also become familiar with a story that is known throughout the West. Similarly, a listening exercise in which you call out instructions to have students go through a series of meaningless motions is not as rich as one in which you give directions to have students walk through a wedding or a baseball game. Of course, there will be occasions when for pragmatic reasons you need to use material with little cultural content—you can't find an appropriate cultural topic, appropriate materials are not available, and so forth—but genuine cultural topics and issues should be brought into the language classroom whenever possible.

The following list of suggestions, therefore, is less a culture course curriculum than it is a series of ideas as to how culture can be incorporated in listening, speaking, reading, and writing courses; therefore the suggestions are organized according to types of language skill practice. To the extent possible, the list is also arranged according to the conceptual difficulty of the tasks.

Arousing Students' Interest in Culture

Because culture covers such a broad range, no matter how well you pack cultural information into your language courses you will still only be able to start students out. Obviously, whether or not they will continue pursuing the issue on their own depends to a large extent on how interested they are in it. Thus, Seelye (1993) suggests that as early as possible in your courses you should try to get students interested in culture. Among the activities he suggests for hooking their interest are the following:

1 Show students where places are on a map. For example, instead of just telling students where you are from, where you went to school and so forth, show them. Having a visual impression of where something is may be the first step to becoming interested in it. (Don't underestimate the power of a nicely colored map to catch the attention of students in classrooms that tend to otherwise offer little visual stimulation.)

2 Locate real natives of the culture for students to talk to. Of course, as a VT you are a fine candidate for this role, so encourage students to ask you about what interests them about your culture. It is also generally refreshing for students to have other representatives of your culture to interrogate, so take advantage of friends and relatives if they come to visit you.

3 Draw on the exotic. There are undoubtedly aspects of your culture that students will find quite strange, and these can often be a good hook for getting students more interested in the culture. Once you have their interest, try to move them past the curiosity show stage by

talking with them about why these "oddities" exist. Generally they make sense within the context of your culture, and learning to search for the logic of a culture is one of the most important habits students can develop.[7]

4 Show and tell. An activity I would add to those suggested by Seelye is the tried and true tradition of "Show and tell." From time to time bring in artifacts from your home culture as starting points for discussion or just for students to look at. Classrooms tend to have a surfeit of spoken and written words, and often not enough objects to look at or touch. This alone—not to mention the touch of the exotic—will often suffice to make your artifact a refreshing addition to your students' day and a nice way to arouse their interest. (You might also encourage your students to bring in things to show you before or after class, thus enhancing your education and giving them a chance to practice speaking.)

Dialogues

From the earliest stages of English study, most students are exposed to dialogues in textbooks. If these dialogues are at all realistic, they should provide a model of not only speech but also of normal patterns of social interaction. Thus, when studying them students should learn how Westerners interact.

As pointed out in Chapter 8, the way to use textbook dialogues as models of culture is to emphasize the functions (e.g., ways to invite, change a topic, politely disagree). When teaching the dialogue, call attention to the pattern of gambits involved, and teach students not only language tools but also how they are normally used. This aspect of dialogues can be emphasized by giving students practice assignments that are organized around functions and moves rather than around language per se; simply by presenting dialogues in this way you will be reminding students of the patterns of interaction underlying the language.

Culture Talks

The most direct way to approach the teaching of almost any aspect of culture is simply to talk about it. Lecture format allows students to learn about cultural background knowledge, beliefs and values, and cultural patterns at the same time as they practice their listening comprehension. The richness of lessons based on culture talks can be enhanced by having students respond by talking/writing

[7]All of the above are discussed in detail in Seelye (1993).

to you about corresponding aspects of their own culture. (For discussion of talks and lectures as a teaching technique, see Chapter 7.)[8]

Explanatory Cultural Discussions

In Chapter 8 we considered a form of small-group exercise in which students are asked to prioritize answers to questions like "What are the five best places to visit in your country?" or "Who are your nation's five greatest heroes?" By asking questions related to culture, you can provide students with an opportunity to practice talking to you and each other about their own culture, a skill that is arguably even more important than being able to talk about a foreign culture. This also provides students with a genuine communication opportunity, and you with a chance to learn about your host culture. (See Appendix B for other culture-related questions.)

With some minor modifications, this kind of exercise can be used to help sensitize students to the problem of considering the background knowledge of an audience from a different cultural background. To do this, ask students to discuss questions that require them to present information about their culture. Then, as they present their conclusions, play the role of the blissfully ignorant foreigner and whenever they assume background knowledge of the culture that you think a typical foreigner might lack, ask them to explain. You might do this directly by asking questions ("And just who is this Yue Fei?"), or perhaps more subtly by using facial expressions (perhaps somewhat exaggerated for comic effect) to let them know when their explanations are over your head or when they are boring you with what you already know. The virtue of this latter approach is that it will remind students to watch their audience for signs as to whether or not their message is getting through clearly.

Interpretive Discussion

This is a kind of speaking class exercise that helps students develop better habits in interpreting the behavior of people from other cultures. It also provides a good forum for discussing cultural differences, especially those in beliefs and values.

To begin the exercise, present students with a situation in

---

[8]Books designed to introduce your country to foreigners are useful as resource material for culture lectures. Examples for the U.S. would include Gary Althen's (1988) *American Ways: A Guide for Foreigners in the United States* (Intercultural Press) and Alison Lanier's (1988) *Living in the USA* (4th ed., Intercultural Press).

which they have a puzzling encounter someone from another culture. Consider, for example, the following:

> You are applying for an important scholarship, and your U.S. English teacher writes a nice recommendation letter for you. You finally get the scholarship, and feel grateful to your teacher, so you buy her an expensive gift. On the day that you present it to her, after class, she refuses to accept it. Why is she refusing?

Once students have had a chance to make sure they understand the situation, ask them in groups to discuss answers to the question. Stress that the goal is not to find "the right answer" but rather to brainstorm and come up with a variety of possible interpretations of the U.S. teacher's behavior. Then have the groups present their theories to the class for discussion. Finally, from your perspective give feedback as to what alternatives seem most likely, trying to give credit to as many suggestions as possible. (For theories that are way off the mark, a smile and "Good guess, but no" will usually do the trick without hurting too many feelings.)

One goal of this kind of interpretive discussion is for students to learn something about the beliefs and values of the culture in question; this is where your responses to students' suggestions are beneficial. However, a second goal is to encourage students to think broadly and cautiously about how to interpret behavior across cultural lines, so it is important that students try to think through the issue themselves before you offer your analysis. It is also best if the exercise does not simply turn into a game of who knows the right answer, lest students lose sight of the importance of thinking of alternative possibilities and instead simply try to memorize pat responses. Also, most actions result from a mix of factors, and there is generally not only one right answer to a question of why someone does or says something.

To compile a good collection of problem situations tailor-made to your situation, listen to stories your friends tell about their cross-cultural encounters or look into your own experience for situations where there were potential or real misunderstandings.[9]

This kind of exercise is challenging both conceptually and linguistically, so it is best used with students at intermediate or advanced levels.

---

[9]Resources for such exercises would include Craig Storti's (1994) *Cross-Cultural Dialogues: 74 Brief Encounters with Cultural Difference* (Intercultural Press), which presents a series of short dialogues containing cultural misunderstandings, and Richard Brislin et al. (1986), *Intercultural Interactions: A Practical Guide* (Sage), which presents cross-cultural problem situations. To a greater extent than the approach presented above, however, both of these works suggest a correct analysis of each encounter.

Texts and Cultural Content

Unlike students in ESL settings, students in EFL settings have relatively few opportunities for direct contact with Western culture and must rely heavily on reading, viewing, or listening to "texts" that contain cultural information in order to build the cultural background knowledge that they need. (Here, I use the term *text* to refer to books, magazine and newspaper articles, advertisements, television shows, films, radio programs—in short, any kind of organized discourse in English that might have cultural content.)

To the extent that you have choice in what students read or view, particularly valuable materials include:

1 Texts that realistically portray contemporary daily life and typical social interactions. Magazines and newspapers, particularly the advertisements, are especially rich in daily life realia and also cover a range of contemporary culture and social issues. Even when magazine and newspaper articles are too difficult to read (or it is too much trouble to get copies made), they can still be adapted for listening exercises. When possible, television programs and films are also an excellent resource.

2 Texts that teach the basic background information of Western culture—history, geography, government, economy, and society. High school textbooks can be a good source of this kind of material (old textbooks can often be purchased for you at a reasonable price by a friend back home). Both printed materials and documentaries are often available at your embassy or consulate in the host country.

3 Books or films that tell the well-known stories of your culture. These are often inherently interesting and usually raise a rich range of cultural issues. Additionally, they are important to know about simply because they are well known. Traditional Western stories would include the Greek and Norse myths, Bible stories, nursery rhymes, Grimm's and Andersen's fairy tales, and legends surrounding figures such as Ulysses, King Arthur, Joan of Arc, Robin Hood, and Davey Crockett. Modern characters who have moved into legend would include figures like Superman, Helen Keller, Babe Ruth, Marie Curie, Martin Luther King, and even Elvis Presley. Of course, many of these stories can be found in film as well as printed versions, and in many countries simplified readers based on the classic works of Western literature are available.

4 The particularly important body of shared knowledge that tells the story of your culture. This story is drawn from the history of a culture, but it is not a cold academic rendering of facts. Instead, it is a rather selective account that focuses on people and events that have special significance in defining a culture. In fact, it is often a rather simplified and "patriotic" version of history. Special attention is usually paid to those people/things/events of which the culture is most proud—its heroes, victories, great achievements, great creative works

and other models of excellence. This kind of shared cultural knowledge is especially important not only because it is widely known, but also because it plays a significant role in establishing the identity of a group and often offers important clues as to the values of the culture. This kind of history is often found in school textbooks.[10]

How does one teach cultural background knowledge? In a sense it is the text itself that does much of the teaching, so your first responsibility is to see that your students study and remember the cultural content of their texts as well as the language. The first step is to point out worthwhile cultural material when it appears in texts. For example, if students are reading a passage about Thomas Edison you need to tell students that he was not only a real person but one who is quite famous and important. The second step is to underscore the importance of learning cultural information by including it on tests, quizzes or whatever when it comes time for evaluation. As noted in our previous discussion of the backwash effect, your choice of what to hold students responsible for sends a strong signal about what you consider important and what is worth their time to study.

This kind of attention to cultural content may seem unnecessary; one might assume that students would learn this naturally. However, my experience both in teaching and the early stages of my own language learning would suggest that when students run across new names, dates, and events in texts it is not easy to tell whether they are widely known or obscure, and students looking for ways to cut corners may ignore names, places, dates, and content in general unless they see good reason to do otherwise.

Obviously learning culture from books, movies and the like is somewhat problematic—the pictures of a culture that they present are often not typical, complete, or entirely realistic. Thus, one of your main duties when dealing with fiction is to help students evaluate how useful a given text is as a portrayal of culture. You may not be able to give a detailed analysis of exactly how typical or realistic a situation is, but you will often be able to perform the very useful function of letting students know whether it is more or less typical of some stream of culture (and, if so, of which one). By approaching the text critically, you will also be helping students form the habit of not simply accepting any portrayal they read about the outside world as unvarnished truth.

Texts as Examples of Culture

Study of texts is not only a way to build background knowledge, but also an excellent opportunity to study the beliefs and values of a

---

[10]This aspect of your culture is important, but it is also potentially sensitive. A nation's identity is often forged in conflict with other nations, thus the story may

culture. To the extent that they are realistic and typical of a major stream of culture, stories are especially useful because they provide examples of people interacting in a cultural context, and there is thus ample opportunity to see how they respond to various situations.

One way to use stories to teach beliefs and values of a culture is through interpretive discussion of the kind introduced above. To adapt this exercise for use with narratives, have students select an incident in a story that they find hard to understand. Consider, for example, a story in which the main character, an old U.S. widow, is invited by her son to go live with him and his family but refuses. Students from many cultures might find the refusal of the old woman hard to understand, so this would be a promising topic. As in the interpretive discussions above, approach the question of the widow's motives by first having students brainstorm possible interpretations in small groups. Also encourage them to rely on evidence from the text as much as possible when seeking support for their theories. This will encourage students to not only read carefully, but also to try to understand a situation from within its own cultural framework rather than drawing theories entirely from their own cultural background. Then, after students have presented their theories, respond by pointing out clues in the text that students have overlooked and also drawing on your own cultural background.

Nonfiction texts such as magazine or journal articles, or even advertisements, can be treated in a similar way. For example, if students are reading an article on the women's rights movement in the West, you might have them consider the question of what would lead to such a movement. In this case, it is the subject matter of the text that becomes the focus of the interpretive discussion. The text itself can also be seen as an example of cultural behavior and become the focus of discussion, particularly if it assumes cultural values and beliefs that are not made fully explicit. Advertisements are particularly amenable to this kind of treatment because of the strong appeal they make to the beliefs and values of the audience.

Interpretive discussion of texts is conceptually more demanding than memorizing cultural data, so this kind of activity is generally more appropriate for students at the intermediate and advanced stages of English study.

Texts as Examples of Genres

A third aspect of culture that should be addressed when working with texts is that of genres, the customary patterns into which

have strong "us versus them" undertones, not to mention substantial elements of boosterism. Thus, although the story should be presented with empathy, it should also be presented with a degree of critical distance.

communication is organized. This is especially important for advanced students in EFL settings because their main opportunity to use English—and main hope for breakthrough—often lies either in reading or listening to the radio, and knowledge of the genre conventions of whatever kind of material they read or listen to will aid their comprehension.

One approach is simply to point out the formulas underlying whatever texts (e.g., films) students are studying in class. A more interesting alternative in advanced classes is to have students try and discover for themselves the formulas of Western texts. I find that this works best if you first prime the pump by having them describe to you the formula for a familiar genre within their own culture. For example, with Asian students I find that asking them to outline the typical kung fu movie works particularly well; romances are another good option. Then, as students read or view Western texts which are fairly typical of some genre, have them be on the lookout for the underlying formula. Then, during discussion, ask them to present their theories as to what the formula might be.

Sensitivity in Teaching Western Culture

The main reason English has such a dominant role in so many parts of the world is that over the last two centuries English-speaking nations have wielded tremendous economic, political, and military power. One consequence of this fact is that the experience of many countries with the English-speaking nations has been less than entirely positive. Westerners have often been invaders, colonizers, or economic competitors rather than friends, and the desire of many people to learn English is complicated by feelings of resentment toward the power and wealth of those countries that English represents. In some cultures, this resentment is expressed openly; in others traditions of politeness will make these attitudes more difficult for an outsider to detect but they may well nonetheless be present. Thus, the teaching of Western culture, particularly if it is presented with strong overtones of Western superiority, has the potential to arouse considerable resistance and hostility.

Unfortunately, VTs are not always very sensitive to this problem. Although few VTs consciously seek to be offensive, you may well be working in a country that is not as wealthy, efficient, or modern as your home country, and in this situation it is hard not to let a note of pride or superiority creep into your voice when introducing your culture. Most Westerners, Americans in particular, also have no memory of serious oppression by an outside power, and so may underestimate the bitterness with which people in many developing nations view their relationship—historical or current—with the West. A second problem is that just the difficulties of adjusting to an unfamiliar culture (*culture shock*—see Chapter 15) often erode VTs' feelings of goodwill toward their host countries, and this makes it more likely that in culture lessons the VT will offend by either explicitly or implicitly suggesting that the host culture is inferior.

Even if you present Western culture in a sensitive way, students may not always be pleased by what they hear. It is not within your power to eliminate all the feelings of local pride or resentment over past injustices that may influence your students' feelings toward Western nations, and no matter how sensitively you approach the issue of Western culture, implied comparisons will sometimes reflect negatively on the host culture. However, it is within your power to see that your culture lessons present a model of fair objective treatment of cultural issues, and that they are not unnecessarily offensive. This will not only help ensure that your lessons are well received, but also that students will learn to approach culture in the same way themselves.

One strategy that will make you more objective in your discussion of culture is to habitually point out that there are both advantages and disadvantages to almost every major facet of a culture. For example, when discussing the advanced U.S. health care system, you should also point out its expense; when discussing the U.S. stress on self-reliance, note that this both contributes to a high level of national productivity and to a willingness to tolerate poverty among those who will not or cannot work hard; when discussing the high rate of U.S. car ownership, mention both the freedom and mobility it allows and the price paid for gas, insurance and repairs (not to mention the problem of air pollution). This habit of always presenting two sides to an issue may seem somewhat artificial, but it is beneficial both because it makes your presentation of issues more objective and because it forces you to think through issues more carefully in order to find two sides. This habit is also, incidentally, good training for both you and your students because it serves as a reminder that there generally is both a good and a bad side to most aspects of any culture, and it is thus a good antidote to tendencies toward cultural chauvinism.

A second way to avoid being offensive in your presentation of cultural issues is to lean toward politeness more than frankness when talking about the culture of your host country. This does not necessarily mean being dishonest, but it may mean avoiding a question or saying less than you might like to. Remember that your role as a guest in the host country means that you follow rules different from those of host country nationals. It is not uncommon for newcomers to a foreign nation to hear host nationals speaking critically of their own country, assume that it is acceptable to chime in with a few criticisms of their own, but then be surprised when even relatively restrained criticisms cause the tone of the conversation to become distinctly chilly. It is a universal human tendency to be more sensitive about criticism coming from outsiders than from insiders, and in most countries the safest initial assumption is that critical comments you make will touch a more sensitive nerve than similar comments made by host nationals.

In general, it is best to behave as a polite guest, especially during the early stages of your sojourn in the host country. Even in your home culture, when invited to someone's home for a meal, you probably try to find something nice to say about the food, no matter what it tastes like. A similar policy regarding culture lessons in your host country has much to recommend it.

14

A Trouble-Shooter's Guide to the Classroom

Thank hese chapters on various aspects of English teaching will close with discussion of a few of the most common problem situations English teachers face overseas. No solutions are promised—I still face the same problems myself—but these suggestions may help you make your load a little more comfortable and manageable.

Overly Large Classes

Classes of 30-50 students or more are not unusual in many countries. For listening comprehension or reading lessons, such a large class is not an insurmountable obstacle; for speaking and writing lessons, however, large classes present very serious problems. In a speaking class of 50 students, it is simply impossible for you to give much individual attention to students, and writing classes of this size mean that you cope either with mountains of compositions or with guilt for assigning students too little writing.

The solution that generally first occurs to language teachers, and that can become a obsessive crusade, is to reduce the size of the class. Unfortunately, this is often not possible. Large classes are generally a result of necessity (e.g., lack of funds, staff) rather than a philosophy of education; most educators the world over would agree that smaller classes are better, and would reduce class sizes if they could. The danger for you in this situation is that if you try to reduce the class size and fail, you may consciously or unconsciously write off the class as hopeless and go into an embittered survival mode rather than doing what can be done to make the class as effective as possible. There are, of course, situations where survival is about all that can be expected, but a large class is by no means necessarily one of those situations.

In all but the smallest speaking classes, students will get most of their practice talking to each other rather than to you. The problem presented by a class of 50 is therefore different from that presented by a class of 20 only in degree, not kind. In both cases, speaking practice should ideally consist primarily of pair and small-group work rather than dialogue between teacher and student. The real problem in large classes is one of management, specifically, of ensuring that students will actually speak English when you are out of earshot. (See Chapter 8 for suggestions on encouraging English use in class.)

If most of the students in a class will not speak English unless you are present, the problem becomes much more difficult because the class must be more teacher centered. In such cases, while trying to solve the attitude problem that keeps students from speaking English in pairs/groups, you may be forced to rely heavily on listening comprehension exercises and teacher-focused question-and-answer exercises. Although less than ideal, such use of class time is by no means the end of the world. The development of listening comprehension skills does contribute to the development of speaking skills, and teacher-focused dialogue can be useful even in a large class if you remember to interact with students in a random pattern so that all the students in the class need to listen and think through responses to questions. Remember, it is the mental process of creating sentences that is the most difficult part of the speaking process, and any practice that forces students to go through this process under time pressure is valuable for the development of speaking skills.

Overly large writing classes are somewhat more problematic in that they almost inevitably require you to work very hard just to respond to a small amount of writing per student. As suggested in Chapter 10, it is particularly important in large writing classes that you make sure that students edit and polish work as much as possible before you go over it, so in-class self- and peer editing is recommended. Putting strict length limits on assignments, and emphasizing the virtues of terse writing, can also help. Finally, stress activities in which students—rather than you—become the audience.

The outrageously large writing class is, incidentally, a situation where negotiation with your school has a relatively high chance of being profitable. Most educators can relate very easily to the problem of high stacks of compositions, but they may have an exaggerated idea of how much being a native speaker of English will lessen the time it takes you to edit a composition. I have known schools to assign all the composition courses in a department to a VT under the assumption that native speakers can correct papers almost effortlessly. Talking about the issue with your school administration and letting them know how much time you spend working on student papers may result in an attempt to lighten your load. If nothing else, you may get a clear statement of how much time you are expected to devote to composition correction. This, in turn, takes some of the onus (and guilt) from you in situations where you have no choice but to give rare or short writing assignments.

Classes With Disparate Skill Levels

A particularly frequent and annoying problem is that of classes in which some students have much better English skills than others. This situation is especially common in night schools and other institutions where students come from a variety of backgrounds, but it is also found in school systems in which groups of students move up the educational ladder together as a class. Because of differences in background, or simply in the diligence with which students study, in some classes you may find that some of the students already know most of the material you plan to cover while others have fallen completely behind in both mastery of the material and skill development. This situation makes lesson planning difficult because it is hard to meet the needs of students at one level without neglecting those of students at another level. It may also produce motivation problems in the class; students toward the top end of the range are bored while students toward the bottom end are dispirited and confused.

As with the problem of overly large classes, the first response is normally to see if the students cannot somehow be redistributed in order to form classes of more equal skill levels. An administration that has little experience with language programs might be unaware of the importance of placing students of roughly equal skill levels together, and even an experienced administration may be unaware of the situation in your particular class, so a negotiated solution is worth an attempt. Where possible, you might campaign for some kind of skill-based placement testing to be used in the process of assigning students to classes, and when this approach works it is definitely the best solution. However, often there is little that can be done to resolve a situation by moving students, particularly when a term has already started, and then the problem becomes one of how to make the best of things.

In classes with mixed skill levels the difference between a teacher-centered class and a student-centered one becomes especially critical. The pace and difficulty of activities in a teacher-centered class will necessarily be dictated by the teacher, and this forces students to march together in lockstep. If, for example, all the students in a class must listen to the same story together, students who could understand more rapid speech have to suffer through an overly slow presentation while their weaker classmates are embarrassed to stop you and ask questions or ask for repetition. This same dynamic holds true for all-class activities such as large-group discussions in which students with stronger English skills usually set the pace and many of their classmates have to sit through an activity that is completely inappropriate for their skill level.

In contrast, to the extent that students work alone, in pairs, or in small groups, they are able better able to work at their own pace. For example, taped listening assignments done at home allow students with better listening skills to complete the activity quickly and move on to something else; other students can stop and listen to difficult segments as many times as they need to. In small-group discussions, students with weaker speaking skills can express themselves at their own level without as much fear that they will be slowing down other students. Thus, one key to dealing with a class with varied skill levels is by making the class as individualized and student-centered as possible.

Another way to approach the issue is through talking about it with your students. Some students may resent the effect that other students—stronger or weaker—have on class progress,[1] so you should remind students that this is a normal part of group learning, not a special curse of your language class. Being reminded of this may help students redirect their efforts from complaining about the situation toward trying to productively deal with it. It also helps to stress that the issue is not necessarily one of good students and bad students. Of course, some students wind up with weak English skills through sheer laziness, but the problem can also result from different levels of opportunity or different learning abilities, so remind yourself and your students that skill levels are just that—skill levels—and not an indication of a student's intelligence or moral character.

It often helps to do a little special public relations work with the students at the upper and lower ends of the class. Let students with unusually strong English skills know that you recognize their high level of ability and then challenge them by giving them a little extra responsibility (as discussion group leaders, for example), or by giving them some difficult but interesting extra projects. You may also suggest that they have a responsibility to help and encourage others in the class, or at least give others a chance to talk. Let less advanced students know that you don't consider their present skill level an indication of lack of ability, but also emphasize that they need to put extra effort into trying to catch up to the rest of the class. Those students who remain below the skill level of the class average will face a constant series of assignments and exercises that are not well-suited to their skill level and will not only learn less from these than will students for whom the level of the activities is more appropriate, but will also find them difficult and painful. It is therefore worthwhile to put in the extra effort necessary to catch up.

All the pep talks in the world are not likely to be of much use to the morale of less advanced students if they are followed by a series of grades that say that they really are at the bottom of the class. Unfortunately, if all of the class assignments and exercises are graded on the basis of general skill level, and if assignments are all graded

---

[1]A special problem here is false starters, that is, students who have already studied English before but who choose to be placed in a class below their skill level. This problem is less common in EFL settings than in foreign language courses in U.S. universities (where students who have had 2 years of high school French often sign up for French 101 in college to review and get an easy grade), but where it occurs it should be taken seriously. The presence of a few false starters in a class skews the curve considerably, and if you do not somehow compensate for this effect, you will be punishing those who are at the level for which your course was intended.

on the curve, less advanced students are unlikely to receive much encouragement from their marks. This is one reason why it is good to grade at least partly on the basis of progress rather than absolute skill level. It is also a good argument for including a content component, such as culture, in a course. It is not necessarily the case that students with advanced language skills have much more Western cultural background than their less advanced classmates, so the inclusion of such an element in a course gives less advanced students at least one opportunity to start from the same place their classmates do.

Even the most student-centered class will have at least some teacher-focused interaction, even if it is only in the giving of directions, and in these interactions you will need to decide the skill level to which you will target your communication. My advice is that you avoid slowing the class down to the pace of the slower students. Although speaking slowly and keeping activities easy may seem to be more humane, in the end it is not. As much as I would like to believe otherwise, the problem with at least some of the weaker students in any class is that they do not put forth as much effort as their peers, and if you slow down the class to the level of the weakest often the lazier students relax rather than endeavoring to catch up. Even worse, this approach discourages those students who work harder. My suggestion is that you tailor communication to a level slightly higher than that of the average student in the class, thus keeping it within the range of a majority of the students but making it challenging.

Class Discipline

Unfortunately, some students have no interest in learning and others are just plain mean, and even extensive efforts to bring such students around may come to naught. However, in my experience, most students are willing to give you a fair chance and are generally well disposed toward a teacher who is reasonably pleasant and works hard. The first step toward establishing class discipline is therefore earning the respect—even affection—of your students.

Earlier in this book we have touched on a variety of factors involved in the process of earning respect, including diligence in teaching and fairness in evaluation. Another factor that may affect student affection for you is your interest in the host culture and language. An all too frequently overlooked reason to study the host language is that this is an important step toward earning the affection of the people you work with; efforts to learn the host language are the most visible and convincing evidence of willingness to identify with the people you work among (see Chapter 15). Cultural sensitivity is also a key part of earning respect—it may well be in inability to win the respect of a class that a teacher's decisions to flout local norms by doing such apparently irrelevant things as wearing shorts and sandals in class or having a casual sex life may come back to haunt him or her.

However, no matter how ideal a role model you become, it is almost inevitable that you will come across students who do things that you perceive as problematic. An important first step in such situations is to try and determine how members of the host culture perceive such behavior, because some behaviors considered improper in your home country might be considered normal, or at least less serious, in the host country. For example, in many countries class attendance is somewhat optional, and failure to show up for class may not be considered inappropriate. There may also be different standards concerning what is considered an appropriate level of attention in class; not all cultures share the assumption that a class should maintain complete silence while a teacher—or especially another student—is speaking. Even such firmly rooted Western taboos as those against burping and farting are not universal. The first time a student loudly burped while I was talking in class in China I took it as a calculated offense, only to discover later that it was no more intended to offend than a cough or sneeze would have been. (Another important example, copying of others' work, is discussed in Chapter 10.) It is thus important that you check first with members of the host culture to find out if a behavior that you find unacceptable is also considered problem behavior within the host culture.

If you determine that the behavior in question is in fact improper, the next step is to find out how such problems are normally dealt with within the culture. Of course, you are not bound to handling the situation the same way a host country teacher would, but it is important that you have an idea of what the normal response would be so that you can gauge whether or not your response might be considered excessive or insufficient. Talking to someone from the host country may be helpful for several reasons. In addition to finding out how he or she might handle the situation, you can get feedback on your planned response, and you may also gain insight as to the origins of the problem. (In many cultures, feedback about your behavior may not be direct, so it is important to be on the lookout for apparently irrelevant casual comments—for example, regarding your dress or the amount of homework you are giving—because it may be within one of these that key information about your own contribution to the problem may be buried.)

Perhaps the most important thing to remember in a cross-cultural situation is to try not to get upset about an issue before getting the facts, and probably not even then. There is a good chance that your interpretation of the situation is not entirely accurate, and the probability that you will handle it inappropriately if you shoot from the hip is even higher.

It may be difficult for VTs, many of whom were only recently students themselves, to mentally shift into a class authority role, but it is important that the need for such a shift not be ignored. A reality of teaching is that you have a degree of power over students, if only because you determine grades, so the question is not one of whether or not you should exercise power in class but of how well you exercise it. Thus, you should give serious consideration to how you will handle discipline problems, and unpleasant punitive options may need to be considered if the situation calls for them.

With regard to specific responses, it is difficult to do more than make a few very broad generalizations—too much depends on the specific problems, personalities, and culture involved. However, here are a few commonsense suggestions. First, before dropping the bomb on somebody, fire a warning shot. One possibility is making a specific statement of the consequences of continued unacceptable behavior— in other words, a threat. The best threats are those that are possible and that you are prepared to carry out; don't threaten to kick a student out of class if you are not prepared to do so or if it is not within your power to do so. It also helps if threats are very specific so that a student does not cross the line again due to ignorance rather than intent. "If you copy again, you will regret it!" is not as helpful to a student as "I will make you do the entire paper over again if I find a single phrase in it that is the same as your girlfriend's."

Second, try not to delay too long before clarifying and dealing with a problem situation. Failure to respond may well allow the situation to become worse, and may also lower the reservoir of respect and support that other students in the class have for you. When your natural desire to avoid seeming like an authority figure tempts you to avoid confrontation, remember that a student's disruptive behavior often influences other members in the class and that you have a responsibility to maintain an environment in which other students can learn. Another problem with long-delayed responses is that they tend to become more spectacular when they finally do appear, and there is a greater danger that you will have lost the objectivity and emotional control necessary to handle the situation in a sensitive and appropriate manner. An early warning disrupts relationships much less than a blow-up a few weeks later.

Finally, anger is a high-risk strategy for dealing with problems. In many cultures, particularly in Asia, public displays of anger are less acceptable and forgivable than in Western cultures, and the consequences of an inappropriate tirade may be severe and long-lasting. This does not mean that in these cultures nobody ever gets angry in public, but it does mean that there are very complex rules as to who can get angry at whom, and when and how this is done; a high degree of cultural awareness and finesse is required to prevent the outburst from being a disaster. Even in cultures that are relatively accepting of anger, its use may still do more to damage relationships than to modify behavior. In general, a serious but calm response will be effective in getting your message across and will better preserve your relationship with the wayward student than an angry scolding will.

Students Who Participate Too Much

We are all familiar with the kind of student who tends to dominate, always being the first to answer a question or offer an opinion. The problem that such behavior can create in a class is that it limits opportunities of other students to participate and may also discourage their willingness to try. For you, the problem is how to control the behavior without discouraging the student; the student who participates frequently is, after all, doing what we wish most students would.

One approach is to simply ignore the eager student's hand when it goes up, and to direct activity to other members of the class. This approach, however, often has the effect of making the eager student more vigorous in efforts to be noticed. Students who talk a great deal tend not be shy or overly sensitive personalities, so more direct approaches may be necessary. One is to speak to these students individually, praising their willingness to participate but asking them to give others a chance. During class then, when the hand pops up again, you might even say: "Jan, I see your hand, but let's see if we can't get someone else to respond first."

Try not to become visibly annoyed with such students. They may already have popularity problems in class (though they may also be class leaders), and your disapproval can give license to other students to be critical. They may also quite understandably feel that chances to practice are not to be wasted and that there is no good reason to let speaking opportunities go if others won't take advantage of them, a view that you should encourage rather than discourage. Your ultimate goal is to encourage other students to participate more rather than to make the overly talkative student participate less, and you may make more progress toward this goal by showing appreciation of the eager student's efforts than by becoming irritated at them.

Students Who Participate Too Little

Teachers often take participation to mean answering questions or offering opinions during all-class activities, and it is generally assumed that this kind of participation is an important part of the learning process. Upon reflection, however, it should be clear that the few moments a semester students spend speaking in front of the whole class are not a significant part of their total speaking practice time, and a student who never volunteers in a large-group setting is not necessarily getting much less practice than his or her classmates. In fact, the only unique benefit of speaking out in front of the whole class is that it trains students to pluck up their courage for speaking in front of large audiences, so I would suggest that failure to speak up in large-group settings should not be considered a serious problem.

In fact, it may be counterproductive to pressure students to participate unwillingly in all-class settings. Most students are, understandably, less than entirely confident of their English skills and are thus already somewhat intimidated in English class. Knowing that they could be called on to publicly perform in front of a large audience increases the level of anxiety, and fear may well become more salient in their minds than interest in learning. If you single out such students by calling on them the result is tension and wasted class time; the reluctant student sits in embarrassed panic, unable or unwilling to answer, while classmates become either more nervous or bored. The only thing that such an exercise accomplishes is putting enough fear into student hearts that they are more likely to do their homework; it achieves little in terms of in-class learning.

The saddest aspect of trial by questioning in class is that it may torment students who are in fact participating; in other words, students who pay attention in class, actively think through responses to questions, and participate actively in pair or small-group activities. These are the most important forms of participation because it is through these activities that students will get the bulk of their English practice. Only a very few highly vocal students will get significant amounts of practice in an all-class forum.

One way in which you can encourage students who tend to speak very little is by providing speaking opportunities that are as nonthreatening as possible, these being pair or small-group activities that don't provide a large audience and allow students greater freedom to speak at a comfortable English skill level. Another way to help is by seeing that topics are within students' range of competence; some topics, particularly those dealing with a student's daily life, can be discussed at a wide range of skill levels, while others (capital punishment, constitutional reform, etc.) can only be discussed by students who have substantial speaking skills and large vocabularies. A third way in which you can help is by gently encouraging. A student is more likely to take the plunge and try to say something to a smiling and interested teacher than to a demanding martinet whose primary interest seems to be ensuring obedience to orders.

Ultimately, however, there is a point at which you have done what you can to provide opportunities and encouragement, and at that point it is up to students to take advantage of those opportunities. One element of treating students with respect is allowing them the freedom to make choices, and beyond a certain point further intervention on your part may do more harm than good by creating fear and tension, or simply by wasting time that could have been better spent on other students who are more willing to respond. Make sure that opportunities and channels of communication remain open, but don't feel guilty about every student who chooses not to speak up in class.

Students as Friends

For quite a number of reasons, it is not unusual for VTs to discover after a few months in the host country that their social life centers heavily around their students and that most of their host country friends are students. This is in part because you will see students on a more regular basis than most other people so there is opportunity for relationships to develop. Also, it is not uncommon for VTs to be close in age to their students; if you are a recent college graduate, you may be closer in age to your students than to most of your host country colleagues. Finally, in some settings you will have something very important in common with your students—you are both relatively new and transient in the community. When this is the case, students are more open to new friendships than people who are long established in the community.

In some ways, forming close ties with your students can be a good thing. As you become closer to your students you will learn more about their background, living and study conditions, and aspirations, not to mention the host culture in general. Having good friends, whether students or not, is also a precious thing in and of itself. However, it can also become a problem if conflict develops between your role as a teacher and as a friend.

One potential problem is that students with whom you become friends may misunderstand the new relationship. In some cultures it is normal for teachers to choose one or more favored pupils who then have special privileges; in others there is no precedent for a Western-style friendship between teachers and students. In these cases you may find your student friends unintentionally—or intentionally—using their relationship with you in a way that you did not intend. A second problem is that as you develop friendships with students you will inevitably become closer to some than others, and this may lead to a perception on the part of other students that you are playing favorites. Often what happens is that you become closest to the students with the best English—these after all are the ones who are easiest to talk to—or to those who are most willing to spend time with you. These students are also often the ones most likely to get good grades (and to whom you will feel inclined to give the best grades). Thus, when grades come out, it is easy for other students to accuse you of favoritism. A third problem is that of favoritism of the highest order—romance. For quite number of reasons, romances between VTs and students are not uncommon. You will probably be lonely at times in your host country, you may well be very attracted to the host culture and its people, and you may simply have a student who you find to be very attractive.

In Chapter 2 the problem of romances between VTs and students has already been mentioned, so I will only reiterate my feeling that in most cultural settings this should definitely be avoided (and even in cultures where this kind of relationship is not frowned upon it is still rich in potential for things to go wrong). With regard to the issue of friendships with students, I hesitate to suggest that potential problems should deter you from having student friends because I know too many VTs whose time in the host country has been enriched immeasurably by friendships with students. However, I also know many VTs whose experience in the host country was marred by a student friendship that went wrong. Balancing the roles of teacher and friend even in your own culture is not easy, and in a culture where you are not very familiar with the rules there is substantial potential for misunderstandings. For this reason a case could be made for exercising at least some restraint in friendships with students, being friendly and enjoying their company but not becoming so close to a special few that they or other students are unclear about roles. The corollary to this is that you should also try to develop friendships with other kinds of people in your host community. This may not happen as naturally as do friendships with students, but efforts in this direction can result in your building friendships with people who are more naturally your peers.

PART III

Living Abroad

15 Adapting to Your Host Culture

- ◆ Adapting comfortably to life in the host country is important not only for your general well-being but also for your teaching.

- ◆ Expectations have a major impact on the level of frustration you feel in a new culture.

- ◆ People commonly experience culture fatigue as part of the process of adapting to life in a new culture.

- ◆ Two of the best ways to speed your adaptation are through learning about the host culture and learning to speak the host language.

The success with which you adapt to life in your host country will not only have a significant impact on how rewarding your own experience is, but will also directly affect your success as a teacher in a number of ways:

1 It will have an impact on your attitude toward the culture in general, and hence toward your students and your work. Put bluntly, VTs who hate life in the host country often find it difficult to maintain enthusiasm for their teaching.

2 It will affect your energy level. The work of VTs who are physically, mentally, and emotionally drained by constant friction with the host culture will almost inevitably suffer.

3 VTs who have a poor attitude toward the host culture often fall into the habit of making hasty overgeneralizations and unfair criticisms. This in turn makes the VT less than ideal as a role model of cross-cultural communication and understanding. Also, a teacher with a negative attitude towards the host culture may do more damage than good in terms of building their students' interest in learning English and its culture. Students may pick up on the sense of hostility and respond to it in kind.

4 Finally, VTs who have learned little about the host culture are at a disadvantage as teachers because they will not be able to interact as effectively with students or school staff. Often your ability to teach effectively depends as much on your skills in reaching out to a recalcitrant student—or making friends with the cranky old man who has the key to the audiovisual equipment room—as it does your ability to explain an idiom, and your success in building and maintaining good relationships with people will be directly affected by your success in adapting to the culture.

There are, of course, many joys of life in a new culture—the delights of friends, new foods, scenic beauty, and the sheer fascination of a new way of life—and it would be a tragedy if anyone were to finish this chapter with the feeling that an experience abroad is a trial to be withstood as stoically as possible. In fact, it may be one of the best experiences of your life. However, below I focus mainly on problems because in my experience most people don't need much advice on how to enjoy a good time.

Cultural Adaptation and Expectations

Repeated bouts with frustration and disappointment can eat away at one's sense of well-being and make adapting to a new environment a more draining experience. VTs in many countries often experience frustration over low efficiency, disappointment at the slow speed with which friendships with host nationals develop, and a host of other annoyances. What problems like these have in common is that the mental and emotional stress they cause is created as much by the expectations you bring with you as by the conditions in the host country. Take camping as an illustration. Conditions in a wilderness camp are generally far more primitive than those in most host countries (assuming the camper is backpacking rather than living out of a Winnebago), but problems such as the absence of hot showers are generally taken in stride because the camper doesn't expect hot showers. If, however, the same camper were to enter a Holiday Inn room and discover that the shower didn't have hot water, the response would probably be less bucolic.

Thus, one important aspect of preparing to enter a new culture, and of adapting to it after arrival, is careful consideration of your expectations. As Weaver (1993) points out in a discussion of cross-cultural adaptation: "It seems that if we do not anticipate a stressful event we are much less capable of coping with it" (p. 138), and unexamined or unreasonable expectations virtually invite dissatisfaction. It is not possible to present an exhaustive checklist of all possible areas in which you need to check your expectations before venturing into unknown lands, but a brief discussion of a few key areas may highlight some of the kinds of problems VTs often encounter and help get you in the habit of examining the role that your expectations may play in making situations frustrating.

I. Efficiency: VTs in many host countries fight running battles with their host institutions in an effort to get things done faster. Modern Western culture considers time, hence efficiency, very important, and has thus devoted considerable effort to creating conditions and training people to ensure that things can be done quickly. This will not necessarily be the situation in many host countries, for a variety of reasons. Perhaps the host culture values interpersonal relationships more than efficiency. Perhaps your host country is still in the process of modernization and even though it now has some of the machines that facilitate work in the West people may not yet have fully adapted to a work style centered on using and maintaining them. Perhaps the host culture actually works very efficiently, but you have not yet learned how to get things done. For whatever reason, unrealistic expectations vis a vis efficiency are a major potential source of frustration for VTs in many host countries.

2. Organization and disorganization: VTs sometimes have unrealistic expectations as to how well the host institution has planned for them. It is not uncommon for VTs to think of the people in a host institution as "them," a monolithic group that presumably thinks as one organic whole. Many VTs also fall into the habit of viewing themselves as the primary focus of the host institution's attention, an assumption that is encouraged by the fact that many host institutions treat their Western teachers as VIPs. It can thus come as a nasty surprise if you discover that different people in the host organization have very different—and perhaps conflicting—expectations of you, and that they have not spent the time necessary to come to complete consensus as to exactly what your teaching mission is.

3. Appreciation: Many VTs are willing to accept minimal salaries and make other sacrifices because their primary motive for going abroad is a desire to serve the host country (again perceived more or less as a single unit), but then expect residents of the host country to appreciate the sacrifice the VTs are making. Disappointment often occurs when VTs encounter people in the host country who don't show much appreciation for their contribution (Stewart & Bennett, 1991). Of course, on reflection, many people in any given host country have little or no idea why you are there, and may assume that your motives are not in the least altruistic. It is also not uncommon for the help and advice of overseas experts to be viewed with mixed feelings by many host country nationals. In many host countries, your living standard will also be higher than average for a person of your age and experience, a situation that will drastically alter the view many host nationals take of your sacrifice.

A special variation of this problem that VTs sometimes meet arises from different understandings of what their role is. Many VTs perceive themselves not only as language teachers but also as modernizers and reformers. They consider the traditional methods used by their host country colleagues as less than ideal—if not downright backward—and take it on themselves to correct the situation. Often they are encouraged in this misperception by host nationals who decry the poor quality of local teaching approaches and praise Western methods. However, VTs who launch out on a campaign of reform often meet stiff resistance, and it may be only after considerable frustration that they discover that the school views them as useful mostly because of their native control of English, not because of their credentials in language pedagogy. Praise for Western teaching methods often contains a strong element of politeness and may not indicate much real desire to change.

4. Living conditions: Of course, in poorer host countries, most VTs don't expect all the luxuries of home, and many are pleasantly surprised at how well they are taken care of. However, it is also not unusual for VTs to find that there are aspects of daily living that fall below their expectations. Common problem areas are temperature control, sanitation levels, and food. For example, many Westerners have never had the experience of being uncomfortably cold or hot for long periods of time—and of having no warm/cool place to retreat to. An unfortunately common sight in such situations is an indignant Westerner insisting to a host national that it is too cold (hot, wet, whatever) for anybody to tolerate, forgetting that the host national may well bear the exact same problem every day. (Of course, a VT who is new to difficult conditions may need special treatment in order to keep functioning as a teacher, and martyrdom is not necessarily in and of itself a virtue. However, the danger in this rationale is that if carried too far the message it tends to send is that Westerners deserve better living conditions than host nationals.)

5. Relationships: One of the most delightful aspects of life abroad is the opportunity for friendships with people of a different culture. However, in many cultures significant friendships take longer to develop than they do in the West. North Americans in particular are accustomed to developing close (though often transitory) relationships quite quickly, much faster than close relationships develop in many cultures. One source of frustration for many Westerners can thus be the slow pace at which friendships develop. A related disappointment often occurs if a "friend" turns out to have been interested in gain to be had from a relationship with a Westerner, or if it becomes clear that a friendship has very defined and unexpected limits.

6. Adaptation: Many people assume that the hardest part of adapting to a new culture is getting through the initial shock, and that it will then get progressively easier. This is not entirely untrue, but for reasons that will be discussed below the hardest part often occurs some months after arrival in a new culture. In fact, one of the factors that can contribute to so-called culture burnout is the expectation that things should be getting easier, and frustration when they only improve slowly. A common related expectation is that once you are living in the host country you will pick up the language and culture rather quickly and easily, and disappointment results when learning the language and culture turn out to require a substantial investment of effort.

It is virtually impossible to approach life in a new culture with no expectations at all. Neither is it possible to be so well informed that all of your expectations are accurate. However, it is possible and useful to consider potential problem situations that you may encounter so that you are mentally prepared. Getting as much accurate information as possible about what life will be like in your new culture is also of great value. However, perhaps the most important safeguard is just to be aware of the role expectations play in creating frustration and disappointment. In a frustrating situation, sometimes simply realizing that your expectations are part of the problem is a major step toward improving the situation. The old metaphor of the half-full glass is trite but true: If you focus on the fact that the glass is not full, you will undergo more emotional wear and tear than if you are thankful that there is any water in the glass at all. There may be real hardships and problems in your new life in your host country, and altering the way you look at these problems will not make them all go away, but adjusting expectations can often help reduce your sense of frustration and disappointment.

The Adaptation Process and Culture Burnout

Culture Shock and Culture Burnout

You have probably heard the term *culture shock* and may understand it to refer to the jolting experience of suddenly being thrust into a new culture. This initial impact, however, is not the real problem most people face in adapting to a new culture. There are certainly many new things to adjust to in a new country during the first weeks and months of one's stay, but for most people difficulties during this initial period are more than compensated for by the excitement and joy of being in new surroundings and discovering new things. The more difficult phase for many people arrives later in their stay in the host country, the period after the newness of the experience has rubbed off but before adaptation has progressed very far. Those who have investigated culture shock explain it in a variety of different ways, but there is a growing tendency to view the problem as one of exhaustion more than shock, and to speak of culture fatigue rather than culture shock.[1] It is this view that I will assume in the following discussion, although I prefer the term *culture burnout* because the word *fatigue* seems to me a bit too mild. The advantage of viewing culture burnout as a process of physical, mental, and emotional fatigue is that it not only helps people make sense of what is happening to them, but also implies (correctly, I believe) that the problem is manageable. I find it

---

[1]See Barna (1994), Grove and Torbiorn (1993), and Seelye (1993) for discussion of culture shock as a process of fatigue. For other views, see Kohls (1984) and Weaver (1993).

helpful to describe the problem as one of an empty emotional gas tank resulting from the following formula:

decreased energy intake + increased energy drain = burnout

DECREASED ENERGY INTAKE

Moving to a new country cuts you off from many of the people and things from which you are accustomed to drawing strength and refreshment. You will no doubt be leaving behind friends and family members whose loss will deprive you of an important source of comfort. You may also be leaving behind a job that gave you a sense of self-esteem and confidence in your abilities, a home or possessions that gave you a sense of security, and hobbies or pastimes that provided relaxation. Because you are moving to a place where you probably don't speak the local language, you will also be limiting your access to TV, books, movies, and other cultural products that provided both stimulation and recreation. In short, you are drastically cutting down on the number of things in your life from which you draw energy.

The early days of life in a new country tend to be as exciting and interesting as they are draining, so the loss of these old sources of refreshment may not be felt immediately, and ultimately many of these sources of refreshment will be replaced by new ones. However, as you settle in and life becomes more routine, there will probably be a time when the excitement of a new life has worn off but you have not yet found new friends, job satisfaction, hobbies, cultural outlets, or whatever you need to sustain you emotionally. During this period, the energy supplies in your emotional gas tank aren't being replenished as much as they are at home.

INCREASED ENERGY DRAIN

Until you have gained a comfortable mastery of life abroad, life in your host country will also place greater demands on your reserves of energy than life at home would. One problem is that you may have to cope with more physical drain, even if only because any move to a new place involves considerable running around in the process of setting up a new home (and this in a place where lower efficiency levels make getting things done much more work than you are used to). It is also common for people in a new country to get sick more often than they would at home. A second problem is that many of the tasks that you could perform almost unconsciously at home require a lot more thinking in a new country, hence more mental drain. Part of the problem is that you have to relearn many of the basics of living, even in simple tasks like buying food or stamps. Also, if you are in a country where English isn't widely spoken and you don't speak the host language, each effort to communicate involves considerable mental effort.

However, most experts agree that the greatest problem is emotional drain. In a new culture, you are often in uncomfortable situations where you don't fully understand what is going on or don't know what to do. You may also find that in areas of your life where you were previously sure and confident—for example, your work or social skills—you are not able to perform at your normal level of efficiency. Even as simple an act as buying a stamp at the post office can become an emotional trauma for fear that the clerk will say something you don't understand, leaving you unsure of what to do next while at the center of an impatient, pushing crowd. On top of it all, as a novice to the intricacies of etiquette in the new culture, you will probably make a fool of yourself more than once. It is when these unusual demands on your reserves of energy, patience, and good humor cause them to run low—and when you have not yet found adequate new sources of refreshment—that you are afflicted by culture burnout.[2]

Symptoms of Culture Burnout

Symptoms of this adjustment problem vary, but among the most important are:

1. Decreased patience and increased irritability: As your energy level decreases perhaps the most predictable result is that your reserves of patience and good humor become depleted. Over time, it becomes a little harder to roll with the punches, and you may find that you are less patient with problems than you were when you first arrived. It is not unusual to subconsciously feel that while you adjust to the host culture, it should be adjusting to you just as much, and that over time you are more justified in a less forgiving response to problems or mistakes.

2. An increased tendency to be critical of the host culture: Annoyances that you were initially able to ignore or tolerate often grow over time into more serious grievances. As you are affected by culture burnout, you may also find yourself quicker to leap to negative conclusions when puzzling or unpleasant things happen in your relations with host nationals. These grievances then get passed around in the form of war stories and

[2]For a more sophisticated model of the culture fatigue experience, see Grove and Torbiorn (1993).

regularly hauled out to prove broader (often negative) generalizations about the host culture.

3. Withdrawal from contact with the host culture into a small community of other outsiders: It is generally harder to make friends with host nationals than with other foreigners with whom you have more in common, so VTs quite naturally tend to drift into self-contained little expatriate communities. At a deeper level, interaction with the host culture may call your ideas, values, and way of life into question, and it is generally less exhausting to socialize primarily with a community that does not present these kinds of challenges. Unfortunately, complaining about the host country often becomes the staple topic of conversation among ex-pats and the result is generally reinforcement of negative attitudes.[3]

These symptoms of culture burnout are not only problems in and of themselves; because they tend to separate you from the host culture, they also slow down the speed with which you learn how to function comfortably and efficiently in the host country. These problems are particularly serious for a language teacher because they tend to pull you towards exactly those cross-cultural attitudes that you should be trying to teach your students to avoid. It is thus important that you do what you can to prevent culture burnout.

Dealing With Culture Burnout

Different people have very different experiences with culture burnout . Some are virtually incapacitated, going through a period of extreme withdrawal and hostility toward the host culture; others experience little or no trouble. It seems safest to say that, though the intensity of the problem can vary widely, most people will have to fight the problem of exhaustion and decreased emotional energy sometime during their stay abroad. Fortunately, there are steps you can take to at least minimize adjustment problems.

1 Continue to explore new aspects of your environment. One factor that often contributes to culture burnout is boredom, often caused by routine. It is quite natural during the early stages of adjusting to a new environment to first learn how to get by in a limited daily routine of essential places (often consisting of a home-school-dining hall triangle of some kind), and it is not unusual for people to then spend much of their time within this safe narrow range. This has the advantage of

---

[3]See Kohls (1984) for other symptoms.

limiting your emotional energy output because life within the routine is easier, but it also tends to become stale after a time, and when this happens you lose the refreshing and invigorating effects of new discoveries. Even minimal efforts to keep expanding the range of your routine—walking home a new way, eating in a new place, looking for a new store—do much to keep life in your host country interesting and stimulating.

2 Avoid overloading your work and activity schedule, especially with regular commitments. It is not unusual for VTs to be led by volunteer spirit to take on an unreasonable workload of in- and out-of-class activities during the first few weeks abroad when they are still fresh and energetic, only to be unable to sustain such a high level of output over longer periods of time. As you calculate the amount of work you expect to do, do not assume that you will be able to maintain the same level of efficiency and output in a new environment that you can in a familiar one. After all, if you later discover that you have extra energy to burn, you can add other commitments; it is generally easier to make new commitments than to break existing ones, and does not create the bad impression that you do not keep your word.

3 Allow yourself strategic retreats into your own culture. Some people who go abroad do so with the intention of immersing themselves in the host culture, hoping that by only associating with host nationals and only speaking the host language (except in English class, of course) to come out of the experience fluent in the language and culture after a fairly short time. This approach does work for some people, but it can also be a recipe for burnout. There is much to be said for allowing yourself occasional vacations from the host culture, be they afternoons with an English novel or an evening with friends from your home country.[4]

4 Try to maintain a positive attitude and not to give in to the tendency to constantly find fault. Kohls (1984) suggests that rather than complaining it is more productive to look for the logic underlying those features of the host culture that seem strange or unpleasant; merely seeing that the host culture is reasonable is a major step toward making peace with it.

5 Get to know the people, culture, and language of the host country, which is ultimately the most effective long-term cure for culture burnout. Knowing the host country well does not necessarily mean that you will fall in love with it, but familiarity with the language and culture considerably increases the chances that you will find rewards to balance out the trials of your stay. It also makes life easier by reducing misunderstandings and by decreasing your sense of alien-

[4]Weaver (1993) suggests that associating with other people who have gone through culture burnout is very helpful, provided that the meetings don't degenerate into gripe sessions.

ation. Finally, study of the culture and language will also help you become a better teacher. It is to the study of the host culture and language that we turn next.

As we have already seen, the term *culture* covers a very broad range of things, everything from great poets to the closing time of the local market, and almost anything that you learn about your host culture will help in your adaptation process. However, some kinds of information will be of more immediate value than others.

Learning the Culture of the Host Country

1. Daily life survival information: This category needs little discussion because both you and your host institution know you need to learn about such things as eating, shopping, and transportation, so provision is often made for you to get this kind of information.

There is much to be said for trying to become self-sufficient as soon as possible because as your ability to take care of yourself increases so will your sense of self-confidence and general well being. Everything may seem overwhelming at first, so you may be more concerned with completing any given task (even just getting a meal or mailing a letter) than with learning how to do it yourself, and this may result in you falling into the habit of relying on helpful friends to do things for you. While there is little harm in this as a short-term expedient, over the long haul this is dangerous because it will make you a burden on those around you and because it will confine you to a restricted routine that may be as stifling as it is safe. As noted above, such a routine is an invitation to boredom and culture burnout.

2. Do's and don'ts of polite behavior: The need for this kind of knowledge is fairly immediate because from early on in your host country stay you want to create the best possible impression. It is unlikely that host country nationals will expect you to have mastered all the intricacies of local etiquette, and numerous faux pas will no doubt be forgiven with good grace. However, there are deeply felt taboos in every culture that are assumed to be universal standards of decent human behavior, and frequent violation of these will put considerable strain on your relations with host nationals. In contrast, knowing a few basic rules for handling social situations politely will do much to start your new relationships out on the right foot.

One way to quickly learn a few basic rules of polite behavior is to look in books written for tourists that have a section on etiquette. While these will probably only hit a few of the highlights without much depth of explanation, this kind of very basic information is probably what you really need for those first days in your new country. Another way to quickly learn a few of the most important rules to ask host country nationals and fellow expatriates . Host country nationals may enjoy teaching you some of their standards of polite behavior and be favorably impressed by your interest, but may also omit mention of relatively taboo subjects either because they feel it is rude to discuss them or because they assume you already know. For more taboo issues, you may find the advice of other expatriates more straightforward. Finally, however, the best way to learn how to interact is by becoming a good observer. Learn to pay attention to such things as how people act and speak in formal or polite situations, who is treated with special respect, and how people normally behave in daily life.

3. The national story: As noted in Chapter 13, a culture is defined in part by its story, those events, achievements, and people that members of the culture feel to be especially significant. You can easily learn some of this story by reading a little of the history or literature of the host country before arrival. After arrival it may be both more interesting and effective to pursue the issue in the company of host culture friends. Let people take you to museums, historical spots, or cultural events as an opportunity for them to show off their culture to you; the significance of these outings often lies as much in the relationships that are built as the amount of culture and history that you learn. In many countries, simply expressing an interest in these issues will go a long way toward creating a good impression on people. This is especially true in smaller countries or areas with a strong regional culture because people in these areas don't expect outsiders to take much interest in them and are often doubly pleased when someone does.

4. Beliefs and values: As Kohls (1984) noted, being able to see the logic underlying the host culture is one way to help you come to terms with it, and to this end study of the beliefs and values of your host culture can be a helpful part of the adaptation process. Insight into why host nationals behave as they do will reduce misunderstanding and enhance your ability to understand and interpret the actions of those around you.

Books on the culture of the host culture provide

productive approach to this area of study.[5] Another way to learn these beliefs and values is through your own observation, but it is important to observe carefully over a long period of time lest your conclusions be drawn more from your preconceptions than the evidence. Perhaps the best approach is through friends or informants in the host culture, people who will give you a good and reasonably frank explanation of why people do the things they do. Cultivating a friendship that allows the host national to give you good feedback may take a considerable investment of time and patience, but if you can establish such relationships you will have an unexcelled window into the host culture.

5. General background knowledge: Knowledge of the history, geography, current affairs, government, society, economy, and politics of your host culture is usually not immediately essential for your daily life there, but over the long run it is helpful to know about these things if only so that you feel that you understand some of what is going on around you.

This kind of information is relatively easy to gain access to. Books, museums, newspapers, and magazines are all possible resources. The visual media should also not be ignored; even if you don't understand the host country language, watching films and TV may be a useful and even enjoyable way to gain insight.

One way to speed up the learning task—and make it more interesting—is to draw on the people around you as resources. Remember that your priority goal is to learn what host nationals know, so it makes sense to approach a topic first through their eyes. For example, you might approach a topic like history by asking several people about the most important events and people in their history, rather than starting with a history book that will tell you far more than most host nationals remember.[6]

6. An area of expertise: In your study of the host culture, one final possibility to consider is choosing some aspect of the culture to become a specialty. Perhaps

[5]See Kohls (1984) for a good list of information resources about other cultures. Also, the Interacts series mentioned in Chapter 2 is an excellent source of this type of information.

[6]Kohls (1984) presents a list of questions you can use in a cross-cultural investigation. See also Bryan Grey, Ken Darrow, and Brad Palmquist (1975), *Transcultural Study Guide* (Volunteers in Asia).

this might be a hobby like cooking or martial arts, or a special area of knowledge such as the national religion or local history, or learning to play a musical instrument unique to your host country. What makes this kind of study special is that by focusing in one area you can gain a degree of mastery in some aspect of the culture, maybe even getting to the point where host nationals respect your accomplishments. The advantage of this—other than the pleasure and recreation that it provides—is an enhanced sense of self-esteem. It simply feels good to know that there is some area of life in the host country where you are above average, and having some kind of contact with the host culture that is enjoyable and rewarding can be a helpful antidote to the negative attitudes that often develop as you cope with burnout.

Learning the Host Language

To Learn or Not to Learn: Costs and Benefits

Many people assume that once they are living in a foreign country, picking up the language will be relatively easy and fast, much less painful than foreign language classes in high school or college were. This is not entirely untrue: study of a language in the country where it is spoken is generally much more rewarding than study at home, and it certainly offers more opportunities for practice. However, this does not mean that language study in your host country will be cost-free—even there, learning the language requires a substantial investment of time and effort.

I would argue that for almost any VT it is worthwhile to develop at least survival skills in the host language: ability to shop, deal with social courtesies, ask where things are, use the post office, and so forth. The rewards for achieving this level of skill are immediate and significant, and failure to learn at least basic language skills for getting by will leave you in a constant state of dependency on others (or on your ingenuity in nonverbal communication). Over time, the cost this exacts in mental and emotional drain will both diminish the quality of your experience abroad and make emotional survival and adaptation much more difficult.

However, once you have learned enough of the language to deal with the necessities of daily life, the question of whether or not you wish to continue is a real one. From this point on the gains made in language mastery are slower and come at a higher price; it doesn't take as much work to go from point zero to survival language skills as it does from the survival level to the point where you can carry on social conversation. So, after many VTs reach the survival language point, their language study tends to slow down or even grind to a halt. At this point, you may find yourself asking whether putting in so much additional time and energy is worthwhile.

One main reason to seriously consider striving for a higher level of language skill is that this will greatly enhance your chances of successful adaptation to the host culture. Obviously, ability to speak the language reduces the wear and tear of daily life in your host country by making communication easier. Also, the more you can understand of what is going on around you, the more comfortable and at home you will feel in the host culture. This, in turn, translates into reduced emotional drain from constant uncertainty and confusion. Finally, facility in the host language opens up whole new possibilities for access to the host culture, and this makes possible friendships and insight that can do much to restore your interest, excitement, and sense that being in the host culture is as rewarding as it is demanding. Over the long run, this is the best single way to counteract culture burnout.

The price of not investing the time and effort to achieve a higher level of skill is permanent alienation from the host culture, and often longer and more severe bouts of culture burnout. This prediction may seem a bit strong, and I do recognize the fact that there are host country situations where it is possible for a monolingual English teacher to survive quite happily for long periods of time. However, even in these cases satisfaction must be achieved within a limited range because lack of facility in the host language will deny access to some of the population and culture, often most of it, and all too often monolingual expats are forced back into a community of others like themselves.

A second benefit of continued language study is that as you study the host language, you will learn a lot about the process of language learning and about effective strategies for language study. All language learners are different to some degree, so study methods that work for you may not be so good for others, but firsthand experience with different learning strategies is still one of the best ways to ascertain how effective they might be, and a teacher who has firsthand experience as a language student is generally far more sensitive to these kinds of real-world problems than one who has spent little time on the students' side of the desk. Knowledge of the host language will also directly benefit your teaching by helping you understand why students have some of the problems they do. Not all student mistakes are related to their native language, but some are, and knowledge of the host language will help you more quickly focus on problem areas common to all of the students in the class.

Let me tentatively suggest that there may be a third important benefit of sustained language study. VTs from Western nations often have only limited experience with foreign language study, and many have never achieved a significant level of proficiency in a foreign language. In fact, the main thing that many VTs learned in high school or college foreign languages classes was that language study can be hard work. Rubin and Thompson (1994) make the interesting observation that "if an individual's first experiences with a foreign language were not particularly pleasant or successful, he or she will tend to expect the next language learning experience to be just as stressful and unfruitful as the first" (p. 8). It would seem reasonable to assume that these negative experiences would color one's language teaching as well as language learning. A teacher who has never experienced any success or reward in language study may find it difficult to be emotionally convinced that such success is possible, and such teachers may not really expect students to achieve a high degree of proficiency. This lack of expectation may, in turn, be communicated to students through teaching practices that focus more on the rules students have to play by to get a good grade than on proficiency itself. I do not mean to suggest that a someone who does not speak a foreign language cannot be a good English teacher. I do suggest, however, that the enthusiasm and proficiency-orientation of a language teacher for whom rewards and success in language learning are not an emotional reality may not be as strong as those of one who is at least beginning to experience those rewards and success in his or her own language study.

Speaking a foreign language well enhances your credibility as a language teacher, but the primary issue is not how fluent you become; rather, it is the question of whether or not you have credentials as a language learner. If nothing else, lack of foreign language skills simply looks bad in a language teacher and provides a permanent reason to be defensive. Without credentials as a language learner, you have to apologize too often.

Learning the Host Language

As suggested above, language study in your host country may be easier in some ways than in language courses at home. For one thing, your environment will reinforce your language study and provide ample opportunities to practice. For another, you will have many chances to use what you learn, and in many cultures your attempts to speak the language will be rewarded with praise and enthusiasm.

There are, however, also some special problems involved in trying to learn the host language in many countries. The first is that there may be few or no language courses for you to take, especially if you are in an area where there are not many other foreigners, so your study may need to be pursued in less formally structured ways. There may also be few books or other materials available, particularly for intermediate study. Finally, you will probably be teaching on a full-time basis and have to look hard to find time for language study. In short, language study in the host country will probably require greater initiative and discipline from you than study in a course at home would, but you can also look forward to greater progress and rewards if you find the time to study and practice.

Based on the conditions described above, let me make a few suggestions as to how to pursue language study in your host country:

LANGUAGE

One issue you will face in many countries is that of which language or dialect to learn. Many countries have both a national language and a variety of local languages or dialects (that are often completely different from the national language). If you work in an area where a regional language is spoken, you may thus face a hard choice between the national standard and the regional language.

On the side of the national standard, it will probably be easier to locate study materials and you will be able to use the language over a wider area. People may also expect you to learn the national standard, and you may meet resistance—or simply confusion—if you don't. On the side of the regional language, this is often what you hear most around you and have more opportunities for practicing; in fact, it may be that you would have very little chance to use the national standard in your area. The other advantage of learning the regional language in some areas is that people will respond to you more favorably. This is particularly true in areas with a strong regional culture and sense of local pride; in such areas, the national standard may be viewed with very mixed emotions as a kind of foreign language (perhaps imposed from the outside by force).

My own practice in such situations has been to focus on the national standard but also pick up a smattering of the local language, but much depends on the local situation and your own language study goals. However, as you consider the issue, don't overlook the feelings those around you have about languages because this will have a major impact on how much reinforcement and encouragement you get in your study.

STRUCTURING A PROGRAM OF STUDY

One of the main problems in not having an organized language course is that lack of structure—not to mention examinations—makes it easy for your studies to drift off course and eventually dwindle into good intentions. It is therefore especially important that you have a clear idea of where you want to go and how you want to get there.

Setting goals is generally not a problem in the beginning because the need to achieve survival speaking and listening skills is so obvious. However, once that level of skill is reached harder choices have to be made. It is here that the principles of planning for "breakthrough" may be helpful to you (see Chapter 3). Assuming that you have limited time, choosing to focus your study efforts on the pursuit of one or two skills will enable you to progress in those areas more rapidly and feel more reward for your efforts. This, in turn, will make it more likely that you will keep studying during the intermediate stages during which rewards are fewer and plateaus more common.

It is also helpful to most people to have structure in their study program. In foreign language classes, this is generally provided by textbooks and other study materials. In a situation where you do not have a textbook, you may need to rely more on a study plan to provide structure. Marshall (1989) suggests a program structured around a "study cycle." This involves working through a series of steps on a regular basis:

1 Plan what kinds of topics and situations you want to learn about.

2 With the help of a mentor (tutor), work up a dialogue for dealing with that topic or situation.

3 Have the mentor tape the dialogue, and then practice it.

4 Go out and practice in the community.

5 Return and evaluate your experience with the mentor.

Such a cycle, or some variation of it, will not only provide structure for your study but also result in you slowly but surely producing your own language study materials, tailored to your goals and needs.

MATERIALS

As noted above, one of the advantages of studying a national language is that at least introductory study materials will more likely be available. For regional languages and dialects materials may be more difficult to find, though often a dictionary or primer has been written at some point in history by a missionary or scholar. (You may only be able to find these in university libraries at home.)

If you need to make your own materials from scratch, taped materials developed with the help of a tutor following the lines suggested above would be useful for beginning and intermediate speaking and listening. For reading, it is good to start out with materials such as maps and signs that are of immediate use and provide rapid reward for your efforts. To build toward reading more substantial texts you might work with children's books. Although the content may not always be intellectually stimulating, such materials are relatively easy, often have pictures to help you create context, and may contain widely known stories that will help you build cultural background knowledge.

At advanced levels of study, the problem of finding materials is less severe because you can begin working with material intended for adult host culture audiences.

TUTORS

Finding a good language teacher is not always easy. There may not be many people around who have experience teaching the local language to foreigners, so when others help you look for a teacher they may turn to those whose experience is in teaching the language as rhetoric or literature. They will also probably assume you want someone who will take all of the initiative in presenting lessons for you. Needless to say, candidates selected in this way may not be ideal—you may find yourself as an audience of one for lectures on schoolbook texts.

Assuming that you want to take control of your own language program, what you want is someone who will answer your questions, patiently talk with you in the target language, and generally cooperate with you in carrying out your plan. Thus, while it is important that your tutor's speech be fairly representative and standard, the qualifications you are looking for may have as much to do with personality and sensitivity as with credentials in language teaching.

One issue that is often sticky is how to pay your tutor. In many cultures, a direct weekly or monthly payment might be culturally awkward. Hence, you will need to seek advice as to what kind of arrangement is culturally comfortable, fair, and doesn't place you in a greater position of obligation to the tutor than you desire. If direct payment won't work, you might suggest payment through a third party, an exchange of language lessons, occasional gifts from you to your tutor, or some other arrangement. Finding a suitable method of compensation may take some effort and ingenuity, but it has the advantage of not only protecting you from accumulating a huge burden of obligation but also setting your relationship on a clear basis. Arrangements that are more casual have a tendency to drift into irregularity or friendly chatting (often in English).[7]

WHEN TO START YOUR STUDY

It is usually best to start your language study as soon as possible, perhaps even before arrival in the host country. One reason for starting early is that language you learn early in your stay will probably be drilled into you permanently by months and years of practice; that which you learn in the last month you will probably lose. Another

[7]See Marshall (1989) for a more detailed discussion of the problems of working with tutors.

reason to have some host language skills as early as possible is that it will enable you to start at least some of your relationships in the host language. One interesting fact of human language behavior is that once two people establish a relationship in one language, they will generally continue to communicate in that language. As an English teacher, you will inevitably spend much of your time with teachers and students who will speak to you in English, and it may be hard to find opportunities to practice the host language. If you delay your study of the host language for several months, your social life will tend to fill with people who speak to you in English, and host nationals who can't speak English will become accustomed to not speaking to you at all. If, on the other hand, you learn to speak at least some of the host language during the first months of your stay, you are more likely to have some relationships with people who don't speak English or who prefer to speak to you in the host language.

16 Afterword: On Becoming a Professional

Many people who go abroad to teach English do so less out of a burning desire to teach English than because they want to experience life in another country. However, many discover that English teaching is an unusually enjoyable profession offering a range of rewards. First, because of the worldwide interest in English an English teacher can find work and live in a very broad range of countries and cultures.[1] Secondly, English teaching is often an especially fulfilling and meaningful form of work because promoting knowledge of English can make an important contribution not only to students' personal development and career opportunities, but also to a nation's modernization efforts. Finally, the raw material of the language teaching profession—language, culture, and communication—is inherently interesting. As an English teacher working abroad, you have the opportunity not only to teach this material, but also to learn it first-hand through interaction with people of other cultures. Thus, it seems only appropriate to close this book with a few words on steps to take if you find that EFL teaching is a career that you wish to pursue on a professional level.

The first step would be to look into a degree program in language teaching. As of this writing (1995), good first places to look for information in the would be:

1 Teachers of English to Speakers of Other Languages, Inc., 1600 Cameron Street, Suite 300, Alexandria VA 22314 (USA). TESOL's comprehensive listing of ESL/EFL programs, *Directory of Professional Preparation Programs in TESOL in the United States and Canada* (edited by Ellen Garshick) is updated every few years, the 1995-1997 edition being the most recent.

---

[1]See Susan Griffith (1991) *Teaching English Abroad: Talk Your Way Around the World.* (Oxford, Vacation Work) for a sample listing of English teaching jobs abroad.

2 British Council, Medlock Street, Manchester M15 4AA (UK). The English Language Information Section publishes a list of course programs.

3 The National Centre for English Teaching and Research, Macquarie University, Sydney NSW 2109 (Australia).

Obtaining a professional degree in an ESL/EFL-related field makes you eligible for a broad range of English teaching positions, but it certainly does not exhaust the possibilities for professional training. A second highly beneficial way to prepare for a career as a language teacher is through your own continued foreign language study. Although such study is recommended by most ESL/EFL degree programs, limitations of time mean that it is often not accorded a great deal of emphasis. As pointed out earlier, experience as a language learner helps you grow in your understanding of language learning strategies, the affective side of language learning, and of language in general and English in particular. EFL professionals should make language study a part of preparation for teaching, and—much like a coach or piano teacher—we should continue to stay in shape by regularly practicing the art of language learning. If we learn one language and then rest on our laurels, it is easy for us to grow stale and forget what it is like to be on the other side of the teacher's desk. It is thus necessary that we continue to study, both deepening our skills in languages we already know and occasionally going back to the beginning by learning a new one.

A third important area of study and experience that benefits EFL teachers—and arguably ESL teachers as well—is cross-cultural communication and adaptation. As argued in Chapter 13, many if not most of the situations in which your students will use English will involve cross-cultural communication of some kind, so an understanding of the special problems of communicating across cultural lines is very beneficial to a teacher. Also, if you go on to a career as an EFL teacher you will almost by definition often be living in situations where you need to adapt to a new culture, and many of your students may eventually need to go through the same adaptation process themselves if they go abroad. Thus, your ability to understand and explain that process will be of great value to you as an EFL teacher.

All of this may seem a rather tall order to handle, and it does in fact take years of dedicated work to become prepared in all of the ways mentioned above. The good news, however, is that even in your first year teaching overseas you will make considerable progress in learning the skills that will speed you on your road to a professional career. Even for those of you who have no long-term EFL ambitions, the cross-cultural, language teaching, and foreign language skills that you can develop in a year of teaching abroad will not only make you better prepared for a wide range of careers, but also enrich your life in ways that you probably cannot now imagine.

The Goals Menu: A Starter Kit for Course Planning

The following menu of English course goals is intended to help you begin thinking through some of the goals which you might select for a course. By necessity it is general, and is intended as a starting point rather than a final plan.[1] Reminders:

- ◆ It is good to have both short-term and long-term goals for a course. The former are limited goals that can be accomplished during the course; the latter are ultimate goals toward which students will have to work over a long time.

- ◆ You should have both content and proficiency goals for most courses. In other words, students should improve both in what they know and in what they can do. A natural source of content in English courses is Western culture.

I. General (for all kinds of courses)

   A. Encourage students' interest in English study.

   B. Help students begin to take a more active approach to language study, setting their own goals and choosing their own study approaches.

   C. Help students develop discipline in language study.

[1] In setting goals for speaking, listening, reading, and writing, I am indebted to the ACTFL Proficiency Guidelines, although the system I propose above is simpler in that, as elsewhere I this book, I have only made division into three levels instead of the five used in the ACTFL system. The ACTFL Guidelines are not a set of goals in themselves, but they provide a helpful basis for considering instructional goals. The ACTFL Guidelines are available through the American Council on the Teaching of Foreign Languages (6 Executive Blvd, Upper Level, Yonkers, NY 10701), and can also be found in Omaggio Hadley (1993) Appendix A.

D. Build students toward a good balance of English skills. What makes up a "good" balance depends greatly on the situation, but for many learners it would look something like this:

Stronger in listening than speaking

Stronger in reading than writing

Larger receptive vocabulary than productive vocabulary

Stronger knowledge of vocabulary than of grammar

II. Speaking Goals

A. General (all levels). Help students improve in:

1. Ability to express meaning

2. Flexibility and creativity in dealing with communication problems (e.g., finding another way to say something when you don't know the right word)

3. Vocabulary

4. Grammatical accuracy

5. Fluency

6. Accuracy in pronunciation

7. Interpretation (English to host language or vice versa)

8. Ability to interact in culturally appropriate ways

B. Beginning Level. Help students learn to:

1. Deal with predictable classroom communication

2. Handle simple courtesies

3. Ask and answer basic information questions

4. Use vocabulary for talking about self, family, school, environment, daily routine and activities

5. Use basic grammar structures (e.g., wh-questions, a few basic verb tenses, plurals)

6. Construct short, simple sentences with a fair degree of accuracy

7. Achieve intelligible pronunciation

C. Intermediate Level. Help students learn to:

1. Deal creatively with daily communication situations (to begin to go beyond use of memorized material)

2. Sustain a conversation

3. Tell stories, express an opinion, explain

4. Cope with communication problems by clarification, circumlocution

5. Use vocabulary for discussion of:

   meeting needs (e.g., shopping, health, transport)

   personal information (e.g., history, plans)

   one's home/town/city/region/country

   profession, topics of personal interest

6. Use vocabulary accurately and appropriately

7. Accurately construct short or simple sentences

8. Construct more complicated sentences, though with less accuracy

9. Develop sufficient fluency to sustain rhythm of daily conversation

10. Develop clear (though probably accented) pronunciation

11. Handle common social interactions in linguistically and culturally appropriate ways

D. Advanced Level. Help students learn to:

1. Handle most normal communication situations fluently

2. Explain, persuade, negotiate proficiently

3. Be able to speak in "paragraphs"

4. Quickly resolve misunderstandings, communication problems by clarification, circumlocution

5. Handle unexpected situations, especially problematic cross-cultural situations

6. Use vocabulary for discussion of:

   current affairs, news, social issues

   profession

   own culture and Western culture

7. Use vocabulary properly (level of formality, connotation, grammar)

8. Make few grammar errors that impede comprehension

9. Achieve clear (though probably accented) pronunciation

10. Handle a broad range of situations in culturally appropriate ways

11. Find opportunities to practice speaking outside class

III. Listening Goals

A. General (all levels). Help students improve in:

1. Comprehension of oral English

2. Ability to guess. Ability to determine meaning from language (bottom-up skills) and determine meaning from context, nonlanguage clues (top-down skills)

3. Comprehension of fast or unclear speech

4. Interpretation

5. Vocabulary (receptive)

6. Ability to hear and derive meaning from grammatical structure

7. Cultural background knowledge

B. Beginning Level. Help students learn to:

1. Follow classroom instructions

2. Understand measured, clear speech

3. Comprehend aurally material learned visually from the textbook

4. Comprehend simple information questions (wh-questions, yes/no questions)

5. Use vocabulary for understanding:

   classroom language

   social pleasantries

   discussion of self and daily routine

6. Hear and understand basic grammar structures (e.g., past tense endings, plural endings)

7. Expect cultural patterns for the most common social interactions (e.g., classroom activities, greetings, leave-takings)

C. Intermediate Level. Help students learn to:

1. Understand clear speech at normal speed in face-to-face communication

2. Comprehend aurally material learned visually from the textbook

3. Develop skills for clarifying in conversation when they don't understand

4. Use vocabulary for understanding:

daily social interactions (e.g., shopping, transport)

discussion of personal information

discussion of own/teacher's home/town/region/country/culture

discussion of profession, personal interests

5. Hear and understand basic grammar structures

6. Use context clues to guess (top-down strategies), particularly when listening to more difficult language

7. Expect cultural patterns for a wide range of social interactions

D. Advanced Level. Help students learn:

1. Understand native speech at normal speeds

2. Understand nonstandard speech (accents, unclear pronunciation, reduced forms)

3. Understand discussion not directed at self (overheard conversation)

4. Understand radio programs, TV, and films in English

5. Understand and take notes on lectures

6. Use vocabulary for comprehension of a broad range of topics including current events and profession

7. Develop cultural background knowledge assumed by media news (e.g., place names, names of famous people, historical knowledge)

8. Understand nuances and implied meanings in conversation (e.g., sarcasm, hints)

9. Understand cultural patterns and expectations for common types of discourse (e.g., lectures, stories, news programs, various film and TV genres)

10. Find enjoyable opportunities to listen in English (e.g., radio programs, TV, films)

IV. Reading Goals

A. General Goals (all levels). Help students improve in:

1. Intensive reading, that is, carefully extracting maximum meaning from a text

2. Translation

3. Extensive reading, that is, quickly getting the gist of a text

4. Use of top-down strategies to increase depth of comprehension, including implied meanings, bias, tone

5. Vocabulary (receptive)

6. Grammar

7. Reading speed

8. Ability to guess vocabulary from context

9. Ability to guess around unfamiliar vocabulary

10. Cultural background information

B. Beginning Level. Help students learn to:

1. Become familiar with alphabet

2. Recognize spelling-sound correspondences

3. Read short simplified texts (often from textbook) slowly (bottom-up strategies)

4. Make preliminary guesses as to what a text may be about (top-down strategies)

5. Recognize and use vocabulary as found in textbook

6. Grammar for reading classroom materials and other simple texts

7. Use a dictionary

C. Intermediate Level. Help students learn to:

1. Read relatively simple material quickly while still understanding and retaining main ideas

2. Slowly decode more difficult texts

3. Start building a large receptive reading vocabulary

4. Attend to vocabulary use (level of formality, connotation, grammar) when reading intensively

5. Decode grammatically complex sentences

6. Predict and guess using knowledge of world, knowledge of discourse structures (top-down strategies)

7. Skim and scan

8. Use dictionary effectively

9. Guess around unfamiliar vocabulary using context clues

10. Develop basic knowledge of Western literary culture. Might include knowledge of myths, Bible stories, and other well known stories

11. Develop basic factual knowledge of Western history, society, and culture

D. Advanced Level. Help students learn to:

1. Read a broad range of material (magazines, novels, general interest books, books on profession) with little or no dictionary use

2. Read relatively unimportant or easy material quickly, skimming where desirable

3. Extract main ideas, flow of thought, logical organization from a text

4. Build a large receptive vocabulary

5. Attend to vocabulary use when reading intensively

6. Decode grammatically complex sentences

7. Read actively—predicting before and while reading, guessing from context, skimming over unimportant material

8. Understand Western literary culture

9. Understand Western history, society, and culture

10. Enjoy reading (find reading material in which they are interested)

V. Writing Goals

A. General (all levels). Help students improve in:

1. Ability to communicate in writing

2. Range of vocabulary

3. Accurate usage of vocabulary

4. Grammatical accuracy

5. Translation

6. Ability to edit and revise

7. Ability to write quickly

8. Knowledge of proper forms for written communication

9. Knowledge of cultural knowledge, beliefs, and assumptions of Western audience

B. Beginning Level. Help students learn to:

1. Write down spoken language—dialogues, messages, personal letters, lists (material that requires little formal organization)

2. Take dictation

3. Use proper conventions of writing (capitalization, spelling, punctuation)

4. Fill in forms

5. Develop adequate vocabulary for writing about self, immediate environment

6. Check word usage, spelling in a dictionary

7. Understand and use basic grammar

C. Intermediate Level. Help students learn to:

1. Write proper form for letters—personal and business.

2. Write journal entries

3. Write personal narratives

4. Write creatively

5. Organize expository paragraphs and short compositions

6. Take notes

7. Develop and use vocabulary for above objectives

8. Check word usage, spelling in a dictionary

9. Write most common grammar structures accurately

10. Proofread for errors

11. Revise compositions to improve organization, general effectiveness of communication

12. Write with sufficient speed and fluency to produce multiparagraph texts in relatively short times

D. Advanced Level. Help students learn to:

1. Use expository writing skills for academic, business purposes

2. Write for professional purposes

3. Write narratives

4. Do creative writing

5. Write multipage compositions

6. Acquire vocabulary for the above

7. Develop good organization, ability to develop points to achieve coherence

8. Avoid or find most grammar errors

9. Adjust explanations/attempts at persuasion to take into account knowledge/beliefs of Western audience

10. Find opportunities to practice writing outside class (correspondence with friends or pen pals, creative writing.)

B Culture Topics List

The following list of topics and questions can serve as a database of ideas for oral skills classes, but you could also draw on it to create material for listening, writing, and perhaps even reading lessons (if you feel like writing little culture notes on the board for your students). If you choose to use it as material for speaking and listening lessons, let me suggest a basic activity format on which you can design your own variations.

1 Choose an item and modify it as necessary to make it appropriate for your class. Many of the items below are already structured as tasks, but you may need to modify the task type to fit your lesson. Basic task types include making a list, prioritizing a list, describing steps in a process, making a choice, or listing advantages and disadvantages.

2 Briefly introduce the topic and task, and then have students discuss in small groups. This phase of the activity gives students practice in talking about their culture and explaining it to an outsider, in expressing and discussing personal opinions, and in developing problem-solving and discussion skills. It also helps students expand the range of topics that they are comfortable discussing. Some topics will lead into sustained discussion that might take the whole class period; others are best used for quick warm-up or closing activities.

3 Ask a representative of each small group to report to the class at large, and open the issue to general discussion. This phase of the activity allows groups to share ideas, and also gives the small-group discussions a sense of closure.

4 Comment on the point in question from the perspective of your own culture. This phase not only gives students listening practice, but also gives them a chance to learn more about your culture. In Steps 3 and 4 of the activity, contrasting and comparing students' cultures and yours will make the issue much more interesting.

Warning: Some of the topics below are quite sensitive and should be used with caution, if at all. Especially sensitive topics are marked with an asterisk (*).

Daily Life

Animals

- What is the most useful kind of animal? (Or most dangerous? Nicest?)
- What animal best symbolizes your country? Why?
- In your country, what qualities do given animals represent?
- Is it a good thing to keep pets?

Clothing

- What is the proper clothing for a teacher? (Or business person? Official?)
- How has fashion in your country changed over the past 10 years?
- In your country, how does clothing mark social class? (Or region? Income level?)
- What advice would you give a foreigner about dressing to stay warm in winter? (Or cool in summer?)

Daily Schedule

- What is a normal daily schedule for a worker? (Farmer? Student? Official? Teacher? Etc.)
- Describe your ideal daily schedule.
- What is a normal schedule for eating meals? (When, what, and how much?)
- What is the normal pattern for sleeping?

Food

- In order of priority, list the most important foods in the local diet.
- Who should buy/prepare food?
- What are five especially nutritious foods and what are they good for?
- What are the most famous dishes of this region? What makes them special?

♦ If you had to prepare a banquet for a guest from another country, what would you prepare?

Games

♦ List five popular children's games.

♦ List five popular games played by adults.

♦ Step by step, describe how to play a popular game that is unique to your country/region.

Hobbies

♦ List the five most popular hobbies in your country. (Why are they so popular? How do you pursue them?)

♦ Should people have hobbies? If so, what are the best ones to have?

Housing

♦ Prepare to give a description of a typical dwelling so that your teacher can draw it on the board.

♦ What are the steps for getting housing in your country?

♦ Is there any way in which housing especially reflects your culture? (Or history? Topography?)

♦ What are the steps for moving to a new home?

Hygiene

♦ What are the five most important things parents should teach children about hygiene?

♦ How often do people bathe, when, and how?*

♦ How do you clean your teeth and when?[1]

---

[1]This question may not seem very promising, but in many countries, you will get quite a reaction when you try to explain dental floss.

Identification

◆ List the most important kinds of IDs/documents people in your country are required to have.

◆ For what kinds of things does one need an ID in your country?

◆ What are the steps involved in getting an ID?

Jobs

◆ Describe the steps in a normal job search.

◆ What are the three best ways to get a job?

◆ Describe a typical job application/interview process.

◆ What are the five most desirable kinds of jobs? (Or least desirable? Most prestigious?)

◆ What are the top three jobs you would want your child to have?

◆ What is the procedure involved in changing jobs?

Medical Care

◆ What are the steps for getting medical care in your country?

◆ What five tips would you give a foreigner in your country on how to stay healthy?

◆ What are the best steps to take if you have a cold? A fever? A stomach ache?

◆ What were the most important lessons your mother (parents, grandparents) taught you about staying well (healthy)?

Plants

◆ List five plants (e.g., trees, flowers) and what they symbolize in your culture.

◆ What plant best symbolizes your country and why?

◆ What are five kinds of plants (e.g., trees, flowers) that everyone in your country would recognize?

◆ Give five rules for raising healthy plants.

Recreation

◆ List the most popular leisure time activities in your country.

◆ What are the most common kinds of parties? (Or social gatherings? Activities?)

◆ Is it better to work lots and have more income or work less and have more vacation?

Shopping

◆ For a foreign visitor, list the most common kinds of stores in your country and what you would buy there.

◆ What is the best strategy for bargaining in a local market?

Space

◆ If you had an office, what would be the best way to arrange the furniture (e.g., desk, chairs)?

◆ For receiving guests in a living room (or meeting room), what is the best way to arrange chairs?

◆ How far should you stand from your boss (or mother, same sex friend, opposite sex classmate) when talking to him or her? How far is too far? Too close?

Sports

◆ What are the three most popular sports in your country?

♦ What sport best symbolizes your country?

♦ Prepare instructions to teach your foreign teacher how to play a sport unique to your country or region.

Time

♦ For an appointment (or a dinner, a date), how late can you be without needing to apologize? (How early?)

♦ List five situations where it is polite to be late.

♦ What is the best time of day for studying?

Traffic and Transport

♦ For a foreign teacher, prepare a list of the most important traffic rules. (Which of these are people most likely to break?)

♦ List 10 tricks for biking/driving on crowded roads.

♦ Design a plan for improving transport in your city (or country, county).

♦ Give a foreigner five pieces of advice on how to buy a good bicycle (or motorcycle, car).

♦ What are the steps for getting a driver's (e.g., car, motorcycle, bicycle) license?

Travel

♦ What are your country's top tourist attractions?

♦ If you could go on a 10-day trip in your country, what places would you visit?

♦ If you had to arrange a 10-day trip for a visitor to your country, where would you have him/her go?

Weather

♦ Describe the most perfect possible kind of weather? (The worst?)

◆ What are five tricks for staying cool in the summer? Warm in winter?

◆ What are five tricks for coping with high humidity? Very dry climates?

◆ List necessary precautions for staying safe in a typhoon (or blizzard, hurricane).

The Cycle of Life

Birth

◆ List customs surrounding birth.

◆ Describe how birthdays are celebrated.

Children

◆ Is it better to err on the side of strictness or leniency with children?

◆ What are the best ways to deal with a child who is misbehaving?

◆ Who should be primarily responsible for taking care of children? Wife? Husband? Grandparents? Relatives? Daycare center?

◆ What are the most important lessons to teach young children at home? Older children?

◆ Is childhood the best time of life?

◆ Should children be given chores? If so, what? Paid for them?

◆ What obligations do children have to their parents later in life?

Dating/Mating

◆ What are the normal ways to find (meet, win) a partner?

◆ What are the characteristics of the ideal boyfriend? Girlfriend?

◆ What are the advantages and disadvantages of matchmakers? (Blind dates?)

◆ What are the most common problems faced in finding (choosing, winning) a partner?

◆ Write a definition of *love*.

Marriage

◆ What procedures does one normally go through to get married?

◆ What are 10 basic rules for a happy marriage?

◆ What are the characteristics of the ideal wife? Husband?

Divorce

◆ List circumstances under which divorce should be acceptable.*

◆ Describe the procedures for getting a divorce.*

Friends

◆ Where (how) do people in your country make their best (most) friends?

◆ Write a definition of *friend*.

◆ List the kinds of help you can always expect from a friend.

◆ List situations where you can say no to a friend who asks for something. (When is it impossible to say no to a friend who wants something?)

Old Age

◆ Describe the typical day of a retired teacher (or official, farmer).

◆ Describe the budget of a typical retired person (or teacher, worker).

♦ What do you want to do most when you retire?

♦ In order of priority, list the people/agencies which have responsibility for taking care of people when they become old.

♦ Should old parents live with their (grown) children? (Advantages? Disadvantages?)

Funerals

♦ What are procedures and customs for funerals?*

Rites of Passage

♦ At what age is a person considered a baby? A child? An adult?

♦ How old is young? Middle aged? Old?

♦ When does someone become an adult? What marks the difference between an adult and a child?

Men and Women

♦ What jobs are best suited for women? For men? For either?*

♦ What duties should men have at home? Women?*

♦ Is it better to be born a man or a woman?*

Chatting

Interacting

♦ List the five most common topics people chat about.

♦ In your culture, is there a difference between chatting and gossiping? If so, describe what the difference is.

♦ List the five most common topics people gossip about.

Eating

♦ At a banquet (at someone's home for dinner) how can you politely avoid eating something you don't want to eat?

♦ For a foreigner going to a banquet, list the five most important rules for eating politely.

♦ What are the five rudest things a person can do at a meal?

Drinking

♦ Explain the rules of toasting to a foreigner.

♦ List/describe the circumstances under which it is hard to refuse to drink. (Who? What situation?)

Functions in Communication

♦ How do you introduce people?

♦ How do you make an invitation? How can you politely refuse an invitation?

♦ How do you strike up a conversation with a stranger? When is it appropriate/not appropriate to strike up a conversation with a stranger?

♦ How and when do you apologize?

♦ How and when do you compliment? How does one respond politely to a compliment?

♦ When is it necessary to say something like "Excuse me"?

♦ How does one disagree politely?

♦ How do you give advice? In what kinds of situation do people often give advice?

♦ How do you interrupt someone? When is it acceptable/not acceptable to interrupt?

♦ List five good excuses you can use to refuse an invitation. What are the so-called rules that underlie the excuses?

Gifts

♦ On what occasions should gifts be given? To whom? How should they be presented?

♦ What makes a good gift?

♦ When should you say no to a gift?

♦ When is a gift a bribe?*

Language Learning

♦ What do you like most (least) about language study?

♦ What is the best way to:
learn a language?
improve your listening/speaking/reading/writing?
improve your grammar in writing/speaking?
improve your reading speed/comprehension?
study for a test?
memorize vocabulary?

♦ What are the most important things you should learn about a foreign culture?

Parties

♦ List the different kinds of parties people have in your country.

♦ Describe the normal sequence of events at a party.

Politeness

♦ List five "golden rules" to help a foreigner know how to be polite in your country.

♦ List five rude things a foreigner should never do in your country.*

Problem Solving

♦ What should you do if:
you buy an expensive appliance, and it doesn't work when you get home?

your boss makes an unreasonable demand?

you are angry at your friend and you want to let him/her know it?

you have a guest who you want to leave?

you want your employer to increase your salary?

you want permission from your parents to marry someone they don't like?

Society

Business

◆ List the advantages (disadvantages) of business as a career.

◆ What are the ingredients that lead to success in business?

◆ List the key qualities of an effective advertisement.

Cities

◆ What are the major social problems facing cities?

◆ What are the most important advantages/disadvantages of living in a big city?

◆ Should there be controls on who can move to cities?*

Economy

◆ List the advantages (disadvantages) of a capitalist economy (or socialist economy).*

◆ Describe the tax system in your country. (What kinds? Who needs to pay? How is the amount determined? How are they collected?)

Education

◆ Describe the path a student must follow through the educational system to eventually reach university. (Tests?)

◆ Describe the ideal teacher (student).

◆ What are the best parts of student life? The worst?

Farming

♦ Describe the normal schedule of the farming year (e.g., seasons, crops).

♦ What are the steps for planting and harvesting the main local crop?

♦ What are the advantages and disadvantages of life as a farmer?

Industry

♦ List the most important national/local industries.

♦ What are the advantages/disadvantages of industrialization?

♦ If you could establish a new industry in your area, what kind would it be?

♦ In your area, should polluting industries that will bring in jobs be encouraged?*

Government and Politics

♦ Outline a lecture explaining the structure of your government to a foreigner.

♦ What are the advantages/disadvantages of democracy? Other political systems?*

Languages and Dialects

♦ Draw a map showing the different languages and dialects in your country.

♦ What language serves as the national standard and why?

♦ List the languages spoken in your country in order according to prestige.*

♦ If you could speak another foreign language, which would be best?

♦ If you could learn another language/dialect spoken in your own country, which one would be best?

Law and Order

♦ List five crimes and the penalties for them.

♦ What are the advantages (disadvantages) of a career as a lawyer? Policeman? Judge?

♦ Describe the procedure of a typical trial.

Science

♦ For a foreign visitor, describe how and in what kinds of institutions scientific research is carried on your country.

♦ What are the most famous centers of scientific research and learning in your country?

♦ What are the advantages (disadvantages) of a career as a scientist?

Social Problems

♦ List five of the most serious social problems in your country.*

♦ List causes that underlie them.*

♦ How should they be dealt with?*

The Nation

Holidays

♦ What are your most important national/regional holidays, why are they celebrated, and how?

Geography

♦ Make a map showing the topography of your country or region.

♦ List several ways in which the geography of your country/province affects life there.

History

♦ Write a short outline of the most important events in your country's history.

♦ What are your country's greatest national achievements?

♦ What are the most important symbols of your nation/culture?

♦ Describe your flag and its significance.

Cultural Borrowing

♦ What has your culture borrowed from other countries?

♦ What have other cultures borrowed from your culture?

♦ Is cultural borrowing good or bad?

♦ What kinds of things should/should not be borrowed from other cultures?

Famous People

♦ Who are the most important famous people of the past? Of the present?

♦ What is the best/easiest way to become famous?

♦ List your greatest national heroes and the values they represent.

National Issues

♦ What are the top five most controversial issues in your country?

♦ For an issue now being publicly debated, describe the two sides of the argument.

Stereotypes

♦ List the ways in which people in your country learn about foreigners.

♦ Describe the typical foreigner.*

♦ Describe the typical person from different regions in your country.*

Creative Arts

Arts

♦ List your country's most famous artists or artworks.

♦ What makes something a great work of art (or music, drama)? List the criteria by which it is judged.

♦ Describe the process by which artists are trained.

♦ How should artists be trained? Describe the process.

Entertainment

♦ List your country's best known entertainers.

♦ What are the most popular forms of entertainment?

Genres

♦ What are your country's most popular types of movies/books/TV shows?

♦ Describe the formula of a popular type of movie/book/TV show.

Literature

♦ Introduce your country's greatest works of literature to a foreigner? (What are they? What makes them great?)

♦ List your country's most popular traditional stories and their characters?

♦ What values are reflected in your country's greatest literary works?

♦ What are your country's funniest works of literature? (Or most boring? Most satirical?)

♦ If you could recommend one book to a foreigner who wants to learn about your country, what would it be and why?

Music

♦ List, in order, your country's most popular kinds of music. Among young people? Older people?

♦ Does your region have any special kinds of music? What makes it special?

♦ What instruments do people in your area most often learn to play? How?

Television

♦ How much television do most people in your country watch? Who watches most?

♦ List, in order, the most popular kinds of TV programs.

♦ Are increased levels of TV viewership good or bad?

Philosophy, Religion, and Values

♦ List your country's greatest thinkers and their most important ideas.

♦ List the main religions in your country and describe the beliefs of each.*

♦ Should children be trained to be more obedient or independent?

♦ List situations in which adult children should be obedient to their parents. (Or should not be obedient to their parents.)

♦ What are the advantages and disadvantages of being rich?

♦ What are the characteristics of the ideal woman? Man? Father/mother? Child? Leader?

♦ In a society, is it better for people to be more independent and self-sufficient or more mutually reliant and supporting?

313

♦ Define *success.*

♦ List situations where the rights of the group are more important than the rights of the individual, and situations where the rights of the individual are more important than those of the group.

♦ What is the most important thing in life?

♦ If you were 80 years old looking back on your life, what would you most want to see? (Have accomplished? Have become?)

♦ What are the advantages and disadvantages to an office situation where the boss tries to treat everyone as equals?

C Books to Consider Taking With You

Below are books that I would recommend to a VT for a small EFL reference library. These are books which accessible to the general reader and appropriate to an EFL setting. Recommendations are restricted to books that are useful even if students do not have a copy of the text and flexible enough to be of use in a wide range of settings and student skill levels (hence the absence of reading textbooks or listening materials). I have also tried to recommend books that are easily available, relatively inexpensive, and as light as possible.

Azar, Betty. (1989). *Understanding and using English grammar.* Englewood Cliffs, NJ: Prentice Hall Regents.

Azar's grammar books contain straightforward explanations of grammar structures, accompanied by charts, examples, and a multitude of exercises (some of which are set up so that they can be done orally). A good resource both for learning and teaching grammar. (This is actually one of a series of three books: *Basic English Grammar* is aimed at lower lever students, and *Fundamentals of English Grammar* at intermediate students. However, I would recommend *Understanding* if you can only carry one.)

Bowen, J. Donald, Madsen, Harold, & Hilferty, Ann. (1985). *TESOL: Techniques and procedures.* (2nd ed.). Rowley, MA: Newbury House.

A good volume on the theory and practice of language teaching. Very practical, easy to read, and full of concrete examples.

Brown, Douglas. (1991). *Breaking the language barrier.* Yarmouth ME: Intercultural Press.

A readable discussion of how to learn languages. Good attention to affective factors, and constant emphasis on how learners must form their own strategies for success.

Brown, Douglas. (1994). *Teaching by principles.* Englewood Cliffs, NJ: Prentice Hall Regents.

Probably the best single introduction to the general issues and practice of language teaching. Readable as well as insightful.

Cross, David. (1991). *A practical handbook of language teaching*. London: Cassell.

This practical introduction to language teaching explicitly assumes an EFL setting (Cross draws heavily on his African experience in teaching large classes of younger learners). Very specific on the nuts and bolts of in-class teaching techniques.

Klippel, Friederike. (1984). *Keep talking: Communicative fluency activities for language teaching*. Cambridge: Cambridge University Press.

An excellent cookbook of speaking activities.

Kohls, L. Robert. (1984). *Survival kit for overseas living: For Americans planning to live and work abroad* (2nd ed.). Yarmouth, ME: Intercultural Press.

A brief, readable, and insightful discussion of the process of learning to live in another country. The various lists in the book, including the list of culture topics in Chapter 14 and the list of American values in Chapter 8, are also very handy as teaching resources. Despite the explicit American focus, most of the general principles would apply to anyone from a Western background.

Raimes, Ann. (1983). *Techniques in teaching writing*. Oxford: Oxford University Press.

A brief clear introduction to the teaching of writing.

Rubin, Joan, & Thompson, Irene. (1994). *How to be a more successful language learner* (2nd ed.). Boston: Heinle & Heinle.

An excellent, brief introduction not only to language learning strategies but also to the nature of language. Easy reading, highly recommended.

Sion Christopher. (Ed.). (1985). *Recipes for tired teachers*. Reading, MA: Addison-Wesley.

A collection of ready-to-use activities for days when you and your students need a break. (There is also a second volume, *More Recipes for Tired Teachers*.)

Seelye, Ned. (1993). *Teaching culture: Strategies for intercultural communication* (3rd ed.). Lincolnwood, IL: National Textbook Company.

This is intended primarily for foreign language teachers in the U.S., but is both a useful discussion of the issue of culture teaching and a good collection of activity ideas that could be modified for an EFL setting.

Stewart, Edward, & Bennett, Milton. (1991). *American cultural patterns: A cross-cultural perspective* (rev. ed.). Yarmouth, ME: Intercultural Press.

Although slightly technical, this short volume is a good introduction to the values and assumptions of American culture, and is very helpful in thinking through the issue of what a culture is.

Ur, Penny. (1981). *Discussions that work: Task centered fluency practice*. Cambridge: Cambridge University Press.

An excellent introduction to how to conduct discussions, and lots of good activity ideas.

Ur, Penny. (1984). *Teaching listening comprehension*. Cambridge: Cambridge University Press.

Practical discussion of the basic issues in listening comprehension, and a good collection of tasks for the listening classroom.

Ur, Penny. (1988). *Grammar practice activities: A practical guide for teachers*. Cambridge: Cambridge University Press.

A conveniently referenced collection of activities for grammar practice. Many are communicative activities that could serve as a useful supplement in speaking/listening classes. Note: This does not teach grammar to the teacher.

A final note: TESOL, Inc. publishes a collection of books called the New Ways Series. Each volume in the series is a fine compilation of activity ideas, contributed by practicing language teachers, on one particular aspect of teaching. As of early 1996, the series included books on listening, vocabulary, reading, grammar, speaking, writing, teacher education, and teaching young children. More books are in production. Available from TESOL, Inc., 1600 Cameron Street, Suite 300, Alexandria, VA 22314, USA. Tel 703-518-2522. Fax 703-518-2535.

D References

These are other works I have referred to in this book. All are books (or articles in books) that are easily available, so you might peruse the list for further additions to your English teaching library (especially if you have a generous allowance for books and luggage).

Abbott, Gerry, & Wingard, Peter. (Eds.). (1981). *The teaching of English as an international language.* Glasgow, Scotland: Collins.

Barna, Laray. (1994). Stumbling blocks in intercultural communication. In Larry Samovar & Richard Porter (Eds.), *Intercultural communication: A reader* (7th ed.). (pp. 337-346). Belmont, CA: Wadsworth.

Carrell, Patricia, & Eisterhold, Joan. (1987). Schema theory and ESL reading pedagogy. In Michael Long & Jack C. Richards (Eds.), *Methodology in TESOL: A book of readings* (pp. 218-232). Rowley, MA: Newbury House.

Carruthers, Rod. (1987). Teaching pronunciation. In Michael Long & Jack C. Richards (Eds.), *Methodology in TESOL: A book of readings* (pp. 191-200). Rowley, MA: Newbury House.

Damen, Louise. (1987). *Culture learning: The fifth dimension in the language classroom.* New York: Addison-Wesley.

Eisenstein, Miriam. (1987). Grammatical explanations in ESL: Teach the student, not the method. In Michael Long & Jack C. Richards (Eds.), *Methodology in TESOL: A book of readings* (pp. 282-292). Rowley, MA: Newbury House..

Faber, Barry. (1991). *How to learn any language.* New York: Citadel Press.

Fox, Len. (1987). On acquiring an adequate second language vocabulary. In Michael Long & Jack C. Richards (Eds.), *Methodology in TESOL: A book of readings* (pp. 307-311). Rowley, MA: Newbury House.

Gairns, Ruth, & Redman, Stuart. (1986). *Working with words: A guide to teaching and learning vocabulary.* Cambridge: Cambridge University Press.

Gower, Roger, & Walters, Steve. (1983). *Teaching practice handbook: A reference book for EFL teachers in training.* Portsmouth, NH: Heinemann.

Grove, Cornelius, & Torbiorn, Ingamar. (1993). A new conceptualization of intercultural adjustment and the goals of training. In Michael

Paige (Ed.), *Education for the intercultural experience* (2nd ed.). (pp. 73-108).Yarmouth, ME: Intercultural Press.

Hendrickson, James. (1987). Error correction in foreign language teaching: Recent theory, research and practice. In Michael Long & Jack C. Richards (Eds.), *Methodology in TESOL: A book of readings* (pp. 355-372). Rowley, MA: Newbury House.

Hughes, Arthur. (1989). *Testing for language teachers.* Cambridge: Cambridge University Press.

Kaplan, Robert. (1986). Culture and the written language. In Joyce Valdes (Ed.), *Culture bound* (pp. 8-19). Cambridge: Cambridge University Press.

Lewis, Michael. (1993). *The lexical approach: The state of ELT and a way forward.* Hove, England: Language Teaching Publications.

Lewis, Michael, & Hill, Jimmie. (1985). *Practical techniques for language teaching.* Hove, England: Language Teaching Publications.

Littlewood, William. (1984). *Foreign and second language learning: Language acquisition research and its implications for the classroom.* Cambridge: Cambridge University Press.

Long, Michael, & Richards, Jack C. (Eds.). (1987). *Methodology in TESOL: A book of readings.* Rowley, MA: Newbury House.

Madsen, Harold. (1983). *Techniques in testing.* Oxford: Oxford University Press.

Marshall, Terry. (1989). *The whole world guide to language learning.* Yarmouth, ME: Intercultural Press.

McKay, Sandra. (1987). *Teaching grammar: Form, function and technique.* Englewood Cliffs, NJ: Prentice Hall.

McLaughlin, Barry. (1987). *Theories of second language learning.* London: Edward Arnold.

Murray, Denise. (Ed.). (1992). *Diversity as resource: Redefining cultural literacy.* Alexandria, VA: TESOL.

Nunan, David. (1989). *Designing tasks for the communicative classroom.* Cambridge: Cambridge University Press.

Omaggio Hadley, Alice. (1993). *Teaching language in context* (2nd ed.). Boston: Heinle & Heinle.

Oxford, Rebecca. (1990). *Language learning strategies: What every teacher should know.* New York: Newbury House/Harper & Row.

Paige, Michael. (Ed.). (1993). *Education for the intercultural experience* (2nd ed.). Yarmouth, ME: Intercultural Press.

Richards, Jack. (1990). *The language teaching matrix.* Cambridge: Cambridge University Press.

Samovar, Larry, & Porter, Richard. (Eds.). (1994). *Intercultural communication: A reader* (7th ed.). Belmont, CA: Wadsworth.

Scarcella, Robin, & Oxford, Rebecca. (1992). *The tapestry of language learning: The individual in the communicative classroom.* Boston: Heinle & Heinle.

Stevick, Earl. (1988). *Teaching and learning languages.* Cambridge: Cambridge University Press.

Taylor, Barry. (1987). Teaching ESL: Incorporating a communicative, student-centered component. In Michael Long & Jack C. Richards (Eds.), *Methodology in TESOL: A book of readings* (pp. 45-60). Rowley, MA: Newbury House.

Valdes, Joyce. (Ed.). (1986). *Culture bound.* Cambridge: Cambridge University Press.

van Ek, J.A. (1987). The threshold level. In Michael Long & Jack C. Richards (Eds.), *Methodology in TESOL: A book of readings* (pp. 78-85). Rowley, MA: Newbury House.

Walters, Keith. (1992). Whose culture, whose literacy? In Denise Murray (Ed.), *Diversity as resource: Redefining cultural literacy.* Alexandria, VA: TESOL.

Weaver, Gary. (1993). Understanding and coping with cross-cultural adjustment stress. In Michael Paige (Ed.), *Education for the intercultural experience* (2nd ed.). (pp. 137-168).Yarmouth, ME: Intercultural Press.

About the Author

Don Snow holds an MA in ESL from Michigan State University and a PhD in East Asian Language and Culture from Indiana University. He has taught language and culture in the United States, Taiwan, the People's Republic of China, and Hong Kong, and has worked with a number of organizations that send volunteer teachers abroad. At present he is a Co-Worker for the Presbyterian Church USA and serves as the overseas coordinator for a program through which language teachers from many nations are invited to teach in China by the Amity Foundation. When not working on language teaching materials or visiting teachers in China, he dabbles in the study of the written forms of Chinese dialects.